ROUTLEDGE LIBRARY EDITIONS:
BUSINESS AND ECONOMICS IN ASIA

I0130350

Volume 1

THE ACCOUNTING SYSTEM
OF NATIVE BANKS
IN PEKING AND TIENTSIN

THE ACCOUNTING SYSTEM OF NATIVE BANKS IN PEKING AND TIENTSIN

LI CHIEN MING

Routledge
Taylor & Francis Group

LONDON AND NEW YORK

First published in 1941 by Hautes études, Tientsin
Reprinted in 1982 by Garland Publishing, Inc.

This edition first published in 2019
by Routledge
2 Park Square, Milton Park, Abingdon, Oxon OX14 4RN

and by Routledge
52 Vanderbilt Avenue, New York, NY 10017

Routledge is an imprint of the Taylor & Francis Group, an informa business

British Library Cataloguing in Publication Data
A catalogue record for this book is available from the British Library

ISBN: 978-1-138-48274-6 (Set)
ISBN: 978-0-429-42825-8 (Set) (ebk)
ISBN: 978-1-138-35308-4 (Volume 1) (hbk)
ISBN: 978-1-138-36486-8 (Volume 1) (pbk)
ISBN: 978-0-429-43106-7 (Volume 1) (ebk)

Publisher's Note
The publisher has gone to great lengths to ensure the quality of this reprint but points out that some imperfections in the original copies may be apparent.

Disclaimer
The publisher has made every effort to trace copyright holders and would welcome correspondence from those they have been unable to trace.

The Accounting System of Native Banks in Peking and Tientsin

Li Chien Ming

Garland Publishing, Inc., New York & London
1982

Bibliographical note:
this facsimile has been made from a copy in
the University of Chicago Library.

Library of Congress Cataloging in Publication Data

Li, Chien Ming.
The accounting system of native banks in Peking and Tientsin.

(China during the interregnum, 1911–1949)
Text in English; tables and forms in Chinese.
Reprint. Originally published: Tientsin : Hautes
études ; Shanghai : Université l'Aurore, 1941.
(Economic studies, no. 19)
1. Banks and banking—China—Accounting. I. Title.
II. Native banks in Peking and Tientsin. III. Series.
IV. Series: Economic studies (T'ien-chin kung shang
hsüeh yüan. Shang k'o) ; no. 19.
HG1707.L5 1982   657'.833   80-8827
ISBN 0-8240-4682-X   AACR2

For a complete list of the titles in this series.
see the final pages of this volume.

All volumes in this series are printed on acid-free,
250-year-life paper.

Printed in the United States of America

THE ACCOUNTING SYSTEM
OF NATIVE BANKS
IN PEKING AND TIENTSIN

HAUTES ÉTUDES

INDUSTRIELLES ET COMMERCIALES

FACULTY OF COMMERCE

工商學院
商科

Economic Studies

No. 19

THE ACCOUNTING SYSTEM OF NATIVE BANKS IN PEKING AND TIENTSIN

經濟論文 第十九冊

京津銀號業之會計制度

By

Li Chien Ming

李建名著

HAUTES ÉTUDES

Race Course Road

TIENTSIN

UNIVERSITÉ L'AURORE

Avenue Dubail

SHANGHAI

1941

FORWORD

I can only commend very heartily the very complete study given by Mr. Li Chien Ming on the Native Banks in Tientsin and Peking.

Such a comprehensive work on this subject was so far lacking and it will certainly be appreciated by all those interested in business in China.

It may sometimes be considered that the Native Banks are an unnecessary and costly link between small Chinese traders and the larger Chinese and foreign banks but one must admit that it would be extremely difficult to do without them even now and that it will be so for many years to come.

The native banks are not an artificial but a truly natural creation based on Chinese conceptions and habits not only of trade but also of living in general. They are very close to their customers from every point of view and this is the main reason of their strength.

Their small capital and their close connections with their customers are a reason for their usual specialisation, but the inherent risk is reduced by their associations which in a way realise what modern banks try to obtain by the dissemination of their investments.

The very extensive work of Mr. Li Chien Ming will certainly be of great interest to all doing business with Chinese and also to all interested in Chinese life in general as it gives an accurate insight in one of its important activities.

G. Véron

PREFACE

During the past few years there has been a substantial development in native bank practice. Originally, the books of accounts kept by the Shansi bankers were recorded by primitive methods of book-keeping, but with the introduction of the cash-journal method by Allen Shand in modern banks, some of the native banks employing former employees of modern banks as chief accountants are reforming their accounting system after the cash-journal method which is characterized by the cash-journalizing principle and the preparation of receiving and paying slips or vouchers as original evidences of the business transactions.

To-day most of the native bankers, being attracted by the advantages of modern accounting as it is practised by many business concerns, on the one side and being pressed by the enforcement of income-tax, which asks for an exact figure of the taxable income, on the other side have finally chosen to do away with their traditional methods of book-keeping. However, partly due to the influence of the modern banks and partly due to the business conservatism which shows reluctance to resort to professional experts for designing a suitable system of accounts, the native banks are generally adopting the slip system without the least modification, with the consequent burden of operating expenses due to increased clerical work and change of book-keepers.

It cannot be overlooked, however, that the business operations of most native banks are not the same as that of modern banks, if not altogether different. The former, generally having smaller capitalization and fewer employees, naturally handle less business and have limited activities; and in many cases a native banker is practically no more than a customer of modern banks.

But the cash-journal method is devised to meet the complicated bussiness functions of modern banks. The slip system has proved

PREFACE

satisfactory in highly departmentalized business organizations, yet in an office of limited size, like that of most native banks, it is practically a luxury. While the modern bank accounting is developed on an intelligent basis, the unnecessary expense of its installation and maintenance must be guarded against. It is totally mistaken to regard the slip system as a cure-all for the bankers' ills. The adoption of new accounting system invariably involves additional expense, which is justified only where it pays for itself in the value of the information secured.

The "four-pillars" method used by the native bankers in the preparation of their financial statements, corresponds to assets, liabilities, profit and loss. The "Ho-lung-men" system of closing books of account corresponds to periodic extraction of trial balance and is practically double-entry in principle. Thus, with only a slight improvement in the theory and practice of native banks accounting, the old method may be made use of smoothly and efficiently with less clerical trouble and expense.

In view to study the existing accounting system of native banks, there has been much demand for a complete exposition of the business practice of native banks in Tientsin and Peking, which would serve as a guide to further studies of the subject. This work could be done only by a well-bred investigator, having good connection with native bankers and sufficient knowledge of accounting; Mr. Li Chien Ming, who has now completed this task was well qualified to conduct the research and to materialize it into a book of exposition and suggestions that should be helpful to both researchers and practitioners everywhere. He has had the opportunity of interviewing a large number of authoritative native bankers in Tientsin and Peking, so that the thesis which is here presented is in fact the result of an exhaustive study, discussion and deliberation until it has actually become an expression of qualified opinions and accepted practice.

Li Pao Chen.

Tientsin, July 1941.

AUTHOR'S PREFACE

The significance of native banking is obvious throughout China, but there is no book, either in Chinese or in English, for recording the accounting system of these enterprises. Only a few books concerning the organization and business operations have been published. This is the motive for writing this essay, but the scarcity of references made the task more difficult. Most of the materials were collected through personal interviews with native bankers both in Tientsin and Peking during the last year.

My purpose is to show to the public the specific features of native banking and its accounting system, and to give useful suggestions to the enterprises. On account of the restrictions of time and circumstances, only two districts are included. It is believed that a part of valuable materials has been left out. Moreover, owing to the scope of the subject, data concerning old, interesting methods of organization and management of native banks, especially the "Lu Fang" (爐房), "P'iao Hao" (票號) and their associations, which were described by old and famous native bankers, had, perforce, to be omitted.

I must, in any case, express my grateful acknowledgement to Rev. François Théry, S. J., Dean of Faculty of Commerce; and Mr. Li Pao Chen (李寶震先生), Professor of accounting; and other Professors of the Hautes Etudes, for their suggestions and corrections to this text. The same thanks must be given to several native bankers, to the Chairman and other officers of Native Bankers' Associations in Tientsin and Peking, who kindly supplied me with practical and statistical data, and models of various forms used by native banks.

C. M. Li.

Hautes Etudes,
   Tientsin.
August 5th 1941.

CONTENTS

CONTENTS

CONTENTS

CONTENTS

TABLES AND FORMS

TABLES AND FORMS

CHAPTER I.

GENERAL SURVEY OF THE ENTERPRISES

I. Historical Survey

Native banking is a prominent factor in both the Tien-tsin and Peking money markets. Locally, the native bank is called Yin Hao (銀號), which literally means "Silver Shop" or firm. This enterprise has originated from many sources such as money exchangers or Ch'ien P'u (兌錢攤), (錢舖), metallic ornaments stores or Shou Shih Lou (首飾樓), P'iao Hao(票號), Lu Fang (爐房) etc. [1] [2] The origins of the money exchangers and metallic ornaments stores are hard to trace on account of the insufficiency and inaccuracy of records that have been handed down to us from ancient times. [1] Since the capital was removed to Peking, the 19th year of Yung L'e (永樂) (1421 A. D.) in the Ming dynasty (明朝), the business both in Tientsin and Peking improved gradually, following the increase of population. [2] So, more financial organizations were established, but they were so simple that they could not attract the attention of the people at that time. [1]

After the foundation of the Ch'ing dynasty the financial organs were reformed, and many Piao Hao and Ch'ien Chuang(錢莊) were established to deal with deposits, loans and remittances, and to act for Treasury. [4] Their style was in embryo. Many years after, the native banks came up and took their place. When modern banks arose, they were much affected, but due to the stable foundation of the enterprise, and the old business custom of the past hundred years, they still assist in monetary operations on a very large scale.[1] Thus many native banks are still subsisting and even, in recent times, their number has increased.

Turning to the evolutionary process in native banking development, it was affected not only by internal factors, but also by the economic and political influences. Peking was the capital of the Ming and Ch'ing dynasties and of earlier Chinese Republic; on the other hand, Tientsin became a great commercial port eighty years ago. Furthermore the geographical connection of Tientsin and Peking is very close, thus the conditions and evolution of Tientsin and Peking native banks are very similar. In order to make it clearer in mind, the development of the enterprises will be illustrated period by period in the following:—

1. *Primitive Period*—Before the time of Chia Ch'ing (嘉慶) of the Ch'ing dynasty, the financial organizations were not sound. There were only money exchangers (換錢舖) and metallic ornaments shops. The main business operated by money exchangers was only for exchange of metallic coins and notes which were called "Chih Ch'ien" (制錢), "Yin Ting" (銀錠) and "Ch'ien T'ieh" (錢帖). The amount of deposits and loans was small; even they were operated by a few shops, because the large part of investments were still handled by large capitalists in that period of feudalism. Although the metallic ornaments shops dealt also with money exchange, "Yuan Pao" (元寶) melting, and accepting deposits, this was still an accessory business, the manufacture of ornaments being the main one. The influences of these two kinds of organizations on the money market was small until the Piao Hao were organized.[1] The "Lu Fang" existed already in this period, but they dealt only with melting silver like the silversmiths.[5] So this time may be called the primitive period.

2. *Piao Hao Period*—The Piao Hao, being also called "Piao Chuang", were commenced by Shansi people in the Ch'ing dynasty. There are five hearsays about the origin of Shansi native bankers. They are as follows:

(1) During the reign of Shun Chih (順治) (1644-1661), the

rebel Li Ch'uang (李闖) was defeated, and he lost all his treasures robbed in the Shansi Province in his rout. A large part was got by a certain Mr. K'ang (康氏) who set up in trade and erected the first P'iao Chuang in the Capital of Shansi to facilitate money transfers. Large profits were made, and many branches were established later on. Thus other rich men of Shansi followed his example.[6 7]

(2) In the time of Ch'ien Lung (乾隆) and Chia Ch'ing (嘉慶) (1735-1819) a merchant in P'ingyao (平遙) Shansi, Mr. Lei Li T'ai (雷履泰), who was trusted by a capitalist, Mr. Li of Ta P'u Village (達蒲村), established the Jih Sheng Ch'ang Paint Shop (日升昌顏料舖) in Tientsin.[1] He felt difficulties in transporting his silver bars from Tientsin to Szechuan for the payment of the paint verdigris. Then he invented the method of remittance by erecting a branch shop in Szechuan. All the money of the merchants at that time moving between two places was able to be handed more conveniently by Jih Sheng Ch'ang for remittance. More and more merchants and officials entrusted him large amounts of money, so the shop made much profit. The Jeh Sheng Ch'ang Piao Hao (日升昌票號) was established formally in P'ingyao in the second year of Chia Ch'ing (1798),[1] and a large number of branches were distributed in many provinces.[5] In addition, it is said that the regulations of Piao Hao were made by two famous scholars Mr. Ku Ting Lin (顧亭林) and Mr. Fu Ch'ing Chu (傅青主).[6]

(3) On account of the lean soil, dense population and difficulties of living in Shansi, the people were obliged to trade in other districts. The Piao Hao was established to help them to remit their money from other places.[x]

(4) "Making money" was the main belief of most of the Shansi people. They were never afraid of any trouble happening in their business. So one may believe that the Piao Hao were started by them.[8]

(5) Salt, iron, silk and coal were the natural resources in Shansi. Large quantities were transported to other provinces, and in return big sums of money were earned. The Piao Hao were establish-

ed for the purpose of financing the trade."

Of the above five sayings, the first two are verisimilar and the second one is more reliable. We have no doubt on that the initiator of the Piao Hao was found in Shansi. In the 19th. year of Chia Ch'ing (1814), a second Piao Hao named Wei T'ai Hou Hao (蔚泰厚號) was established, and gradually more Piao Hao were founded. During that time, they could be classified into three groups, viz. "Ch'i" (祁) "Tai" (太) and "Ping" (平)." The Piao Hao which were situated in Ch'i district (祁縣) were called "Ch'i group", such as "Ta Shên Ch'uan" (大盛川), "Ta Tê T'ung" (大德通), "Ho Shên Yuan (合盛元) etc; those in T'aiuKu district (太谷縣) were "Ch'ih l T'ang" (志一堂), "Ta Tê Yü" (大德玉), "Hsieh Ch'éng" (協成) and "Ch'ien Ta" (乾大), which belonged to the "T'ai group". "Wei T'ai Hou", "P'ai Shên Ch'uan" (百盛川), "P'ai Ch'uan T'ung" (百川通), "Hsieh T'ung Ch'ing" (協同慶), "Wei Shên Cheng" (蔚盛長), "Hsin T'ai Hou" (新太厚) and others were in Pingyao, so they were called the "Ping group". At first they dealt with remittances accessorily as a secondary business, but gradually specialized in them." The Ch'ien P'u and Lu Fang cooperated with them.

(3) Boom Period—In the reigns of Hsien Fêng (咸豐) and T'ung Chih (同治) (1851-1874), all the poll and land taxes over the whole country had to be transported to the national exchequer in Peking, the capital of the Ch'ing dynasty. The problem of transporting silver bars or Yuan Pao was a very difficult one. The methods of remittances were not much developed then. Only wooden bars cut into two pieces, and in each half of which were hidden ten Yuan Pao weighting five hundred taels (兩) were used. When the two pieces were fitted and closed together, they were bound up by iron strips. This was called "Ch'üeh Mu" (殼木) or "Huan Kang" (黄槓) in colloquial language." The officials had to deliver those "Ch'üeh Mu" to any one of the twenty-six official Lu Fang in Chu Po Shih (珠寶市) to be melted into standard silver. Because it was regulated by the Government that the Yuan Pao without the die of one of the twenty-six official Lu Fang could not be circulated in the

market or handed to the exchequer.[2][5][11] Therefore the business of deposits, loans and remittances operated by the Lu Fang developed extensively at that time.[12]

Meanwhile the number of Piao Hao situated in Peking was also increasing on account of the prosperity of their business. Remittances from other provinces were preferably used instead of transporting silver, for the sake of convenience and safety. The managers of the Piao Hao often inter-communicated closely with the officials and merchants who entrusted them big sums of money for remittances, loans and deposits, which were called "Wei Ti" (為替), "T'ai Fu" (貸付) and "Yu Chin" (預金) respectively by the Shansi native bankers in the former time.[6] The business of the Ch'ien P'u was also developed in the same way.

If we turn to Tientsin, we find that the conditions there were similar to those in Peking. In the tenth year of Hsien Fêng (咸豐) (1860) after the war with British and French allied forces, Tientsin was opened by treaty as a commercial port where many foreigners resided. It suddenly became the commercial centre of North China where all goods were collected and distributed. The commerce made new advances, and the financial market of that city was more active than in the past. The Piao Hao succeeded admirably in their business, and the organization of Ch'ien P'u and Shou Shih Lou improved on account of great strides being made in their business.[1]

Later on, foreign firms and banks were established for negotiating currencies on behalf of foreign merchants, but the Chinese merchants still relied upon the Ch'ien P'u and P'iao Hao for their business operations. Thus the business of the original native banks became gradually prosperous. Before the year "Keng Tze" (庚子) (1900), there were more than three hundred Ch'ien P'u and thirty Piao Hao in Tientsin.[1]

(4) *Period of Depression*—During the rebellion of the "Yi Ho Tuan" (義和團) in the year "Keng Tze" (庚子) (1900) all were ruined. Nearly two hundred Piao Hao and Ch'ien P'u, both in Tientsin and Peking, went bankrupt. That was the first stroke in the

history of Tientsin and Peking financial organizations. Although the commercial market recovered very soon after the fighting was at an end, in fact the money market still remained inactive.[1]

After the negociations of peace with the eight allied armies, Mr Yuan Shih Kai (袁世凱) established the "Kuan Ch'ien Chu" (官錢局) for the purpose of setting in order the money market and guiding it into the right path. The conditions were entirely renewed. Later on, a few Chinese banks were founded such as the Commercial Bank of China (中國通商銀行) in 1902, the Bank of the Board of Finances (戶部銀行) in 1904, which was changed into the Ta Ch'ing Bank (大清銀行) in 1908, and the Bank of China and many other banks buring the Republic.[7][11] The Tientsin money market took a new appearance. Nearly all the Government's deposits were absorbed by these banks, which shared also a part of the business of remittances. Fortunately the foundations of P'iao Hao and Ch'ien P'u were stable, and they were little shaken immediately. In the last few years of the Ch'ing dynasty, there were still thirty four P'iao Hao, and more than twenty important Ch'ien P'u in Tientsin.[1]

The Ch'ien P'u and P'iao Hao in Peking were much affected by the stroke and a number of firms were eliminated. In the period from the twenty-sixth to the thirty-fourth year of Kuang Hsü (光緒) (1900-1908), the silver dollars appeared in the money market, and the Lu Fang were ordered by the Board of Finance (戶部) to close down their business. Although many petitions were sent to the Board of Finance for their continuance, it was in vain. Then all the Lu Fang were changed into native banks in the first year of Hsüan T'un (宣統)(1909).[5][14]

During the Chinese Revolution of 1911, all the markets were in a wild confusion. Many Ch'ien Hao (錢號) went bankrupt due to the political upheaval. This may be considered as the second stroke in the history of money business in Peking and Tientsin. In this period, most native banks were in straits.[1]

(5) *Period of Reformation* → This period contains the years from the beginning of the Republic up to now. After the

revolution, most P'iao Hao in Tientsin abandoned their business on account of the competition of native banks, so there were not more than twenty P'iao Hao left. But in the second year of the Republic (1913), the Peking Ch'ien P'u were flourishing and, two or three years later, the business of the P'iao Chuang of Peking also became more prosperous. Nevertheless, the P'iao Hao suffered another blow in losing about one million dollars through extending credit to Japanese opium merchants in 1920 (民國十年).[1] Hence they occupied no longer the dominating position in Tientsin and Peking. The only P'iao Hao existing in these two cities nowadays are "Ta Tê T'ung" (大德通) and "Ta Tê Hung" (大德恆).[1][14]

As regards the competition of modern banks, it started seriously from 1915 (民國四年). Modern banks were established one after another. They took a large part of business from the native banks.[1] After the issue of fiat money, and exchange control by the three national banks, the position of native banks fell down suddenly. Made alive to the danger by these failures, the native bankers came up to cooperate among themselves and reformed their organization in order to rival the banks in business. In the years 1930 to 1935 (民國十九年至二十四年) there was a tendency to concentration of native banks, especially in Peking. Most Lu Fang, P'iao Hao and Ch'ien Chuang changed their name into that of native banks.[14][15] But the money exchangers did not take part in the movement.

After the Sino-Japanese incident of 1937, the business conditions in the two cities were changed. The whole business centre was moved to the French concession in Tientsin. On account of the depression of banking operations, the native banks rose up and increased in number. Hitherto there are about three hundred native banks in the two cities. Since the assessment of income tax was published, the native banks were forced to change their accounting system, which was partly improved by a few auditors. In the recent two years, a part of the terminology, methods of organization and accounting system of modern banks have been adopted by a number of Tientsin and Peking native banks, and there are a very few newly-organized native banks which are organized in a manner completely similar to modern banks. So, in this period, all the native banks have changed or improved a great deal.

II. The different groups of native banks

Due to the fact that the native banks originated from various sources, there were different groups which dominated according to the periods. In general, each group is named from the native town of the manager, not of the proprietor of the native bank. The customs and methods of operating business used by the managers coming from the same native town are always similar, so the group is formed. Customarily, if the business of a native bank is commenced in the native district of the manager, it is said to belong to the local group or "Pen Ti Pang" (本地帮),[14] otherwise it belongs to the foreign group or "Wai Pang" (外帮) or "K'o Pang" (客帮).[15] A native bank in Tientsin, having a Tientsin citizen as its manager, belongs to the local group, but it would belong to the foreign group if it were doing business in Peking.[16]

The main groups in Tientsin and Peking are: Tientsin group (津帮), Peking group (京帮), Shêng-Chi group (深冀帮), Shansi group (山西帮), Paoting group (保定帮) and Shantung group (山東帮). There is only one native bank of the Shanghai group (上海帮) in Tientsin. (See Appendix). Formerly there were still a few other groups such as Hochien group (河間帮), Honan group (河南帮), Kuang group (廣帮) etc... At present, the most numerous group is the Shêng—Chi group, for the number of native banks of this group in Tientsin exceeds largely that of any other group. In Peking, the predominating one is the local group, which contains a large part of the Shêng — Chi group. Most of the native banks of this group deal with regular business.[16]

The local group of Tientsin is next in number to Shêng — Chi group; it does less remittance business. In both Peking and Tientsin, the Shansi group plays a considerable part exceeding in importance all the rest.[17] Meanwhile, there are also a few different groups in either Tientsin or Peking. Most of them are less important.

1. **Tientsin group** — This group formerly was divided in two parts, viz. Eastern streets (東街) and Western streets (西街), differing by the location and the nature of their business. The former group did business in Kung Nan Ta Chieh (宮南大街) and Kung Pei Ta Chieh (宮北大街) which are at the east of the old city wall. Those situated west of Chin Shih Street (針市街) Ku I Street (估衣街) and Chu Kan Hsiang (竹竿巷) belonged to the Western Streets group. The main business operated by Eastern Streets group was speculative transactions, like purchases and sales of silver and gold, foreign currencies, securities, Japanese Yen, etc... The Western streets group dealt only with regular business as deposits, loans, discount of bills and others. Sometimes they bought or sold securities, or silver and gold bullion, for their customers.[17]

Since the incident in 1937, the native banks mostly moved their offices to the French concession. The Western group disappeared, and of the native banks of the Eastern group only a few were left. Before the blockade of British and French concessions in 1939, a large part of the native banks crowded in the French Concession. There was no native bank in the Italian Concession until the time of blockade.[18] At present, the names of Eastern and Western groups are no longer used, but they still exist in fact.

2. **Peking group** — In the 28th. and 29th years of Kuang Hsü (光緒), there were three kinds of organizations which were engaged in the business of native banking, viz. Lu Fang, Ch'ien P'u and P'iao Chuang. Twenty-six official Lu Fang and other private Lu Fang were all gathered in Chu Pao Shih (珠寶市). The nature of their business was similar to that of the Western streets group in Tientsin. All the transfers of the native banks were settled in that place; even other commercial banks had to go there for settlement. But they carried no speculative transaction. It was the centre of the money market at that time, and it is so even now.[5 14]

The Ch'ien P'u in Ch'ien Men (前門) were the organs for money exchange. The nature of their business was just the same as that of Tientsin Western streets group. In the second year of the Republic (1913) these enterprises were very prosperous, and the best known at that time were Yuan Ho (元合), Tien Chü Fêng (天聚豐) etc... Before merging into native banks, the last one was called "Yung Tsêng Ho" (永增和). Purchases and sales of Japanese Yen and Russian rubles were their chief business.[14]

The P'iao Chuang were scattered all over Peking. The main centres were "Ta Mo Ch'ang" (打磨場), "Ts'ao Ch'ang Chiu Tiao" (草場九條), "Ts'ao Ch'ang Shih Tiao" (草場十條), "Hsüeh Chia Wan" (薛家灣), etc...This kind of enterprises was derived from the Shansi P'iao Ho as mentioned before; so their business was mainly in remittances. Besides, there were many small P'iao Chuang which had no certain place for their business offices. The staff of the small P'iao Chuang often operated in small hotels called "Tien" (店) where they used to live. Those Tien were "Yü Lung" (裕隆), "Tung Tai" (同泰), "Shang Ku" (尚古) and some others. The most popular ones at that time were "Jih Shêng Ch'ang" (日昇昌), "Wei Ch'ang Hou" (蔚昌厚), "Tah Tê T'ung" (大德通), "Tah Shêng Ch'uan" (大升川) and "Yü Yuan Yung" (裕元永).[14]

The Lu Fang worked as an intermediary between the P'iao Chuang and the Ch'ien P'u, so that all of the transfers had to be made in the Lu Fang, which were changed into native banks earlier than others. In 1935 (民國二十四年), these three kinds of enterprises tended to merge and most of them were changed into native banks. Now they are all called native banks; the main influence on the money market is still invested in the Lu Fang of Chu Pao Shih (珠寶市).

3. **Differences between the Tientsin and the Peking group**—In recent years the methods of business operation and the accounting systems of the Peking and the Tientsin groups have partly become similar to each other, especially in the bank accounting system adopted. But there is one peculiarity: in Tientsin an instrument should be used for transfer among native banks, it is called "Poh Mar" (撥碼); in Peking it may be made orally "Tui Hua" (對話).[19] A detailed study

of these two sorts of transfers will be given in Chapter III.

The local group in Tientsin is called "Tso Chuang" (作莊). Among the native banks transfer orders can be made for any amount, even though there is no deposit. But the balance should be paid by cheques or "foreign paper"(番紙)in the next morning; if a native bank fails to do so, its credit will be lost. The Peking group in Tientsin is called "Pan K'o Pan Chuang" (半客半莊), and the amount of the transfer orders sent by them cannot exceed the total sum of their deposits in other native banks. A few native banks of the Peking group are allowed to draw transfer orders for any amount as those of local group, but they are also obliged to settle the balance in the next morning.[10][19]

In Peking, there is no special instrument of transfer. Native bankers may ask any sum of money only by telephone, and the amounts paid and received in transfer should be settled in the very night. It is usual that the transfer has to be paid against deposits; overdrafts are not often allowed.[10][19]

As to the business done by native banks of the Tientsin and Peking group, we may state that speculative transactions are more often done by the Tientsin group, while the managers of the Peking group are rather conservative.[5]

III. Organization and Management

The organization and management are various in different native bank groups according to the conditions of their business. Formerly they were very simple, but nowadays they have developed on account of the increase of their business, and especially they are influenced by the modern banking system.[11] So there is a trend towards unification. In any case, the larger native banks are organized in a similar manner.

1. **The essentials of establishment**—There are four essential elements in a native bank, which are as follows:—

a) *Proprietors*—The native bank is a business firm, organized more or less as a family affair by a wealthy person or a small group of rich people, who assume as partners full liability for all the engagements of the native bank. "Their liability is not limited to the amount of capital subscribed. This unique feature on the part of the owners accounts for the success of the native bank in gaining the confidence of the Public".[20][21]

If the capital is invested by only one person, it is called a sole proprietorship, and the proprietor bears an unlimited liability. When the proprietors are two or more persons, it is a partnership whose members according to law bear a joint and several liability. Formerly the proprietor was called "Tsai Tung" (財東) or "Tung Chia" (東家); now it is mostly called "Ku Tung" (股東).[16][21] There are also a few native banks organized as companies (公司) according to law.[22]

b) *The management*—The manager in native banks is the most important employee, who has the full power of controlling the whole enterprise. Even the proprietor has no right to interfere with him, according to old custom. If the manager is a man of ability, the business will be prosperous; otherwise, the whole business will be in danger. So the manager should be chosen very carefully.[3][21]

Formerly the manager was called "Chang Kuei" (掌櫃), but now is usually called "Ching Li" (經理). If he controls several branch-banks, he is called "Tsung Chang Kuei" (總掌櫃) that means "general manager." Associated to the manager, there are sometimes a vice-manager (副理), assistant manager (襄理), superintendent manager (監理), whose duties are to superintendend the whole business, to deal with the social affairs and to act for the manager when the latter is absent.[33]

According to custom, there may be two kinds of managers: either the proprietor assumes himself the management, this system is called "Tzu Tung Tzu Huo" (自東自夥); or the manager is appointed by the proprietor.[31]

c) *The capital*—The capital represents the investment of the proprietors. It is used as the fundamental operative instrument by which the business of the enterprise can be commenced and developed. Usually the extent of the business varies with the size of the capital invested; but, on account of the unlimited liability of the proprietor, all his assets are in fact included in the capital of the enterprise.[31][34]

Two kinds of capital are available to native banks, viz. the Capital proper and the Hu Pên (護本). The latter is a kind of special long-term deposit of the proprietor, which the enterprise is entitled to use freely in the same manner as the capital.[31][34] (Refer to Chapter II.)

d) *The commercial name of the enterprise* — This name is called "P'ai Hao" (牌號) or "Chao P'ai" (招牌) or "Chang Hao" (商號) in native banks. It is the one which represents the whole enterprise in business. In Chinese business circles, words meaning moral qualities, prosperity or good luck are often used, such as, "Tê" (德), "Fêng" (豐), "Li" (利), "Ch'ang" (昌), "Shun" (順) etc.[31] (See Appendix)

When the above four essentials are fixed, a contract is redacted by both the proprietors and the manager. All the important parties together with guarantors should sign on it. In the contract, the name of the proprietors, the commercial name, location, capital of the native bank, the name of manager and other important employees, their remunerations, the period of reports on the business and financial conditions, the proportion of sharing profits, the extent of business and other particulars should be mentioned. (See Appendix I)

2. **Other employees and their duties** — The internal organization of the enterprise comprises many employees, each one of whom was formerly known under a different name. Now-a-days the names used are the same as in the commercial banks, but the duties remain unchanged.[15]

A) *The chief accountant* (總會計)—He was formerly called "Chang Cho" (帳桌) or "Tsung Chang" (總帳). His duties are to make records of all accounts and reports as well as to calculate interests.[12][35]

B) *The accountants* (會計)—Their old name was "Pang Chang" (帮帳). They are assistants to the chief accountant. Each one of

— 13 —

them is responsible for a part of accounts.[11][25]

C) *The business Clerk* (营业) — He was formerly called "Tso Kuei" (坐柜). He is responsible for negotiating any transaction with outside persons.[11][25]

D) *The Cashier* (出纳) — All payments and disbursements are made through his hands, and he should also keep the valuables and documents of the enterprise.[21][23][25]

E) *The circulating Clerk* (交际) — The old names were "Shroff" (跑街) or "Tsou Chieh" (走街). He is a very important employee, who has great influence on the increase or decrease of the amount of deposits. He is responsible to raise the number of customers and amount of deposits, to investigate the business conditions and the amount of capital of business firms in relation with the bank, in order to fix the maximum amount of overdraft and the limit of unsecured loans. His ability influences the business a great deal. It is a system different of that of modern banks.[11][23][25][30]

F) *The Clerk in charge of general affairs* (庶务)—He is the staff member who takes charge of all expenses, such as the purchase of stationery, fuel, food, furniture and fixtures and other expenditures.[11][25]

G) *The Secretary* (文牍) — He is responsible for letter writing, sending or receiving telegrams.[23][25]

H) *The "Wai Chuang"* (外庄) — He is the one who conducts the remittances and transfers with branches.[11][25]

I) *Apprentices* (练习生)—They were called "Hsueh T'u" (学徒) formerly. Usually the transfer orders, cheques, and "Po Tiao"(拨条) (Refer to chapter III) are prepared by them.[11][25]

On the whole, the number of employees varies with the needs of the enterprise. Usually the number of accountants and of circulating clerks is greater than that of other employees. The "Wai Chuang" are more numerous in the native banks which deal mainly with remittances.[3][11][22][23][25]

3. Administration and Remuneration—

The staff of a native bank may be classified into three

categories, such as apprentices (學徒), "Hsiao Tung Shin" (小同事) and "Ta Tung Shih" (大同事). The first catagory only works for practice and as assistants. The second one is promoted from the first after two or three years' experience. The last kind are the employees of long experience and are responsible for important business. All the above three categories are under the direct control of the manager.[25]

It is a custom that an apprentice is introduced by either the manager or a relative or friend of the proprietor. After three or four days' trial he will enter the staff, if he is accepted by the manager. In recent years, a few native banks applied the method of examination, but they are still very rare. "Hsiao Tung Shih" are often promoted from the apprentices, and the "Ta Tung Shih" are commonly engaged by the manager.[25]

The termination of employment depends upon many causes. If it is due to business stagnation, the employee is discharged at one of the Chinese festivals (年節); if the employee's work is not good, or he disobeys the regulations, the manager may dismiss him at once. The termination at the time of a festival is usually made through a notice from a person sent by the manager, stating "T'ing Hsin Hui Kuei" (聽信回櫃) or "T'ing Hsin Tsai Hui Lai" (聽信再回來) etc., which means not to come back without further notice. It may be also notified to the introducer for transmission to the employee. If there is only a negligence, or if the introducer is very important in the native bank, the employee may be forgiven and recalled: it is called "Chü Hui" (據回). As regards the termination of the contract of the manager or a "Ta Tung Shih", a card called "Tz'u T'ieh" (辭帖) is used, and the two words "Tz'u Hsieh" (辭謝) means "dismissed with thanks" are written on it. This is sent together with a card of the enterprise to the person who is discharged.[25]

The salaries are different according to the grade. An apprentice, during the first one or two years, receives no salary but, at the end of each business year, the "Kuei Sung" (饋送) is given, which depends on the record of his work and the amount of the profits earned by the enterprise. The salaries of "Hsiao Tung Shih" are small, commonly half or one or two dollars every month. The "Chia Ch'ou" (加籌) means the amount of money that the employee is entitled to overdraw every month, and this total will be deducted from the "Kuei Sung" (餽送) at the end of each year. There are also a few differences in "Chia Ch'ou" (加籌): "I Hsin Pan Ch'ou" (一薪半籌) means that an amount equivalent to half of his monthly pay may be withdrawn and "I Hsin I Ch'ou" (一薪一籌) means that an amount equivalent to his full monthly pay may be withdrawn each month.[25]

The monthly salary of the Ta Tung Shih is from ten to thirty dollars, and they can get a special share of profits without any condition, for the purpose of encouragement. This is called "Ch'ih Fu Ku" (吃浮股). Suppose it is said "Two per cent", that means two per cent of the net profit. The manager, sub-managers, etc, earn higher salaries evidently, from forty to more than one hundred dollars, and they can also overdraw and enjoy the "Ch'ih Fu Ku".[25]

The "Kuei Sung" is just a bounty which is distributed by the manager on a lucky day (吉日) at the end of each year. The amount of "Kuei Sung" depends on the total profit and the amount of salary. Besides, a bonus (花紅) is given, if the net profit earned is more than in other years. There is another case where the manager may give to an excellent employee a sum as a special bounty; it is called "Po Tze Kuai" (脖子枴) by native bankers.[25]

4. The Native Bankers' Association—It is a union of native bankers which manages the public affairs, which each member cannot do by himself. The roles of the former native banker's associations in Tientsin and Peking were twofold: one was to fix the prices of metallic money, the rates of exchange, and the quotations of securities, and the other was to dispose of public affairs, disputes, and to represent the members in negotiating with third parties, as well to receive orders and to send messages from and to the Government. Formerly the first role was more important, but gradually it ceased, either because the business vanished or because the market departed from the association. So at present, this association is organized in view of the second rôle.[27] [28]

Although its duties have diminished, the association still occupies a very important position among native banks. The liability of a native bank is unlimited as mentioned previously, and the volume of business operated is often far more than the capital invested. So the credit is the most significant foundation for dealing in the money market. If the credit of a native bank is impaired, the relations with other native banks will be broken off. The association is responsible for preventing such unfavourable eventualities.[27]

In Tientsin, this organization was called "Ch'ien Hao Kung So" (錢號公所) in the reign of Chia Ch'ing (嘉慶), and changed its name into "Ch'ien Yeh Kung So" (錢業公所) in the 26th year of Kuang Hsü (光緒) (1900). In the first year of Hsüan T'un (宣統) the name used was "Tientsin Ch'ien Shang Kung So" (天津錢商公所), but during the 19th year of the Republic it became the Tientsin Native Bankers' Association (天津市錢業同業公會) in accordance with the Law on Industrial and Commercial Guilds (工商同業公會法).[27]

An investigation of the 24th year of the Republic (1935) shows that only forty-seven members, about one third of the total number of native banks, were enlisted in the association (142 native banks).[27] But in the recent years, it was ordered by the Government that all the native banks should be members of the association. So there are up-to-now two hundred and twenty-nine old native banks, and ten new ones have applied for membership. (See Appendix)

In Peking, it was organized by more than twenty Lu Fang in the reign of Kuang Hsü (1875-1908) (光緒年間) and it was called Lu Fang Association (爐房公會). Gradually the number of members increased, and the name was changed into the present name: Peking Native Bankers, Association (北京市錢業同業公會). In the 24th year of the Republic (1935), most P'iao Hao and Ch'ien P'u became members of the association. At present, nearly all the native banks joined the association. There were sixty-eight members in April 1941.[29] (See Appendix.)

IV. The Present Status

The present conditions of Peking and Tientsin native banks are more prosperous and uniform than before, on account of the overwhelming majority of native banks being members of the native bankers' association. Maybe there are a very few native banks omitted in the Government's investigation, which are not enlisted. But they are only regarded as informal native banks. The money exchangers (兌換業), who carry on a different business, have their own association which is outside the scope of this essay.

Most of the following data are collected from the Peking and Tientsin Native Bankers' Association and refer to the end of April 1941 (民國三十年).[30]

1. *The regional distribution on native banks in Peking and Tientsin*

The number of native banks varies very often, for even in a period of one month, there may be a few native banks going bankrupt or newly opened. But at the end of April 1941, the native banks existing in Tientsin were two hundred and twenty-nine in number, not including ten newly opened native banks, and there were sixty-nine in Peking. The number of native banks of each group will be shown as follows:—

Table I. The Distribution of Different Groups in Tientsin and Peking

		Tientsin	Peking
Shêng-Chi group	（深冀帮）	95	61
Peking group	（京　帮）	23	
Tientsin group	（津　帮）	83	—
Shansi group	（山西帮）	14	8
Paoting group	（保定帮）	8	—
Shantung group	（山東帮）	5	—
Shanghai group	（上海帮）	1	—
	Total	229	69

From the above figures, we may see that the Shêng-Chi group dominated both in Tientsin and Peking. The Tientsin group comes second in the Tientsin area. It is evident that the Shansi native bankers had lost their importance, especially in Peking. (See Appendix)

With regard to the places where the native banks are situated, the French concession is the centre of the Tientsin market, and the Italian concession is the next. The old centres of Eastern and Western streets groups have lost their original position. (See Table II)

Table II. The Local Distribution of Native Banks in Tientsin

Areas	The Number of Native Banks	Percentage
French Concession (法租界)	119	51.97
Italian ,, (義租界)	76	33.19
British ,, (英租界)	12	5.24
Japanese ,, (日租界)	11	4.80
Tientsin Municipal Area	11	4.80
Total	229	100.00%

In Peking the main centre is Ch'ien Men Wai (前門外) where the Lu Fang were gathered formerly. There was no big geographical change caused by military events; thus the distribution is still similar to that of Lu Fang and Ch'ien P'u of former times. (See Table III)

Table III. The Local Distribution of Native Banks in Peking

Areas	The Number of Native Banks	Percentage
Ch'ien Men Wai （前門外）	64	92.75%
Ch'ien Men （前 門）	2	2.90%
Tung Tan P'ai Lou （東 單）	1	1.45%
Chung Wen Men Wai （崇 外）	1	1.45%
Nan Chang Chieh （南長街）	1	1.45%
Total	69	100.00%

2. *The volume of capital investment* — The total amount of capital invested in Tientsin native banks is fifteen millions and eight thousand dollars, and three millions seven hundred ninety-six thousand dollars in Peking. In Tientsin native banks, the largest amount of capital is four hundred thousand dollars, and the smallest amount is twenty thousand. Generally the capital of most banks is around fifty thousand dollars, and next to them come the banks with one hundred thousand dollars. The approximate arithmetical average is about sixty-five thousand dollars. In Peking, the largest and smallest amounts of capital of native banks are two hundred thousand and three thousand dollars respectively, The larger number is found for banks with one hundred thousand dollars and next to them for those with fifty thousand dollars. Approximately fifty thousand dollars is the arithmetical average amount. (See Table IV)

According to the above illustration, it is apparent that the amount of capital in Peking native banks is far less than in Tientsin. It shows that the business of native banks is more prosperous in Tientsin than in Peking, independently of the fact that the number of native banks is less in Peking. The minute details of distribution of capital will be shown in the following Table. (Refer to Appendix)

Table IV. The Distribution of Capital Investments

of Tientsin & Peking Native Banks

Ranges (unit $)	Medium	Tientsin		Peking	
		Number of Native Banks	Percentage	Number of Native Banks	Percentage
Below 5,000				2	2.90
5,000— 14,999	10,000			2	2.90
15,000— 24,999	20,000	35	15.29	13	18.84
25,000— 34,999	30,000	12	5.24	8	11.59
35,000— 44,999	40,000	22	9.61	5	7.25
45,000— 54,999	50,000	56	24.47	14	20.29
55,000— 64,999	60,000	26	11.36	5	7.25
65,000— 74,999	70,000	1	0.43	1	1.45
75,000— 84,999	80,000	10	4.37	1	1.45
85,000— 94,999	90,000	—	—	—	—
95,000—104,999	100,000	50	21.85	15	21.73
105,000—114,999	110,000	—	—	—	—
115,000—124,999	120,000	4	1.75	2	2.98
125,000—134,999	130,000	—	—	—	—
135,000—144,999	140,000	—	—	—	—
145,000—154,999	150,000	6	2.62	—	—
155,000—164,999	160,000	2	0.86	—	—
165,000—174,999	170,000	—	—	—	—
175,000—184,999	180,000	—	—	—	—
185,000—194,999	190,000	—	—	—	—
195,000—204,999	200,000	4	1.73	1	1.45
Above 205		1*	0.41	—	—
Total		229	100%	69	100%

*$ 400,000

3. *The volume of business done* — On account of the conservative character and imperfect accounting system of the native
bankers, it is very difficult to investigate the total amount of business
transactions of each bank, even for public services. In accordance
with the figures published in the Tientsin Yung Pao (天津庸報) of
January 24th and 25th 1941 (民國三十年) only seventy-four native
banks out of the 229 made their business volume known. The figures
concerning others cannot possibly be investigated, even in the
Tientsin and Peking Native Bankers' Associations. At any event, these
figures can be deemed as representative of the whole, so that we
see how the business of native banks is carried on, for these seventy-
four native banks are comparatively larger and more important in
Tientsin, their total capital investment is about six million dollars
($5,966,000) and the volume of their business last year (1940) was
about seventy-six milllion dollars ($76,010,603.40). So we may find that
the volume of business for last year was nearly thirteen times the
amount of their capital. Their total profit was over two million
dollars ($2,278,000), which was nearly two fifths of their capital.
(See Appendix)

With regard to the profit and loss of all native banks in
both Tientsin and Peking in 1940 (民國二十九年), the figures are
inaccurate in fact, although they are either published in newspapers,
or reported to the native bankers' association or to public services.
Bankers regard them as their own secret, that no other party can
possibly know. Thus the figures of profit and loss of Tientsin and
Peking native banks are put in the appendix only as information for
reference. From which we can say only that, if the profit reported
by a native bank is large, the native bank has done its regular and
proper business. On the other hand, if the native bank deals in
speculative transactions, the profit reported is usually smaller than
the real figures, so that the secret may be kept. Concerning the
losses, at least they are partially incorrect, for there are many native
banks whose dealings in speculative transactions are only partly
known by the political circles. So fictitious figures are reported

to avoid suspicions. The credit of these banks is often very good, so that figures showing losses cannot affect them. On the whole, the majority of native banks made more profits in 1939 (民國二十八年) than last year (1940).[5]

Notes of the Chapter

1—天津之銀號　王子建,趙赮謙合著（法商學院研究室）P. 1—P..5
2—Personal interview with Mr. C. P. Wei（魏景彭君）
　　　of Tah Chung Bank　　　　　　　　　Aug. 21st 1940
3—楊著中國金融論　楊蔭溥著　（黎明書店）　　P. 274—P. 279
4—中國金融論　張輯顏著　（商務印書館）　　　P. 1
5—Personal interviews with Mr. C.C. Han(韓智齋君),
　　　Manager of Teh Fêng Native Bank; and
　　　Mr. C. F. Wang（王春楚君）　　　　　　March 26th 1941
6—中國錢莊概要　潘子豪著　（華通書局）　　　P. 13—P. 16
7—Binyuan Chu: Banking Practice　　　　　P. 23—P. 24
8—(書名同 4.)　　　　　　　　　　　　　P. 302
9—銀行經營論　朱斯煌著　（商務印書館）　　　P. 14—P. 15
10—Personal interviews with Mr. C.P. Wei（魏景彭君),
　　　Manager of Teh Hûng Native Bank; & Mr.
　　　F.C. Sun（孫芳忱君), Chief-accountant of Teh
　　　Fêng Native Bank.　　　　　　　　　March 23rd 1941
11—Speech of Mr. C. C. Han（韓智齋君), Manager of
　　　Teh Fêng Native Bank, recorded by Mr. J.C.
　　　Pien（邊榮璟君筆記）
12—中華幣制史　張家驤著　（民國大學）　　　P. 50
13—現代世界經濟史綱要　伍純武著　（商務印書館）　P. 317
14—Personal interview with Mr. C.C. Han（韓智齋君）April 13th 1941
15—(書名同 1.) 附錄　　　　　　　　　　　P. 33
16—(書名同 6.)　　　　　　　　　　　　　P. 34—P. 36
17—(書名同 1.)　　　　　　　　　　　　　P. 7—P. 8
18—Personal interviews with Mr. H. Y. Lu,（陸效楊君）
　　　and Mr. P.H. Hsü（徐本河君）of Tientsin Native
　　　Bankers' Association　　　　　　　　March 19th 1941

19—Personal interviews with Mr. C.P. Wei(魏景彭君),
　　　Manager; Mr. C. C. Wan (宛游川君) of Teh
　　　Hûng Native Bank; and Mr. C. M. Ma (馬長
　　　民君)　　　　　　　　　　　　　　　　Feb. 16th 1941

20—(書名同 7.)　　　　　　　　　　　　　P. 200

21—(書名同 6.)　　　　　　　　　　　　　P. 42—P. 43

22—北京銀錢業　劉奇新著　（東方大學論文）　P. 4—P.7

23—(書名同 6.)　　　　　　　　　　　　　P. 54—P56

24—(書名同 1.)　　　　　　　　　　　　　P. 15—P.16

25—(書名同 1.)　　　　　　　　　　　　　P. 49—P. 52

26—Personal interview with Mr. C. S. Chang (張秀
　　　山君), Sub-Manger of Teh Hung Native Bank March 5th 1941

27—(書名同 1.)　　　　　　　　　　　　　P. 52—P59

28—(書名同 22.)　　　　　　　　　　　　　P. 16

29—Personal interview with Mr. S. S. Shang (尚綬
　　　珊君) of Peking Native Bankers' Association April 9th 1941

30—Personal interview with Mr. S. C. Chiao (焦世卿君),
　　　Chairman of Tientsin Native Bakers' Associa-
　　　tion, and Manager of Hsin Shêng Native Bank April 2nd 1941

CHAPTER II.

THE CLASSIFICATION AND ORGANIZATION OF ACCOUNTS

I. The Classification of Accounts

The object of all kinds of business is the acquisition of profit. Opposite to profit is what we call loss. The accounts distribute under specified headings the assets and liabilities of a business concern, in order to calculate the changes in value of these assets and liabilities resulting from business transactions and to determine the profit or loss of the business.[1]

Generally, the accounts are classified into three categories namely assets, liabilities, and profit and loss. The contents of each category vary according to the scope of the business. Ordinary business concerns or factories are interested in buying and selling or manufacturing. They have a large quantity of material assets, such as machinery, stocks etc., and big liabilities, like bank overdrafts, corporation loans and so on. The main items affecting profit and loss are the proceeds of sales and the cost of buying; therefore, the different accounts are classified in accordance with these conditions. But the business of banks and native banks is quite different: their main business is to receive and give credit. The items of credit and debit with third parties are far more important than any others, and the main sources of profit and loss are interests and general expenditures. So the classification of accounts of native banks is different from that of other business concerns,[1][2] even though it is partly similar to that of modern banks.

Formerly the classification of accounts was very simple, only a few headings were used; but nowadays, everything is more complex on account of the development and complexity of the business of native banks. As a consequence, the classification of accounts has been reformed and developed, in order to meet the various needs.[2 3]

Up to now the classification of accounts is not yet unified, because it is fixed by the manager of the native bank according to his own opinion and experience. Sometimes it is similar for various banks if the managers belong to the same group (帮). but sometimes it is not. There are neither books nor records from which the accounting system of native banks can be found, even in Chinese. The only way to get some idea of the system is to collect the headings of accounts used by many larger native banks and to pick up the similar names used in practice. We deem that they are the most suitable to native banks. In recent years, due to the enforcement of income tax, many native banks tried to use the names or methods of modern bank accounting system in the place of the old native bank accounting system; but hitherto there are only a few native banks organized completely on the lines of modern banks.[3 4 5] Then we shall omit them in this essay.

In native banks, the "Hu Pèn" (護本) is a peculiar feature, that is never found in modern banks.[6] It will be included in the section of proprietorship apart from liabilities items, whereas the other items of assets, liabilities and profit and loss will be discussed in the following chapter. These items may, in general terms, be said to be fourfold:

1. **Assets**[1 7]
    Cash
    Gold and Silver Bullion
    Debit Account with other Native Banks
    Investments
    Bills Discounted
    Overdrafts on Credit Account with other Native Banks
    Overdrafts against Securities on Current Account
    Overdrafts on Current Account

Current Secured Loans

Current Unsecured Loans

Secured Loans

Unsecured Loans

Loans guaranteed by Persons or Firms

Forfeited Securities

Debit Account with other Native Banks of outside Localities

Overdrafts on credit account with Native Banks of outside
        Localities

Account with Head Office and Branches

Accounts Receivable

Securities Purchased

Native Bank Buildings

Office Furniture

Suspense Account Dr.

Accrued Interest Receivable

Preliminary Expenses

Maintenance and Repairs

2. Liabilities [7] [8] [9] [10] [11]

Balance Carried from Preceding Year

Profit and Loss for Preceding Term

Profit and Loss for Present Term

Current Accounts

Special Current Deposits

Fixed Deposits

Deposit Receipts

Temporary Deposits

Credit Account with other Native Banks

Overdrawn Account with other Native Banks

Credit Account with other Native Banks of outside Localities

Overdrawn Accounts with other Native Banks of outside
        Localities

Drafts Payable
Account with Head Office and Branches
Account Payable
Securities Sold
Dividend Unpaid
Interest Unpaid

3. Proprietorship

Capital—It is apparent that the capital is the foundation of
the business of every native bank, and it simultaneously belongs to the proprietors; so it is treated as
aliability.[6]

"Hu Pên" (護本)—There are two meanings of "Hu Pên". One
is a special long-term deposit of the proprietor for the
purpose of assisting the circulation of capital. The
native bank should pay a higher interest, but the
proprietor is not allowed to withdraw a part or the
whole of this special deposit, unless both the proprietor
and the manager agree, or the native bank is liquidat-
ed. The native bank may use it just as freely as its
capital. This special deposit is deposited under the
name of "Hu Pên", if mentioned in the contract, or
under any other name according to the proprietor's
will.[7][12][13] It is deemed to be a special kind of capital.

The other meaning is that the proprietor advances a
certain sum of money temporarily for urgent needs of the
native bank. After that period, if the proprietor does not
want to take it back, it will be added to the capital,
but a certain interest has to be paid.[4][5][6] In fact, the
first manner is more convenient.

Reserve Fund (公積金) (厚成) (財神股)—It is the accumulation of net profits after all expenses have been paid,
decided by agreement between the proprietors and the

managers, or provided for by a clause of the contract. The object of this Reserve is to conserve the resources of the enterprise either for the purpose of (1) providing extra working capital or (2) increasing the financial stability of the native bank.[14]

4. Profit and Loss[9]

Interest Received
 Interest on Loans
 Interest on Debit Account with other Native Banks and
   Modern Banks
 Interest on Account with Head Office and Branches
 Miscellaneous Interests

Interest Paid
 Interest on "Hu Pên"[15]
 Interest on Current Deposits
 Interest on Fixed Deposits
 Interest on Credit Account with other Native Banks and
   Modern Banks
 Interest on Account with Head Office and Branches
 Miscellaneous Interests

Remittance Charges
Commissions
Rents Received
Profit and Loss on Investments
Miscellaneous Profit and Loss
Bad Debts
Bad Debts Collected
Preliminary Expenses Written off
Depreciation on Native Bank Buildings
Depreciation on Furniture
General Expenses
Salaries and Wages
Diet Fees

Rents
Taxes
Fares
Stationery Expenses
Water and Electricity
Entertainment Charges
Maintenance and Repairs
Stamps, Telephone and Telegraph Charges
Travelling Expenses
Printing Expenses
Insurance Premium
Policemen Fees or Gratuity Fees
Auditors' Fees
Lawyers' Fees
Newspapers and Magazines Charges
Miscellaneous Expenses

II. The Types and Organization of Accounts

1. Original evidence of transactions

In old Chinese business firms, especially in native banks, the confidence in the staff was the general rule. The proprietor reposed a considerable trust in the manager, and the manager confided in the staff, so that the evidence was of less importance. Even so, breaches of confidence were very scarce. That was the old Chinese business honesty which has decreased little by little. Consequently the evidence of each transaction becomes more important. The kinds of original evidences of transactions, used in recent years, have increased in number, in order to meet the various needs.[15]

(a) "Chě Tze" (摺子)—In Chinese, it is called "Chê Tze" (摺子) or "Cha Tze" (札子) and is used extensively in native banks. It is made of a long and thin Chinese locally made paper, which is folded into many leaves, each of which is about four inches long and two inches wide, with two coloured thicker papers sticking on the first and last leaves. On the face of the first leaf, a label is attached, that it is used for writing the title of the "Chê Tze." Inside the "Chê Tze", the name of the native bank, the year of issue, the series-number of the "Chê Tze" in red ink, and the name of the manager are either written or stamped on the back of the first leaf, and a revenue stamp is affixed on the top. The records are entered on both sides of the leaves continuously. A separate cover is prepared like a small box and the name of the native bank is usually printed thereon.[16]

Fig. I. The forms of a "Chê Tze" and its cover

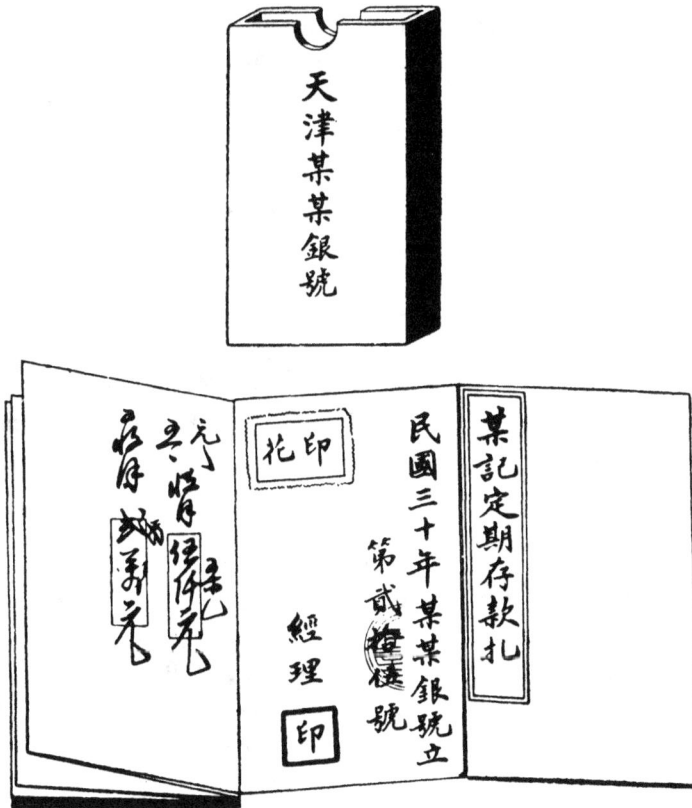

This "Chê Tze" may be used for any kind of deposits, loans, and for the storage and withdrawal of goods in the warehouse of a native bank. It is delivered by the native bank to its customers and each entry is just the same as the entry posted in the "Liu Shui" (流水); the vertical columns of both the "Liu Shui" and the "Chè Tze" are identical. If the "Chè Tze" is used only in part at the end of the Chinese fiscal year, the use may be continued for the following year, but a new revenue stamp should be pasted on it. When a "Chê Tze" is completely filled up, it has to be returned to the native bank which has issued it.[16]

(b) *Cheques and "Poh Tiao"* (撥條)—They are credit instruments used for the withdrawal of money in current-account, and they are usually treated as cash.[17] This kind of instruments may be classified into three categories, viz. cheque, "foreign paper" (番紙), and "Poh Tiao", The forms and names are different, but the nature is identical.[18]

All the three kinds may be bound in cheque-books, "foreign paper" books and "Poh Tiao" books, or they may be in the form of pads. All of them should be numbered consecutively before use, and the series-number of each one should be later accounted for. In the present time, most modern banks use mechanical devices, designed to prevent alterations, in writing cheques;[19] but such devices are used very little in native banks, because it is practically impossible to alter the words written in Chinese black ink by Chinese quill pen, if the figures are written in Chinese capital letters.

Two kinds of cheques are used by the enterprises. One of them is drawn on a modern bank by the native bank (See Fig. II) and the other is used by customers other than native banks or modern banks to draw on the native bank (See Fig. III). These customers are specially called "Wai Hang Chia" (外行家) by the enterprise. The nly difference between the two kinds is that the latter cannot be paid in cash but only used for transfer. If the customer wants to withdraw cash, the two words "Ch'ü Hsien" (取現) should be written on the cheque and the seal of the drawer stamped on these words. This cheque is effective only when the fold of the depositor is brought together to the native bank.[20][21]

Fig. II. The form of cheque drawn on a modern bank by a native bank.

Fig. III. The form of cheque drawn on the native bank by a customer.

銀號向銀行開出之支票

憑票祈付　國幣
第　　　號
此致天津　銀行台照
中華民國　年　月　日
或持票人
元整

外行家向銀號開出之支票

支票

憑票祈交　國幣
第　　　號
中華民國　資號台照　年　月　日
只能撥交取現不憑
或來人
元整

The instrument used by the native banks for drawing on foreign banks is called "foreign paper" (See Fig. IV). There is one thing peculiar, that only a special word, which is fixed by the Chinese comprador of the foreign bank is used in the place of its original title. It is often changed when there is a new comprador.

It is a custom that the character "Chi" (記) is added below the representative word.[30] The following table shows the words used for foreign banks in "foreign paper".

Table IV. The Representative Words of Foreign Banks[32]

The Names of Foreign Banks		The Representative Words	
Chartered Bank of India, Australia, and China	(麥加利)	"I Chi"	義記
Hongkong and Shanghai Banking Corporation	(匯豐)	"T'ung Chi"	同記
Chase Bank	(大通)	"C'hi Chi"	北記
Banque de l'Indo-Chine	(東方匯理)	"Chu Chi"	竹記
Banque Franco-Chinoise pour le Commerce et l'Industrie	(中法工商)	"Chung Fa Chang Fang"	中法帳房
National City Bank of New York	(花旗)	"Shou Chi"	守記
Yokohama Specie Bank	(橫濱正金)	(Formerly:- "Hsin Chi") Nowadays:- "Chen Chin Chang Fang"	(非:信記) 正金帳房
Banque Belge pour l'Etranger Extrême-orient	(華比)	"Ts'ai Chi"	采記
Deutsch-Asiatische Bank	(德華)	"Hsin Chi"	新記

There are two forms of "Poh Tiao": one is used by the modern banks to draw on a native bank (See Fig. V), and the other by the "Wai Hang Chia", the enterprise being the drawee. The form of the lattter is like that of the cheques used by a "Wai Hang Chia".[50] (See Fig. VI)

Fig. IV. The form of Foreign Paper

Fig. V. The form of "Poh Tiao" for Modern Banks.

Fig. VI. The form of "Poh Tiao" for Customers

中華民國　年　月　日
記國幣　　元整
取　計數登摺繳回作廢
銀號向外商銀行開出之番紙（同業用）

中華民國　年　月　日
憑條撥交
國幣
資號台照
第　號　元整
銀行向銀號開出之撥條

中華民國　年　月　日
憑條所交
國幣
銀號台照
第　號
面生要保取現不退
計數不緻容後登摺
元整此致
外行家向銀號開出之撥條

(c) *"Yuan Tiao Ta"* (原條打)—Generally the business concerns use the original receipts or invoices in the same manner as the various kinds of cheques, in order to save time and avoid the trouble of cash payments. This process is also called "Yuan P'iao Poh" (原票撥). The business concern just writes a few words "X X Native bank pay accordingly" (某某銀號照交), affixes its seal under these words and notes the date on the original invoice, which is returned to the messenger of the creditor firm. This messenger can go to the native bank directly and request for payment. The bank is bound to pay if the seal or signature is correct. This invoice should be given back to the debtor concern by the native bank, when the amount paid is entered in the "Chê Tze" of the concern. This procedure is called "Return after payment" or "Chi Shu Chiao Hui" (給數交回) in Chinese.[23]

    Another case of this "Yuan Tiao Ta" can be found in the "Hui Tui Chuang" (匯兌莊) when a "Wai K'o" (外客), who is a customer from an outside locality, comes to demand payment. The "Hui Tui Chuang" usually does not pay cash, but only writes a few words "X X Native bank consider it to be a guarantee and pay accordingly" (某某銀號討保照交), and the rest is just the same as explained in the preceding paragraph.[23]

    (d) *Poh Mar* (撥碼) — This kind of transfer order is used specially in Tientsin. There are two uses of "Poh Mar": the first one is to replace cash when a business concern wants to withdraw or overdraw money according to its "Chê Tze"; it can also be used for transfer when money is paid or received between native banks which are not "Ch'uan Huan Chia" (川换家).[18]

    The form is very simple without any lines or words printed. It is only a piece of Chinese made "Mao Pien" Paper (毛邊紙) approximately two inches wide, and four inches long. The necessary mentions are very few, only the name of the drawee, the amount and the date. No name of drawer is written; he stamps on it a special seal which contains a few unimportant words denoting the nature of the "Poh Mar", such as "Chi Shu Pu Chiao, Tso Wei Fei Chih" (計數不繳.作爲廢紙), "Mo Hao Chi Shu, Ch'u Hsien Pu P'ing" (某號計數.取現不憑), "Chi Shu Pu Chiao, Teng Chang Tso Fei" (計數不繳.登帳作廢) "Wang Lai Chi Shu, Ch'u Hsien Pu P'ing" (往來計數 取現不憑) and so on. Each native bank has its own special seal on which certain words are carved, and only other native banks can distinguish who the drawer is.[18]

    The four different types of "Poh Mar" which are found in the enterprises are "Chao Chiao Mar" (照交碼), "Shou X X Chang

Mar" (收某某帳碼), "Shou Chang Mar" (收帳碼) and "Chien Mar" (見碼). On the "Chao Chiao Mar" it is written "X X Pay accordingly" (某某照交), that means that the name of the native bank written on the order is the drawee. This requests the drawee to pay (See Fig. VII). The second one "Shou X X Chang Mar" means that the payment can be collected from the native bank mentioned on the order which is adressed to the payee (See Fig. VIII). Both of them are used for payment. Thus they are exactly identical in nature although the forms are different.[18]

On the "Shou Chang Mar" the words "Shou Chang" (收帳) are written in order to show that the amount has been received by or transferred to a native bank which is in relation of "Ch'uan Huan" with the drawer. Then the former "Poh Mar" is settled and cancelled after this order has been issued (See Fig. IX). When the drawer and drawee is the same native bank, it issues to a customer the "Chien Mar" which is negotiable among native banks, and the drawer pays or records in the accounts at last. On this order, the words "Chien Mar Chao Chiao" (見碼照交) are written, which mean that any native bank may accept it for transfer.[18] (See Fig. IX)

Fig. VII. The form of "Chao Chiao Mar" **Fig. VIII. The form of "Shou X X Chang Mar"** **Fig. IX. the form of "Shou Chang Mar"** **Fig. X. The form of "Chien Mar"**

(e) *The Receipt of securities pledged.* （抵押品收條）— When the native bank grants a loan on security to a borrower, the receipt which is given to the borrower is called the "receipt of securities pledged" （抵押品收條）. It is printed in duplicate. On both parts the name of the borrower, the quality, quantity and value of the security, the date of maturity and the date of issue, as well as the interdiction to pledge again the goods by giving the receipt as a security are noted on the front side. The records of reimbursements in installments are noted on the back side, with the date of each redemption, the amount received, and the part of the security returned.[54] (See Fig. XI.)

Fig. XI. The form of Receipt of Securities Pledged
Front side

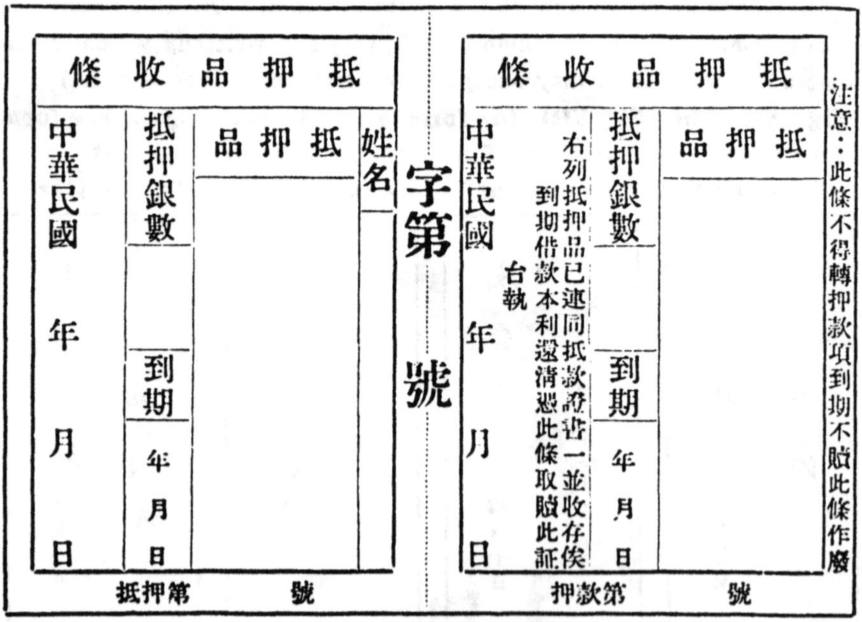

Back side

分 次 取 贖 紀 要							分 次 取 贖 紀 要						
年							年						
月							月						
日							日						
收入金額							收入金額						
付出抵押品							付出抵押品						

(f) *Bills of Exchange* (匯票) — There are three kinds of bills of exchange used in native banks for remittances, viz. the triplicate bill of exchange, the "Tui Tiao" (對條) and the so — called reformed bill of exchange. The first bill on the right side of the triplicate bill of exchange is called "P'iao Ken" (票根) and is sent to the drawee. In the middle is the second bill called "Hui P'iao" (匯票), which is the formal bill of exchange handled by the payee. The counterfoil kept by the drawer is called the "Ts'un Ken" (存根) [20] (See Fig. XII). This is usually a time bill.

Fig. XII. The Form of Triplicate Bill of Exchange

存根
字第　號
第　號　匯至　此向　中華民國　年　月　日　照付　見票遲　實號通行國幣　號認票匯到　天無利照交莫惧是荷　整言明　具

票匯
第　號　匯至　此向　中華民國　年　月　日　照付　見票遲　實號通行國幣　號認票匯到　遺失作廢　面生要保　天無利照交莫惧是荷　整言明　具

根票
字第　號
第　號　匯至　此向　中華民國　年　月　日　照付　見票遲　實號通行國幣　號認票匯到　天無利照交莫惧是荷　整言明　具

The "Tui Tiao" is the simplest form of bill of exchange. Only the name of payee and the amount are written on the middle, where the bill is cut vertically into two pieces like the shape of the teeth of a saw. The date is noted in the last row. It is effective if the seal of the enterprise is stamped (See Fig. XIII). The reason why it is so simple in form is that the amount cannot be possibly found clearly from each separate piece unless the bearer knows it in advance. So it is frequent, when the bearer of this kind of bill of exchange asked by the drawee cannot quote the amount correctly, that the native bank requires a guarantor for the payee.[35]

Fig. XIII. The Form of Tui Tiao

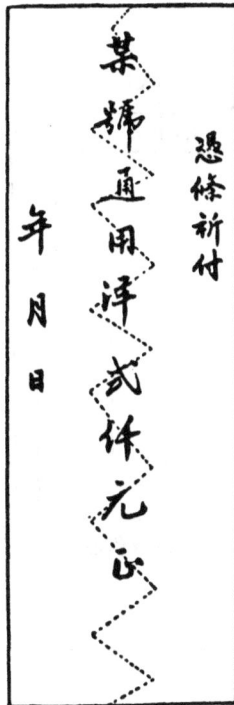

The third kind bears exactly the same mentions as those used in modern banks. It is more complicated than the above forms[36] (See Fig. XIV). As this kind of bills is used commonly both in Chinese and foreign banks, it will not be explained here.

Fig. XIV. The Form of Advice of Bills for Collection

				收款日期			國　　幣									
種類	號數	匯款人	付款人	年	月	日	百千萬千百十元角分									附註

北京　　　　銀號託　　　　收匯欵報單

中華民國　　年　　月　　日　　　　第　　號　第　　頁

上列款項　　貴號照數代收於收訖後通知敝號爲荷此致

..............................台照

北京　　　鋹號具

(g) *The documents of warehousing* (倉庫單據)—There are four kinds of documents used by the native banks, warehouses, viz. the goods receiving voucher, the goods delivering voucher, the warehouse receipt and the bill of warehouse charges; they are similar to those used in modern banks' warehouses. The goods receiving voucher is used to record the goods stored, and the goods delivering voucher for withdrawal of goods; in each of them columns are disposed for quality, quantity, marks and units of goods; the title of the bailor, date, series-number are mentioned and it bears the signature of the chief employee of the native bank and of its warehouse. The former voucher should be filled by the warehouse and sent to the native bank, but the latter one is prepared by the native bank and sent to the warehouse.[17] (See Fig. XV & XVI)

Fig. XIV. The form of goods
Receiving Voucher

天津新生銀號倉庫收貨憑單

戶名	中華民國　年　月　日　庫字第　號						
貨物種類	記　號	數　量	單位	附	註	總號	左列貨物業經收清此致
合　計							倉庫具

倉庫主任　　　　收貨員　　　　記帳員

Fig. XVI. The form of goods
Delivering Voucher

天津新生銀號倉庫發貨憑單

戶名(　　　　)中華民國　　年　　月　　日　　總字第　　號

貨物種類	記　　號	數　　量	單位	附　　註	倉庫	左列貨物希照發此致
合　　計						總號具

副經理　　　　　　主任　　　　　　帳記員

The document given to the bailor is either the warehouse receipt, or a "Chê Tze" of goods stored (存貨摺) which form has been illustrated previously. Both sides of the receipt and its counterfoil are printed. The front side is prepared for recording the date, series-number, name and adress of the bailor, the marks, quality and quantity of goods stored, the amount of insurance premium and of warehouse charges. Two tables are printed on the back side, one for recording the transfers, the other for recording the withdrawal of goods. In the first table, only the date of transfer, the names of the transferor and of transferee have to be entered; in the second the amount of goods withdrawn and of those remaining in the godown, as well as the date of withdrawal, should be recorded. Moreover brief regulations are annexed on the back.[27] (See Fig. XVII)

Fig. XVII. The Form of Warehouse Receipt

A. The Front Side

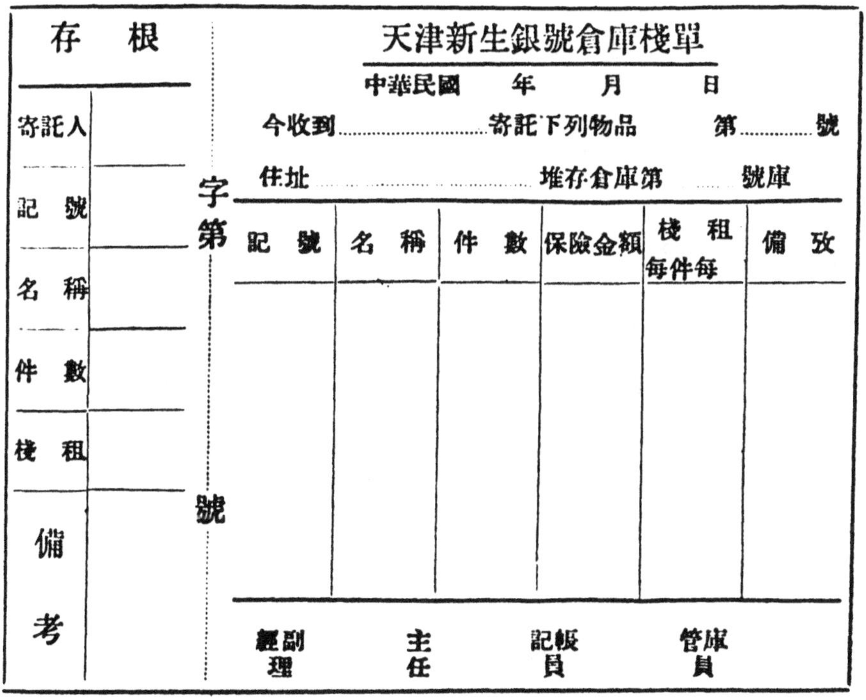

存根

寄託人	
記號	
名稱	
件數	
棧租	
備考	

字第　　號

天津新生銀號倉庫棧單

中華民國　年　月　日

今收到……寄託下列物品　第……號

住址……　堆存倉庫第……號庫

記號	名稱	件數	保險金額	棧租 每件每	備攷

副經理　主任　記帳員　管庫員

B. The Back Side

簡　　　章

一　堆存本倉庫貨物如因潮濕霉爛或鼠咬虫傷 以及天災人禍不可抵抗而受損失
　　者本倉庫不負責任

二　貨主如託本倉庫代保火險時得於棧單內註明倘有意外 按保險公司章程辦理
　　本倉庫不負責任

三　出貨時本倉庫照收存原件交出至其內容變質如何或成色不符 以及殘破短少
　　等本倉庫不負責任

四　貨物存庫發見變質損傷之处 或價值有不足抵交棧租時經本倉庫 通知限期後
　　仍不提取或清結棧租各費本倉庫有自由處分該貨之權

五　本棧單如有遺失須即報明本倉按照本倉庫章程掛失並登報覓保方可補給

過　　戶　　表			
日　　　　期	讓　與　人	受　讓　人	本倉庫簽証
年 | 月 | 日			

過戶表		
月 | 日	讓與人	受讓人

寄　託　貨　物　出　棧　表			
日　　　　期	出　棧　件　數	餘　存　件　數	本倉庫簽証
年 | 月 | 日			

出棧表		
月 | 日	出棧數	餘存數

　　　　The bill of warehouse charges is used for calculating the
charges on the goods stored in the godown: the quality, and quanity
of goods, the original date and number of days of storage, the
carriers' charges paid by the native bank on the bailor's behalf,
are entered in this bill.[17] (See Fig. XVIII)

Fig. XVIII. The Form of Bill of Warehouse Charges

天津新生銀號介庵棧租計算帳單

中華民國　年　月　日

貨物種類	數量	單位	保管時間		棧租			代墊工力			總計	
			起	止	月數 成數 星期 日數	租率	金額	貨物件數 發往地點 工力	率	金額		計

合計

經理副　　會計主任　　營業主任　　復核員　　記帳員

2. Books of Original Entry

The entries are made vertically, and the form and ruling of accounts have changed at different times and are not identical in different native banks. Orginally no lines were printed, but gradually vertical lines were introduced (See Fig. XIX), and in the books of a number of native banks a horizontal line was drawn in the middle of the page, which is divided into two parts (See Fig. XX). At the present time, other horizontal lines are often added according to the managers' or chief accountants' opinion (See Fig. XXI). The inner lines, both horizontal and vertical, in the books of accounts are printed in red color. Nowadays all of these forms are found in different native banks, but the books of accounts with vertical lines or with both vertical and one horizontal line are most commonly used.[38] It is often supposed to be an horizontal line even though there is none. The specimens are shown as follows:

Fig. XIX. & XX. The form of Account—A. & B.

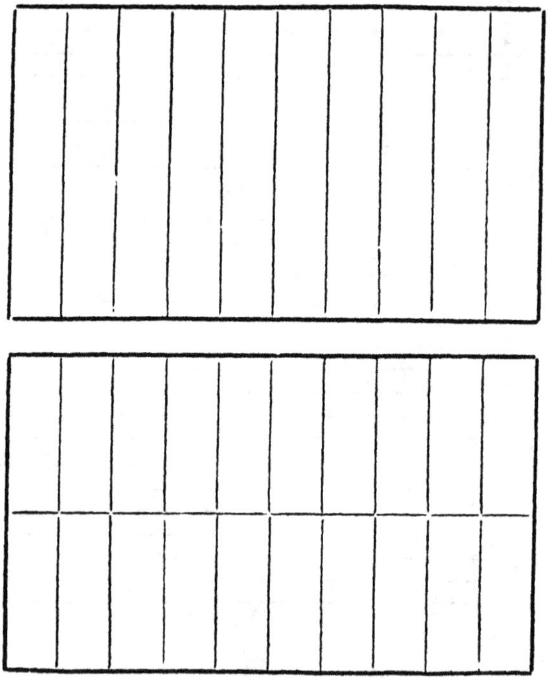

Fig. XXI. The Form of Account—C

It is a custom for accountants of native banks to write vertically, each transaction being recorded from top to bottom in each vertical column. In order to distinguish the receipts and payments, they are written at different levels. This is the reason why a horizontal line is traced in the middle, dividing into higher and lower columns as they are called, for there is no specific name given by Chinese business firms.[18] Two methods are used for recording receipts and payments: the first is to record the receipts in the higher columns, and the payments in the lower ones; the second is the reverse.

In order to show apparently the entry of a receipt or a payment, the word received (收) or paid (付) is added at the top of each entry like "Dr." or "Cr." used in double-entry book—keeping, but the word "Received" (收) may be placed in the higher or in the lower column, and the word "Paid" (付) vice versa, depending on the column chosen for recording receipts or payments. In native banks, these two methods are called "higher column showing receipts lower column showing payments" (上收下付 or 上取下支) and "higher column showing payments, lower column showing receipts" (上付下收 or 上支下取). In the present time the method of "higher column showing receipt, lower column showing payments" (上收下付) is generally adopted.[18] [19] A brief and clear explanation is noted besides the item within the column.[20]

Formerly the words "received" and "paid", in Chinese "收" and "付", were not generally used by native banks, but instead the words "入" and "出" the meaning of which is exactly the same.[12]

The old method of recording transactions with the same firm or person at the same time was to write them in "Su Chou Figures" (蘇州碼)[15] cumulatively in the same column, with or without a very simple explanation (See Fig. XXII). This method was used very often in Peking Chu Pao Shih (珠寶市) during the Ch'ing dynasty.[13] It may still be found sometimes in the old P'iao Hao (票號) of the Shansi group (山西幫) at present.

Fig. XXII. The Old Method of Recording

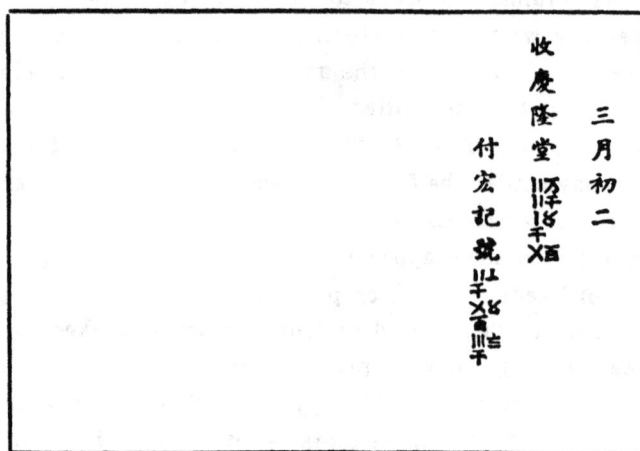

At the end of the Ch'ing dynasty and in the early years of the Republic, when both silver ingots and metallic money were used as media of exchange, there were "Liu Shui" such as journals of silver dollars called "Yang Ch'ien Liu Shui" (洋錢流水), journals of silver called "Yin Tze Liu Shui" (銀子流水) etc. for recording the rates and differences of silver ingots and silver dollars.[31] But they exist no more since the fiat money came into circulation. There was only one book of original entries in which all the transactions were recorded (including cash) in the Ch'ing dynasty, but at end of the Empire it was divided into two main books, which are universally used by all native banks in both Peking and Tientsin, though the names are not uniform. In Peking they are called "Liu Shui Chang" (流水帳), and "Liu Tze" (溜子) in Tientsin.[13]

(a) *"Hsien Chin Liu Shui"* (現金流水).—In the Peking group, it is called "Hsien Chin Liu Shui" (現金流水); in Tientsin, it was formerly called "Hsien Yang Liu" (現洋溜), which name has now been changed into "Hsien Chin Shou Fu Liu" (現金收付溜).[13] As the Peking group is more prosperous and more numerous, the term "Hsien Chin Liu Shui" (現金流水) will be used in this essay. All cash receipts and disbursements are recorded in this book. By cash we mean money, or what represents money such as cheques,[28] or what is called "Foreign Paper" (番紙)[12] by native banks, etc. The principle of the Chinese method of accounting is the double-entry book-keeping in idea, but single-entry in form; it is sometimes more convenient for certain series transactions in native banks.[30] Almost every transaction in a native bank deals with money, hence the records of cash transactions are of the greatest importance; they are similar to the Cash Book of the double entry book-keeping.

The items of receipts and disbursements are recorded in the higher and lower columns respectively, but the date should be written at right, in the first vertical column at the beginning of every day, before any transaction is recorded.[30] It is customary for the accountants of native banks to balance the cash book every day. It is done by adding up the totals of receipts and of disbursements, and the difference between the two mentioned totals represents the amount of cash in hand (庫存) which is recorded in the last column of that day by adding two words "cash in hand" (結存) at the top of the amount, and it is carried forward to the next day.[30]

Fig. XXIII. The Form of Recording in "Hsien Chin Liu Shui"

					收公成號七百五十元 鈔 付茂記五百元 鈔	四月二日	結存四萬〇三百五十元

　　(b) *"Chuan Chang Liu Shui"* (轉帳流水)—This is also one of the two main books of original entry in Native banks. It is often named "Chuan Chang Liu Shui" (轉帳流水) or "Kuo Pi Liu Shui" (國幣流水) by native bankers of the Peking and Shêng-Chi Groups. In Tientsin, "Poh Yang Liu" (撥洋溜) was used previously as the name of the book, but the name of "Chuan Chang Shou Fu Liu" (轉帳收付溜) is adopted in many native banks of the Tientsin group.[12]

　　This book is used for recording all the transactions except cash, that means any transaction without cash payment or receipt, but only through cheques or "transfer orders" or "Poh Mar" (撥碼),[13] or "Tui Hua" (對話),[3] or "Poh Tiao" (撥條), or other documents. Its nature is identical to that of journals in double entry book-keeping. Due to the nature of transfers from one account to another,[13] each item of receipt must have one or more opposite items of payment, and vice versa, the same as in the journal of the double-entry book-keeping.[13] The date should be written at the beginning of every day as in the "Hsien Chin Liu Shui" (現金流水), and a clear and simple explanation should be noted beside each item, especially the name of the native banks from which the "Poh Mar" (撥碼) are received, or the series-number of the cheques and the name of the bank. At the end of each day, the two totals of receipts and disbursements are added up, but there must be no difference; if there is any, the entries have to be checked up until the mistake is found. The mistakes in "Chuan Chang Liu Shui" (轉帳流水) are often caused by either addition or posting. Only one total amount of all payments or receipts is recorded in the column next to the last transaction of the day, with on the top of it, the three words "totally received and paid" (共收,付), because the amount of payments ought to be equal to that of receipts.[5]

There are no vouchers in native banks; therefore all entries in "Ti Chang" (底帳) (Refer to 3. Principal Books) are transferred from either the "Hsien Chin Liu Shui" (現金流水) or the "Chuan Chang Liu Shui" (轉帳流水). Usually, after each transaction has been recorded, this book must be passed to other accountants in order to post it to the corresponding account in the "Ti Chang" (底帳). Two or more "Chuan Chang Liu Shui" (轉帳流水) are often ready and used at the same time when business is brisk; but if one transaction contains several items, or cheques of various banks, they should be recorded in the same "Chuan Chang Liu Shui" (轉帳流水); otherwise checking would be difficult. It is a rule that in each "Liu Shui Chang" (流水帳) the total amount has to be added and noted at the end of each day.[5][13][34]

Fig. XXIV. The Form of Recording in "Chuan Chang Liu Shui"

(c) *"Ying Yeh Kai Chih Liu Shui"* (營業開支流水)—In addition to the above two main books, there is also another book used for recording the expenditures of the enterprise, but it is not used in most native banks; only larger ones have it. This book is kept and recorded by the accountant for general affairs. Its nature is similar to the Petty Cash book of the modern accounting system, but with the difference that all the items are payments, and no receipt is recorded until the total amount is deducted from the gross profit at the end of each year, or half year, or before one of the three Chinese festivals (三節), when this account will be closed. This book is instituted for the purpose of putting aside the miscellaneous small payments which may easily be confused with business transactions[5]. It is customary that a certain amount of money be advanced for expenditures and recorded in the "Hsien Chin Liu Shui", but this amount may or not be recorded in a "Ying Yeh Kai Chih Liu Shui" or temporarily on a wooden board called "Shui Pai"[15] (水牌).

Fig. XXV. The Form of Recording in "Ying Yeh Kai Chih Liu Shui"

					付福食七十元八毛 米一袋	付紙費二元二毛 工商報費	付印刷費四元二毛 小帳	付郵電費五毛 郵票	四月五日

(d) *"Huo Wu Liu Shui"* (貨物流水) — It is used specially in the native banks which have warehouses. All the storings and withdrawings of goods are registered in this book; the receiving and paying of goods stored are recorded in the higher and lower columns respectively; the word "Received" (收) or "Paid" (付) is added on the top of each corresponding transaction. The date and method of recording are just the same as in the "Hsien Chin Liu Shui" (現金流水), but none of the transactions dealing with money can be recorded therein, including the warehouse charges (棧租), insurance premium and so on. At the end of each day, the amount of each kind of goods should be added and balanced separately and the amounts written one by one after the last transaction of the day. The records in the "K'o Hao Ts'un Huo Chang" (客號存貨帳) which is the stock account with individual persons, and "Shang Hao Ts'un Huo Chang" (商號存貨帳) that means the stock account with business concerns, are posted from this book.[37]

Fig. XXVI. The Form of Recording in "Huo Wu Liu Shui"

付跑魁元米五袋	付協盛公司棉紗二十件	收東廣號棉紗一百件	三月一日

3. Principal Books

"*Ti Chang*" (底帳)—This is called variously in native banks "Ti Chang" (底帳) or "Tah Chang" (大帳). It is to be considered as one of the main books of the accounting system of the enterprise, and is corresponding to ledgers of double-entry Book-keeping. The forms of this book are various in different native banks. The most common form is identical to that of the book of original entry. Another form which is also used commonly nowadays, has the first vertical column from the right side double in width, and a short horizontal line traced in the middle of this wider column. The upper column is used for the name of account: the lower one is prepared for particulars; so the word "Particulars" (摘要) is printed on the top of this lower column[5] (See Fig. XXVI). There is another peculiar form designed by an auditor and used by a few native banks, where three horizontal lines are traced at the bottom and form three narrow bands which are used for calculating interests. On the right side of the first are the words "Dr. or Cr." (存或欠), of the second "Number of days" and of the lowest "Product" (積數).[*] (See Fig. XXVII)

Fig. XXVII. The Form of "Ti Chang"—A

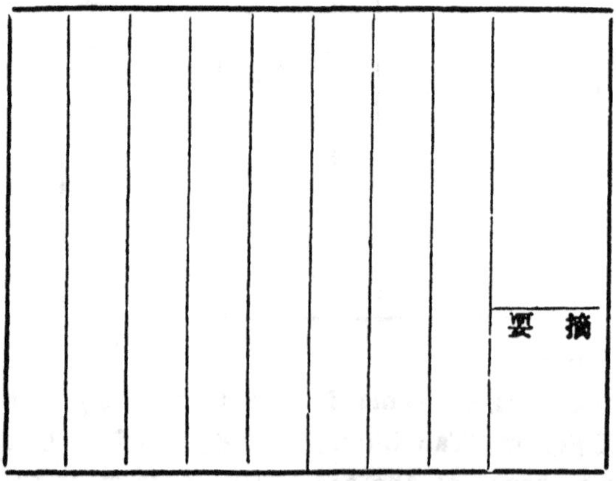

Fig. XXVIII. The Form of "Ti Chang"—B

This form is more complete and convenient, for it is similar to the forms used in modern bank accounting systems, and avoids the defects of the old forms used in native banks; but it is to be regretted that it is not yet generally used.

There are many volumes of "Ti Chang" (底帳): one or more volumes are used for recording each kind of account; they may be subdivided in different titles. On the first page of each volume, an index may be written[4] (See Fig. XXIX), and on the lower edge the name of the account is written (See Fig. XXX), in order to have it readily at hand for reference.[5]

Fig. XXIX The Form of Index of "Ti Chang"

Fig. XXX. Side Title on "Ti Chang"

Every entry in the "Ti Chang" (底帳) is posted from either the "Hsien Chin Liu Shui" (現金流水) or the "Chuan Chang Liu Shui" (轉帳流水). This is similar to the posting in the Italian accounting system, but an entry made in the higher column of the "Hsien Chin Liu Shui" must be entered also in the higher column of a "Ti Chang" and the lower column entries in the "Hsien Chin Liu Shui" must appear also in the lower column in the "Ti Chang".[34] The rule for posting in native banks' accounts is:

"TO POST IN THE SAME COLUMN OF THE INDIVIDUAL ACCOUNT AS THAT WHERE THE ITEMS APPEAR IN THE BOOK OF ORIGINAL ENTRY".

Items of the "Hsien Chin Liu Shui" or "Chuan Chang Liu Shui" have to be reported to the various accounts of the "Ti Chang", when a new transaction is recorded. For the purpose of showing that an entry has been already reported, a red word "Posted" (過) is marked on the top of the item in the book of original entry.[35]

All the accounts of the "Ti Chang" are balanced exactly in the same way as for other books, i. e. the difference between the totals of the two columns is ascertained, the balance is written every day in "Su Chou Figures" (蘇州碼) informally. If there is a debit balance, the amount is placed on the top of the last transaction of the day, preceded by the word "Ts'un" (存). The credit balance is usually calculated at the end of each accounting period, viz. end of each year, or half year, or at the three festivals (三節).[15][36]

When a book of accounts is going to be used up, an entry should be made in the last column of the book to show that the total balance is paid (付), with the note: "transferred to a new book" (更入新帳). If it is a debit balance (收差), a new book is opened, and the balance is posted in the higher column (收方) with the note "transfered from the old book" (由舊帳更來). One thing peculiar is that a counter-entry may be made when the original entry is wrongly recorded. On the top of each of these two entries, a red seal "Ch'ung" (冲) which means "written off" is stamped, whereby the two entries are cancelled.[3][4][37]

The books of accounts used in Native Banks may be classified into four categories, viz., for general transactions, for remittances, for warehousing and for speculative transactions.[38] The titles of accounts are shown as follows:—

A. For general transactions (正規營業) — In native banks these accounts are customarily called "Tso Chia Tze" (作架子) or "Chê Chiao" (摺交).[38]

(1) *Proprietorship account* — It is called "Wan Chin Chang" (萬金帳): the contract of the proprietors and the amount of capital invested, together with the "Hu Pên" (護本), are noted therein. The annual reports should be recorded in this account continuously.[25][39]

(2) *Capital account* — The various names under which the account is known in native banks are; "Tzu Pên Chang" (資本帳) "Ku Pên Chang" (股本帳), and "Tzu Pên Chin" (資本金), as well as "Ken Shêng" (根深) which was the former name. The name of the proprietors and the amount of capital are recorded in it, and it remains constant until the capital is changed.[12][13][80] This book is usually kept by the manager or the chief accountant.[37][39]

(3) *"Hu Pen" account* (護本帳) — It is an account for the records of the proprietors' special long-term deposits, and of the interests for each period. It is usually annexed to the capital account.[12][37][7] But if the "Hu Pên" is not mentioned in the contract, it is entered in the book of fixed deposits accounts.[13][39]

(4) *Reserve Fund account* (公積帳) — It is customarily called "Hou Chêng" (厚成) or "Tsai Shen Ku" (財神股) by native banks but in a few of them special names are used such as "Kung Chi Tang" (公積堂); "Teh Li Tang" (得利堂), "Fu Li Tang" (福利堂) etc., formed by some lucky words,[12] and it is treated as a personal account. Normally a part of the surplus is reserved at the end of every three years, and entered into this account, but in some native

banks, the reserve is recorded at the end of each business year.[12][13][30]

(5) *Fixed deposits account* (定期存款帳)—The name of "P'iao Ts'un" (票存)was used preoviously. All the deposits for fixed periods at a certain rate of interest, deposited by persons, business concerns, persons under designation of household or "Tang" (堂) and so on, are entered in this book.[39]

(6) *Unsecured loans account* (定期放款帳) — In old native banks it is named "P'iao Chi'en" (票欠). It records the loans of the native bank to the business concerns or persons, where a certain period of time is allowed for reimbursement.[30]

(7) *Current deposits and loans account* (來往存欠帳)—It is also called "Wang Lai Chang" (往來帳). This is the record of dates, amounts and interests on money drawn or deposited, and of overdrafts and reimbursements by the customers.[5][26][39]

(8) *Secured loans account* (抵押放款帳)[25][26] — This is used for recording the loans guaranteed by securities pledged by the borrowers.[50]

(9) *Loans with personal security account* (保證放款帳)[5][26] — The records of loans guaranteed by persons or firms of good standing can be found in this book.[25]

(10) *Accounts with other native banks* (本埠同業往來帳)—There are two other names used also in native banks, namely "Ch'uan Huan Chang" (川換帳) and "T'ung Yeh Chang" (同業帳). They contain the debit and credit account with other native banks of the locality.[7][30] All the transactions through "Poh Mar" (撥碼),[31] "Poh Tiao" (撥條) and Native Bank drafts (匯條) are recorded in this account.[39]

(11) *Accounts with other native banks outside the locality*[40] (外埠同業往來帳) — Another title is "Wai Fu T'ung Yeh Ts'un Ch'ien" (外埠同業存欠). The transactions with other native banks in other districts are recorded therein.

(12) *Bank account* (銀行帳)—It includes the records of both debit and credit accounts with modern banks.[39]

(13) *Outside Customers account* (外客帳) — It records the deposits or withdrawals of money by customers from other provinces, municipalities, Hsien (縣) or Chen (鎮).[39]

(14) *Suspense account* (暫記存欠帳)[36] — It may be also called "Ts'an Chi Chang" (暫記帳). All the debit and credit items for the recording of which there is no other suitable account, are entered in this account temporarily.

(15) *Interest account* (利息帳)— called also "Interest received and paid account" (進息出息帳), in which all kinds of interests received or paid are recorded.[39]

(16) *Exchange account* (昜換帳 or 兌換帳) — This account was used formerly for recording the exchange transactions between different Chinese currencies; it is no more used now on account of the unification of currency by the Government.[39]

(17) *General Expenses account* (營業開支流水) — Differently called "Daily Expenses account" (日用帳) and "Diet fees and miscellaneous expenses account" (福食,雜費). All items of miscellaneous expenses of the business appear in this account, such as salaries, wages and bonus, diet fees, travelling expenses, stamps, etc.. It is sometimes divided into many different accounts according to the various items of expenses, when it is necessary.[2 5 39]

(18) *Preliminary Expenses account* (開辦費帳) — It includes all the records of expenses disbursed for the opening of the enterprise.[9]

(19) *Furniture and Fixtures account* (營業用器具帳)[9] — The other name is "Chia Chü Chang" (傢俱帳). It records the price of furniture and fixtures.

(20) *Repairs account* (裝修費)— The expenses disbursed for general repairs of the building and furniture are recorded therein.[5 7]

(21) *Commissions account* (手續費) — where any kind of

commission received or paid is recorded.[25]

(22) *Dividend account*(股利帳)[40]—The name of this account is not uniform; it may be called by similar names such as "Chun I Chin" (純益金) and so on, as the manager of the native bank prefers. The profits of every year to be distributed to the proprietors and the management are entered in this account.[30]

(23) *Balance carried form preceding year*[40] (盈餘滾存帳) — This is the record of the surplus remaining after distribution of profits to the proprietors and manager.[31]

B. For remittances (匯兌)—Under the present conditions, the domestic remittances are much more numerous than foreign remittances,[30] especially in native banks.

(1) *Remittances account* (匯款帳)— Another name is "Receiving and paying remittances account" (收交匯款帳)[25] where all the records of remittances sent to or received from other native banks in other districts may be found.[30]

(2) *Bills account* (遲期帳)— Called also "Chi Tiao Chang" (期條帳), which records the unmatured bills. Sometimes it is annexed to the previous account.[30]

(3) *Foreign remittances account* — Apparently it records the remittances with other banks in foreign countries,[30] but nowadays it is out of use.

(4) *Remittance charges account* (電力帳)— "Yin Li Chang" (銀力帳) is a different tittle used. It is the record of remittance charges and commissions. It is sometimes annexed to the commission account[39] (手續費帳).

C. For Warehousing (倉庫帳)—The accounts used in Godowns or Warehouses which belong to the native bank, are kept both in the native bank and in the godown.[37]

(1) *Individuals storage account* (客號存貨帳)— All kinds and quantities of goods stored or withdrawn by individual persons are

registered in this book.[27]

(2) *Business firms storage account* （商號存貨帳）— It is similar to the Individuals storage account in nature; the only difference is that the bailing is done under the name of a business firm.[27]

(3) *Warehouse charges account* （倉庫費）— This book is divided into three parts, viz. godown charges, insurance premiums and porters' charges. All those charges, either paid or received, are entered in this book.[27]

D. For Speculative transactions （投機業務）—Various names of the same meaning used by native bankers are "Fu Shih" （浮事） and "T'ao Shih" （套事）. On account of the prohibition of speculative transactions by the Government, there is no formal account opened for them, although many native banks still deal mainly in speculative operations. In former times, they were allowed to do so freely, and obviously many accounts were opened.[16] They are enumerated as follows:

(1) *Investments account* （債券帳）— Where all the purchases and sales of bonds and securities are recorded.[33]

(2) *"Chai Ch'uan Sè"* （債券色）— It records the differences between selling and buying prices, as well as the fluctuations of prices.[33]

(3) *Gold Bullion account* （足金帳）— to register the amounts of gold bullion bought or sold.[32]

(4) *"Tsu Chin Sè"* （足金色）— All the differences in settling gold bullion transactions are recorded in this book.[30]

(5) *"Hsien T'ou P'iao"* （現頭票）— This is specially used for recording buying and selling of Japanese currency.[30]

(6) *"T'ou P'iao Sè"* （頭票色）— The fluctuation of prices of Japanese currency are recorded in this book.[39]

(7) *Foreign Currency suspense account* （頭票浮記）— It includes all the transactions in Japanese currency dealt with customers from

outside localities, including persons and firms, and with other native banks.[39]

(8) *"Piao Chin Sê"* (標金色)—It is the record of differences in market-price of Shanghai standard gold (標金).[39]

(9) *"Pu Sê Chang"* (補色帳)—From this account the various balances for receiving or paying gold bullion, Japanese currency, and Shanghai standard gold (標金) in dealings with other native banks can be found separately.[39]

4. Subsidiary Books — "In order to facilitate the entry of the various transactions in their respective accounts, it is necessary that the analysis should, at least to some extent, first be made in books subsidiary to the "Ti Chang." But it should be reminded that the accounting system was very simple in old native banks, and formerly no subsidiary book was kept. Only a few pieces of rough paper were used instead of them. Due to the influence of foreign bank accounting system, the accountants of native banks tried to reform and prepare one or two kinds of subsidiary books; but up to now they are still very scarce in native banks.[25]

A. Investigation tables (調查表) — These tables are used to follow closely the conditions of overdrafts on current accounts. On the top of the table the series-number should be written, and the whole table is divided into nine vertical columns, from right to left according to the Chinese method of writing, prepared for (1) the name of account (2) the address (3) the names of proprietors (4) the capital (5) the names of manager and submanager (6) the name of introducers (7) the names of guarantors (8) the amount of overdraft allowed, and (9) the procedures for account. An example of the form used is given here below. (See Fig. XXXI)[35]

Fig. XXXI. The form of Investigation Table

第　　號 ....

往來手續	透支額	保証人	介紹人	副經理	資本額	股東	住址	戶名

B. The memorandum for important documents preserved (保存要件留底)—It is prepared on the ordinary forms of accounts of the native bank. It records the securities pledged by the borrowers and other important documents, such as the agreements of telephone, water-meter, light-meter, etc.[25]

C. The memorandum for Term Bills (遲期票據留底)—All kinds of negotiable instruments due for future payment are entered in this book, on each page of which three horizontal lines and seven vertical lines are ruled. Each vertical column is divided in two parts; the name of the person who delivered the bill and the name of the drawer are written in the right row, the names of the drawee and payee, and the amount, are entered in the middle row. The date of issue and that of maturity are mentioned in the left row. All the lines and printed words are in red colour. When a bill is settled, a blue seal "Li Ch'i" (理訖) is stamped. But when there is no provision for the bill, or no seal or no stamp on the bill, or no name of payee written, it will not be paid; then a "Tui Hui" (退回) "to be returned" seal is stamped, also in blue colour.[34] (See Fig. XXII.)

Fig. XXXII. The form of memorandum for Term Bills.

交來　立天津 照付　名下國幣　整 字號　日期　月　日　取	交來　立天津 照付　名下國幣　整 字號　日期　月　日　取	交來　立天津 照付　名下國幣　整 字號　日期　月　日　取	交來　立天津 照付　名下國幣　整 字號　日期　月　日　取	交來　立天津 照付　名下國幣　整 字號　日期　月　日　取

5. Subsidiary Records

A. "Shui P'ai" (水牌)—This is one the important subsidiary records used daily. It is made of thin copper plates connected by hinges, each one being approximately eight inches long and five inches wide. They look like a book when folded up, and when expanded, they seem like a long board on which both face and back can be used for records. Though the form and rulings are not uniform, the method is the same. On each leaf, six or more vertical lines and four horizontal lines are carved or printed in black colour. There are two different forms generally used in Peking and Tientsin native banks. The first form is divided in four sections; the titles of the accounts are written in the first section; the second is used for the total amounts of receipts (存), and in the third the total amounts of payments (欠) are recorded[34] (See Fig. XXXIII). The second form is divided vertically in three sections by two horizontal lines ruled on the plate; the middle section is used for writing the titles of accounts, the first and third ones are used for receipts (存) and payments (欠) respectively.[5] (See Fig. XXXIV)

Fig. XXXIII. The Form of "Shui P'ai"—A

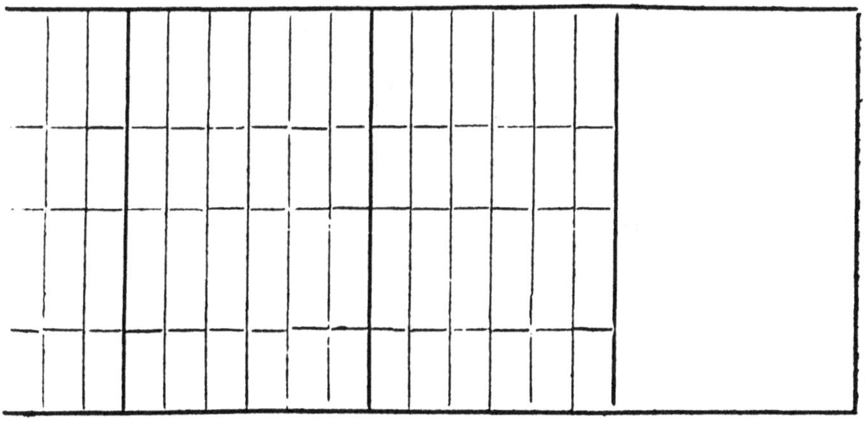

Fig. XXXIV. The Form of "Shui P'ai"—B

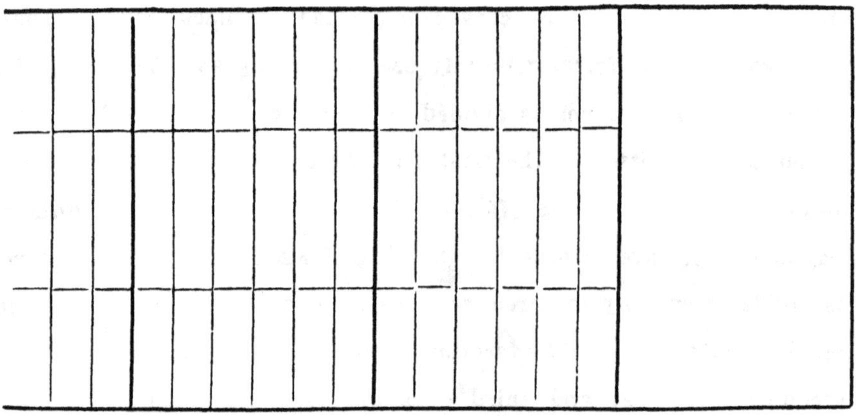

At the end of each day, the total balance of each account of the "Ti Chang" should be recorded in this "Shui P'ai", and the balance of receipts and payments is made out for detecting the errors. In native banks it is called "Ho Long Men" (合龍門), which means putting all balances appearing in the various accounts together, to ascertain the equality of the debit and credit columns.[14] That means that the total of higher columns should be equal to that of lower columns.

It serves three purposes: (1) A proof of accuracy is available to the accountant. (2) It summarizes each account, thus a bird's-eye view of the status and operation of the busines is furnished. (3) It allocates the error to a particular day and so makes it unnecessary to search in the records of any other day, if the "Ti Chang" is not balanced.

If the items of accounts are more numerous, two or more "Shui P'ai" (水牌) can be used accordingly, and it is mostly used for accounts with other native banks.[15] This "Shui P'ai" just serves as the Trial Balance in the double entry book-keeping, but the former one is prepared daily.

B. Memorandum (便查)—The form of this statement is not the same in different native banks, but the theory is identical, for it is used for daily records of the total balances of each account referring to deposits, loans or overdrafts. The balances of all accounts can be known at a glance. Each form is divided into two parts, the upper part is for debit balances (結存), and the lower one records credit balances (結欠). The first vertical column from the right side is "the number of days", the second one is the "date", and the third is "balances". Each part usually contains ten horizontal lines, the last one being reserved for the total of the balances.[35] (See Fig. XXXV)

Fig. XXXV. The Form of Memorandum

結　存	日期	日數	結　存	日期	日數
合　計			合　計		
結　欠	日期	日數	結　欠	日期	日數
合　計			合　計		

C.   Diary Book. （日清）—The method of accounting in native
banks is the double entry in idea: at the end of a certain period
(usually three to five days), a trial balance, called technically "Ho
Lung Men", must be made out accordingly. The purpose of this
book is to check up all the entries in the "Hsien Chin Liu Shui"
and the "Ti Chang". It may be further subdivided into two kinds,
which are mostly used by native banks of the Tientsin group.

(1) *"Yin Kuei Jih Ching"* （銀櫃日清） — Only Cash in hand is
recorded daily in this statement, for the purpose of showing the
total amount of cash in the native bank.[30] Formerly, there were
many kinds of silver, silver coins, token money, etc., which were
all recorded in it (See Fig. XXXVI.); so it was necessary for the
accountant to check up daily the amount of cash in hand. Nowadays
there are only two or three kinds of notes; therefore this necessity
is no more felt and many native banks have dropped this statement.[31]
(See Fig. XXXVII)

(2) *"Chang Cho Jih Ching"* （帳桌日清） — In this statement
the total balance of each category of accounts of the "Ti Chang" and
the "Hsien Chin Liu Shui" is recorded, and their amounts are settled
up every five days. On account of its simplicity, it can be written on
one wooden board. The differences between this statement（帳桌日清）
and "Shui P'ai" （水牌） are as follows:—

a) In the former one, only the total balance of each
category of accounts is taken, while the balance of every account of
the "Ti Chang" and the "Hsien Chin Liu Shui" should be recorded
in the latter.

b) The second one is settled up and brought to date
every day, while the former one is settled up every five days.

At present, this statement is not much used by the native
banks of the Peking and Shêng-Chi groups.

Fig. XXXVI. The Form of "Yin Kuei Jih Ching"

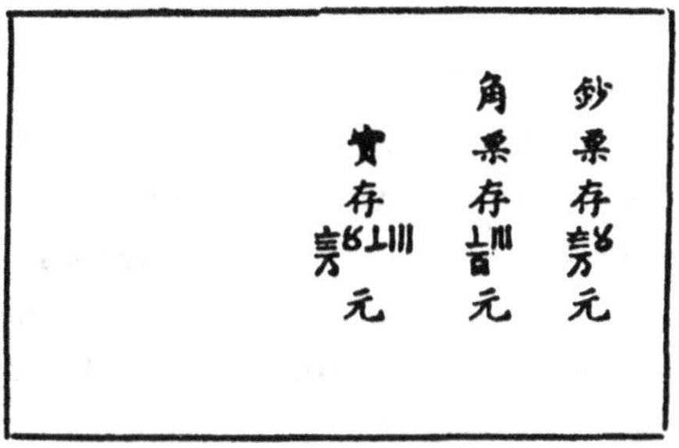

Fig. XXXVII. The Form of "Chang Cho Jin Ching"

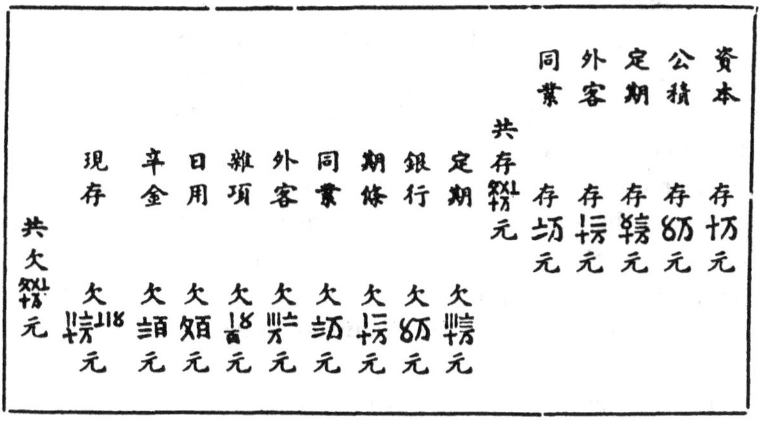

D. Monthly Report (月報)—This statement which is made at the end of each month is used to report the business and financial condition of the whole native bank to the management.[20][30] Usually this statement is entered vertically in a folded red paper; it contains many detail parts, the total of each part and the final balance. The month is written next to the title of "Monthly Report" (月報). It starts with a first group: "Balances Carried down" (舊管), where the amount of each account of capital, "Hu Pên", reserve and various deposits is reported, and a second group "New Receipts" (新收)

includes receipts and gains. A total of the first two groups is written next. The third group "Amounts Paid out" (開除) contains all the payments of interests, sundry expenditures, etc. The loans, advances, overdrafts, value of assets and Cash on hand are separately recorded in the fourth group "New Balance in hand" (實在), and the total of these last two groups is added on the next line. It is evident that the balance of the two totals is the net profit or loss, which, as a custom, is written with a few words of good luck at the end of the statement. This statement is compiled similarly at the end of each month.[2 42] (Refer to Chapter V and Appendix)

E. Annual Report (年總)—This is made at the end of each year and intended to report to the proprietors on the state of the business and the financial conditions of the native bank during the whole year.[33] It is usually written on a long red, folded paper (紅摺), so it is also called the "Red Book" (紅帳)[44] in native banks. The form and arrangement of items are just the same as in the monthly report, but each item is the total of the amounts of the same item during the twelve months, and the net profit or loss to be shared by each proprietor according to the agreed proportion mentioned in the contract, as well as the bonus to the staff, are added. The surplus reserve fund, when agreed to, is added last, if there is a profit in the year.[34 43] So this report may be compared to the financial statements in double-entry book-keeping, but is more complicated. As the purpose is to show the financial condition of the enterprise to the proprietor or proprietors, the items of proprietorship are more important than others.

The method of compiling the above two statements will be illustrated specially in the fifth chapter.

F. Interest Calculating book (打息溜)—This is a long and narrow book without any lines on the pages. It is used for the calculation of interest specially in the Tientsin group, although not by every native bank. The balances of every day in each account, in higher columns (which means "debit side" 存), are copied in this book, and the number of days up to another balance is written under the corresponding balance; then the product of the amount and days is recorded below. The credit balances (which mean the balances in the lower columns 付), are written in another page of the book in the in same way. The amount of interest is entered following each entry; when all the amounts are added up, the total amount of interest for each account can be found more easily.[15] (See Fig. XXXVIII)

Fig. XXXVIII. The Form of Interest Calculating Book

Notes of the Chapter

1—銀行會計　　　顧　準　著　　　（商務印書舘）P. 15—P. 16

2—Personal interviews with Mr. H. P. Ch'ung (种馨
　　浦君), Manager of Ch'ing Fêng Native Bank;
　　and Mr. C. P. Wei (魏景彭君), Manager of Teh
　　Hung Native Bank in Tientsin　　　　　Oct. 10th 1940

3—Personal interviews with Mr. C. P. Wei (魏景彭君),
　　Manager; and Mr. C. C. Wan (宛溢川君) of Teh
　　Hung Native Bank; and Mr. C. M. Ma (馬長民君)
　　in Tientsin　　　　　　　　　　　　Feb. 16th 1941

4—Personal interviews with Mr. H. Y. Lu(陸效揚君),
　　and Mr. P. H. Hsü (徐本河君) of Tientsin Native
　　Bankers' Association　　　　　　　　March 19th 1941

5—Personal interviews with Mr. C. C. Han (韓智齋君),
　　Manager; Mr. F. C. Sun (孫芳忱君) of Teh Fêng
　　Native Bank ; and Mr. S. S. Shang (尚毅珊君) of
　　Peking Native Bankers' Association　　March 29th 1941

6—天津之銀號　王子建, 趙履謙合著 （法商經濟研究室）P. 15

7—Personal interview with Mr. F. C. Sun (孫芳忱君),
　　Chief accountant of Teh Fêng Native Bank in
　　Tientsin　　　　　　　　　　　　　March 31st 1941

8—Shu-Lun Pan: College Book-keeping & Accounting P. 44—P. 46

9—實用銀行簿記　　　謝　霖　著　　　（商務印書舘）P. 38—P. 48

10—北京銀錢業　　　劉奇新　著　　（東方大學論文）P. 19—P. 20

11—Personal interviews with Mr. H. Y. Lu (陸效揚君),
　　and Mr. P. H. Hsü (徐本河君) of Tientsin Native
　　Bankers' Association　　　　　　　　March 30th 1941

12—Personal interviews with same persons as 11.　March 9th 1941

13—Personal interviews with Mr. C.C. Han (韓智齋君),
    Manager of Teh Fêng Native Bank; and Mr. C.
    F. Wang (王春堃君) in Tientsin   March 26th 1941

14—Pitman: Book-keeping Simplified   P. 211

15—Personal interview with Mr. H. S. Chang, (張秀
    山君) Sub-Manager of Teh Hung Native Bank March 5th 1941

16—Visit to Teh Ch'êng Native Bank   Dec. 22nd 1940

17—Patron: Accountants' Handbook   P. 193

18—(書 名 同 6.)   P. 34—P. 38

19—(The same book as 17.)   P. 205

20—(書 名 同 6.)   P. 26, P. 28-P. 29

21—(書 同 名 6.)   附 錄 P. 30

22—Personal interview with Mr. P. H. Hsü (徐本河君)
    of Tientsin Native Bankers' Association   May 10th 1941

23—Personal interviews with same persons as 11   March 9th 1941

24—Personal interview with Mr. F. C. Sun (孫芳忱君),
    Chief-accountant of Tientsin Teh Fêng Native
    Bank   May 4th 1941

25—Personal interviews with Mr. F. C. Sun (孫芳忱君),
    Chief-accountant of Teh Fêng Native Bank in
    Tientsin, and Mr. J. C. Pien (過榮璟君)
    Manager in Peking   April 14th 1941

26—(書 名 同 9.)   P. 15—P. 18

27—Personal interview with Mr. P.S. Chang (張寶善君),
    Chief-Accountant of Hsin Shêng Native Bank
    in Tientsin   April 4th 1941

28—Yeh Shu Yuan: The Method of Accounting used
    in Chinese Business Field   P. 9—P. 11

29—Personal interviews with same persons as 11   Dec. 25th 1941

CHAPTER II

30—(The same book as 28)   P. 16—P. 19

31—(書 名 同 10)   P. 28

32—Pin Yuan Chu: Banking Practice   P. 211

33—(The same book as 28)   P. 26—P. 27

34—Personal interview with Mr. M. T. Wang (王慕
　　唐君), Manager of Chi Tai Native Bank in Peking Sept. 9th 1940

35—(The same book as 28.)   P. 43

36—Personal interview with Mr. C. P. Wei (魏景彭君),
　　of Tah Chung Bank in Tientsin   Aug. 21st 1940

37—Personal interviews with Mr. F. C. Sun (孫芳忱君)
　　of Teh Fêng Native Bank, and Mr. C. P. Wei
　　(魏景彭君), Manager of Teh Hung Native Bank March 22nd 1941

38—(書 名 同 6.)   P. 7

39—(書 名 同 6.)   P. 53—P. 55

40—(書 名 同 9.)   P. 33—P. 34

41—(The same book as 28)   P. 59

42—Personal interviews with Mr. S. S. Shang (倘校
　　珊君) of Peking Native Bankers' Association;
　　and Mr. Y. T. Kuei (桂月汀君) in Peking   Sept. 7th 1940

43—Personal interviews with Mr. T. H. Yü (余天休君),
　　Mr. Y. T. Kuei (桂月汀君), and Mr. S. S. Shang
　　(倘校珊君) in Peking   Sept. 11th 1940

44—(The same book as 28.)   P. 81

45—"Su Chou Figures" (蘇州碼):—

丨 or 一 = 1	亠 or ㄥ = 6
二 or 刂 = 2	㐅 or ㇄ = 7
三 or 刂刂 = 3	㗊 or ㇗ = 8
㐅 = 4	文 = 9
𡿨 = 5	十 = 0 or 10

— 76 —

CHAPTER III

TYPES OF BUSINESS OPERATED & THE ENTRY OF
TRANSACTIONS

The main business of native banks is to deal with money or what represents money, which is the essential medium of exchange in every kind of business. Although modern banks now control a larger part of the original business of native banks, the latter still have their social importance. On account of their more convenient business-hours and simpler procedure, some concerns rely upon them for the supply and circulation of capital.[1] The kinds of business operated by native banks may be classified into four main categories, viz. general transactions (正規營業), remittances (匯兌), warehousing (倉庫) and speculative transactions (投機業務). In fact, while one native bank specializes in one line of business, it may still operate in other lines; but the former can be deemed its main business, and the others are only accessory.[2]

In addition to this, previously a few native banks dealt also in money exchange or selling lottery tickets, but recently money exchanges (兌換業) have been separated from native banks. A money exchange is also called "Men Shih" (門市) in colloquial language of native bankers, and the money exchangers are called "Yin Chien Hao" (銀錢號) or "Chien Hao" (錢號).[3] Therefore, at present, no more native bank trades either in money exchange or lottery tickets; this is reserved to the "Chien Hao" of which no more will be said in this essay.

The technical terms used in native banks for general transactions are "Tso Chia Tzu" (作架子), "Fang Chia Yer" (放架眼), and "Chê Chiao" (摺交). The term for remittances is "Shou Chiao" (收交). The business of a native bank which operates mainly in buying and selling stocks of merchandise such as metals, corn, cloth, together with telegraphic transfers, is called "Hsien Shih" (現市).[4] Speculative transactions are named "Fu Shih" (浮事) or "Tao Shih" (套事). In relation to warehousing, there is no certain term, except the common name "Ts'ang K'u" (倉庫). If a native bank trades both in "Chê Chiao" (摺交) and "Fu Shih" (浮事) or any other kind of accessory business, it is called "Tso Ch'uan Shih" (作全市).[3]

I. General Transactions (正規營業)

This is the main business done by the majority of native banks, especially in the Peking group. It includes deposits and rlans.[1] Native banks make their chief profits out of the interests oeceived in excess of those which are paid.

1. **Deposits** (存款). — The native banks absorb the surplus capital available on the market, thanks to their credit. It is evident that the capital invested by the proprietors is not enough for operating the whole business, and that the floating capital in the market has to be attracted by a handsome rate of interest. These deposits are of the utmost importance to the enterprise.[5]

In the primitive period of the native banks, the deposits were merely the customers' money entrusted for safekeeping; the enterprise had only a right of possession without ownership. Therefore, the native banks had to give back the money originally deposited, and could not pay with other money of the same value, when the depositors withdrew their deposits. The depositors, during that time, received no interest and had to pay a commission, for their purpose was not to make profit, but to commit the responsibility of safekeeping to the native bank. This sort of deposits were similar to safekeeping in modern banks. Nowadays the nature of deposits in native banks is entirely different from that in the olden times. The enterprise has the right of both possession and ownership on the cash deposited. When the money is withdrawn by the customer, the native bank is only liable to pay the same amount, no matter whether or not it is the money originally entrusted.[5]

The money deposited may be transferred or paid in cash by

the native banks. The "Poh Mar" (撥碼), "Poh Tiao" (撥條) and cheque, which represent money, can be transferred easily to any other parties within a certain period without any transfer of real money. This is an economy in the use of money. Moreover, the floating capital is distributed to other people who are in need of it by means of loans. The absorption and distribution of money by native banks has many advantages for certain classes of persons and business concerns, on account of their convenient business-hours and simplicity of procedure. The supply and demand of capital can be adjusted on a large scale through the intermediary of native banks. Besides, the native banks can also eliminate the expenses and risks of keeping money for the owners, if the money is deposited. The above points are the advantages of deposits in native banks.[5]

The deposits of an enterprise may be classified in the following categories:—

(a) *Fixed Deposit* (定期存款) — This is a deposit for a fixed period, at a fixed rate of interest,[16] which are agreed by both parties.[5] The depositor is not allowed to withdraw his money within the period. At the time of depositing, the depositor gives a specimen of his seal or signature, or the native bank gives him a "Chê Tze" (摺子), which will be used as an evidence for the withdrawal of money.[6] At the end of the period, the native bank is liable to pay both principal and interest. It is also called "Chang Ts'un" (長存).[5]

Nearly all the customers for this sort of deposits are individual persons, under their own names, or "Tang" names (堂名) or "Chi" (記); business concerns are very scarce.[78] The periods in native banks are usually three months, half a year and one year;[17] two years is not usual. The rate of interest on fixed deposits is generally higher than that allowed by modern banks, so many customers are attracted;[7] it is also higher than for other kinds of deposits in the native bank. The rate varies according to the period; it is higher if the period is longer, and vice versa.[1] It is a custom in native banks that the depositors should be introduced by another person who is in close relation with the native banks.[7]

When a customer deposits his money in the native bank, the accountant has to record the amount received in the higher column of the "Hsien Chin Liu Shui" (現金流水) and to note the starting date, the period, and the rate of interest. A "Chê Tze" of fixed deposit (定期存款摺) is given to the depositor. At the same time, an account under the name of the depositor should be opened in the "Fixed deposits account" of the "Ti Chang" (底帳), where the entry of the "Hsien Chin Liu Shui" is posted also in the higher column, and the conditions are noted in the column of particulars.[8] (See Example 1)

Example 1:

If the customer tenders a cheque or a "Poh Tiao (撥條) or any other bill for fixed deposit, the entry should be made in the "Chuan Chang Liu Shui" (轉帳流水), just in the same manner as mentioned for the "Hsien Chin Liu Shui", and the number of the cheque, or the name of the drawer, is added in note; but in the lower column, a corresponding entry is made in the name of another native bank from which the cheque or "Poh Tiao" will be collected. In the "Ti Chang", the entry in the "Fixed deposits account" is exactly the same as in the "Chuan Chang Liu Shui", and the entry of the lower column of the "Chuan Chang Liu Shui" is posted in the lower column of the account of the native bank from which the cheque is to be collected.[8] (See Example 2)

Example 2.

When the period expires, the native bank has to pay the principal and interest to the depositor and to collect the income tax for the Government. The accountant ought to calculate the amount of interest, and the income tax which is commonly four per cent, and to make the entries in the "Chuan Chang Liu Shui", as receiving the interest by the depositor, paying out from the "Interest account", and receiving income tax, paying by the customer. It should be mentioned that a brief and clear note must be written beside each entry. In the "Ti Chang", each entry of the "Chuan Chang Liu Shui" has to be posted to its corresponding account.[8] (See Example 3)

Example 3.

定期存款

泉　記　　摘　自二十九年三月十日起息　要定期一年過息一分

三月十日　收一萬元　鈔

三月民國三十年息　十日　收一千元

十日　付四十元　所得稅

民國三十年一月立　韓帳流水　第二册

三月十日

收泉記一千元　年息一分

付付出利息一千元　泉記

收所得稅四十元　泉記

付泉記四十元　所得稅

利　息

三月十日　付泉記一千元

暫記存欠

所得稅　要摘

三月十日　收一萬元　泉記

If the depositor wants to withdraw his money, payment of principal and interest, less income-tax, should be entered in the "Hsien Chin Liu Shui". Meanwhile this same entry is to be posted in the depositor's account in the "Ti Chang" with a note "Cash" (鈔).[8] (See Example 4.)

Example 4.

定期存款

泉　記

摘要　自二十九年三月十日起息　定期一年週息一分

民國三十年　三月十日　收一萬元（鈔）

三月十日　收一千元　息

付四十元　所得稅

付一萬零九百六十元（鈔）

現金流水

三月十日

付泉記一萬零九百六十元　本息

If the customer wants to take back his interest only, and continue his deposit, the accountant should write: paid the principal to the customer, with a note of renewal (轉期), and received the same amount for a fixed deposit, with a detailed note mentioning the date, rate, period etc., in the "Chuan Chang Liu Shui". The interest is paid and recorded in the "Hsien Chin Liu Shui". The entry of another fixed deposit of the same amount is entered in the corresponding account of the "Ti Chang" simultaneously.[8] (See Example 5)

Example 5.

（轉帳流水）

轉帳流水	三月十日	年息一分 收泉記一千元	收所得稅四十元	自民國三十年三月十日起息定期一年週息一分 收泉記一萬元
		付付出利息一千元 泉記	付泉記四十元 所得稅	付泉記一萬元 轉期

（定期存款 泉記 · 現金流水）

定期存款　泉記
摘要 自民國二十九年三月十日起息 定期一年週息一分

	三月十日 收一萬元	三月十日 收一千元	三月十日 收一萬元	平 收一萬元 由三月十日起息定期一年週息一分	現金流水	三月十日
		付四十元 所得稅	付九百六十元 鈔	付一萬元 轉期		付泉記九百六十元 年息一分

Suppose the customer requests to renew his fixed deposit in adding interest for another period, the accountant should record in the "Chuan Chang Liu Shui": paid the total of principal and interest, with a note of "renewal" (轉期), and: received the same amount for renewal of the fixed deposit, with a detailed note to mention the period, rate of interest and date. These two entries will appear simultaneously in the depositor's account of the "Fixed Deposits

Account", but usually a word "Balance" (平) is written on the right at the top of the last entry, showing that the two entries are identical.[8] (See Example 6)

Example 6.

轉帳流水

三月十日

收泉記一千元　年息一分
付付出利息一千元　泉記

收所得稅四十元　泉記
付泉記四十元　所得稅

收泉記一萬零九百六十元　轉期定期一年週息一分
付泉記一萬零九百六十元　轉期

定期存款

泉記　摘要　自二十九年三月十日起息　定期一年週息一分

三月十日　民國三十年　息
十日　收一千元
付四十元　所得稅

三月十日　收一萬元
十日　付一千元

平
收一萬零九百六十元　自三月十日起息定期一年週息一分
付一萬零九百六十元　轉期

(b) *Current Deposits* (活期存款) — There is no limit of time and amount for this kind of deposits.[11] The deposit is repayable to the owner upon demand, and he can deposit any sum of money at any date. This operation is largely practiced by native banks.[5] The depositors are mainly business concerns and merchants from other places; individual persons are not many.[7] The rate of interest is lower than on fixed deposits; furthermore, no interest is paid if an overdraft is allowed, and the rate for overdraft is much higher.[5 6 9 10] This overdraft should remain within certain limits agreed to by the enterprise. It is a custom that, at the beginning of each Chinese business year, the manager discusses with the shroff the maximum overdraft for each business concern. When the limit of overdraft is fixed, the depositor should be informed and the "Chê Tze" (pass-book) for current deposit (往來存款摺) is sent to him.[5 12]

The "Chê Tze" is the chief document on which the amounts received and paid are recorded, and it is kept by the customer. Besides, cheques, "Poh Tiao" (撥條) and "Yuan Tiao Ta" (原條打) or "Yuan P'iao Poh" (原票摺) are used for withdrawals.[13 16]

When money is deposited, an account for the customer in the current deposits account is opened, and particulars are mentioned, such as the rate of interest on deposits, and on overdrafts if such are allowed. The maximum amount allowed for overdraft is noted on another paper or in a subsidiary book. If money is received or paid in cash, it should be entered in the "Hsien Chin Liu Shui", and posted in the corresponding account of the "Ti Chang". Money received is recorded in the higher column, and money paid appears in the lower column both in the "Hsien Chin Liu Shui" and the "Ti Chang".[8 14] (See Example 7)

Example 7.

現金流水　三月十九日　收德康號一千五百元

活期存款　德康號　要摘　三月十九日收一千五百元

　　　　If the deposit consists in a cheque or "Poh Tiao" on other native banks, the amount is recorded in the "Chuan Chang Liu Shui" as received from the customer, and paid to other native bank to which it is committed for collection. The former entry appears in the same manner in the customers account, and the latter one is recorded with the same direction in the pccount of the other native bank in the "Ti Chang".[8] (See Examle 8)

Example 8.

轉帳流水　三月十九日　收德康號一千五百元　付新生銀號一千五百元

活期存款

德康號　要摘

三月十九日　收一千五百元　新華支

本埠同業存欠

新生銀號　要摘

三月十九日　付一千五百元　新華支

Owing to the frequency of transactions with this kind of deposits, the records are various and complex, as many entries for one customer may possibly be made in the same day. The accountant usually makes out the balance between amounts received and paid at the close of each day, in order to check the errors and to calculate the interests on deposits and overdrafts. The balance is written in "Su Chou Figures" on the top of the last entry of that day, with the word "Ts'un" (存) if the total of receipts exceeds the total of payments; when the amount paid exceeds that received, the balance is written under the last entry with the word "Chi'en" (欠) preceding it.[8][25] (See Example 9)

Example 9.

活期存款	興華鹹廠 要摘	一月二日收一千元 傳成支 一月一日付一千五百元 由書帳一册更來 欠絈元	一月二十四日收一千元 鈔 一月四日付三百元 鈔 欠絈元	二月二日存絈元 傳恆票 一月三十一日付五百元 欠順元	十七日收二千元 大通支 存此十 二月二日收一千元	

(c) *Deposits of other modern banks* (銀行存款)— The relations between modern and native banks rae very close, and the native banks frequently collect bills on behalf of the modern banks. But it is very rare that modern banks deposit money for a fixed period. So the nature and entries of this account are similar to those of current deposits accounts. When money is received, the amount is entered in the higher column of the "Hsien Chin Liu Shui", and posted in the corresponding account of the "Ti Chang". The entry is made in the "Chuan Chang Liu Shui", if a cheque has been received (See Example 10). On the other hand, the payment in cash or by cheque is recorded in the "Hsien Chin Liu Shui" or the "Chuan Chang Liu Shui" respectively. The entry in the "Ti Chang" corresponds to that in either the "Chuan Chang Liu Shui" or the "Hsien Chin Liu Shui".[1 7 8 13] (See Example 11)

Example 10.

			轉帳流水
	一月十日	收新華銀行二萬五千元 支號805	
		付大中銀行二萬五千元 新華支	

		新華銀行	摘要	本埠同業存欠
	一月十日收二萬五千元			

Example 11.

			現金流水
	一月十日	付大通銀行一萬元	

		大通銀行	摘要	本埠同業存欠
	一月十日付一萬元			

Formerly this account was entirely separated from the accounts with other native banks, but at present there is a tendency to combine them together in the same class of accounts, though this practice is not adopted by many native banks. In fact, the nature is somewhat different, e. g. the "Poh Tiao" or "Tui Hua" are generally used by native banks, but they are of no effect in modern banks. So, in this essay, the account with other native banks will be examined separately.

(d) *Temporary Deposits* (活期存款) — This kind of deposit is made temporarily by a customer, and the native bank is liable to repay it at any time, while there is no suitable item for recording it. No interest is paid.[11 12] The sources are various as shown in the following:—

(1) The sums collected on behalf of a person who has no suitable deposit account for record.

(2) The money received on account of a transaction where the native bank acts as an agent.

(3) Other deposits without suitable account for recording.

In native banks, this kind of deposits is used commonly for collection of income-tax, accrued interest payable (應付未付利息), remittance payable (應付未付匯款), accrued insurance premium payable (應付未付保費), and so on.[13 14]

Income-Tax — When the interest on deposit has to be paid to a customer, the income-tax should be collected for the Government. The accountant records in the "Chuan Chang Liu Shui": receipt of the income-tax from the depositor, and payment of the same amount for the customer. The next step is to open an income-tax account in the suspense account, and to post the amount received in the higher column, the other entry being made in the lower column of the customer's account.[15] (See Example 13)

Example 13.

The native bank should pay the total amount of income-tax collected to the Treasury at fixed dates. This payment is recorded in the "Hsien Chin Liu Shui" for the whole amount, and reported with the note: cash (鈔) in the lower column of the Income-tax account, which may be closed.[13][15]   (See Example 14)

Example 14.

						所得税 要摘	暫記存欠
付七百十二元一角 杪	收七元二角 張維俊	收二十五元八角 福康號	收三百十六元三角 泉記	收一百十二元六角 福祿堂	十二月三十一日 收二百五十元三角 新記		

Accrued interest payable — This item has been introduced recently in the accounts of a part of the native banks; there was no such account in former times. It is ordinarily used for recording interests on fixed deposits at the end of the Chinese fiscal periods, though the interests should be paid only afterwards. It is customary according to the conservatism of the old native banks that the whole amount of interests are deemed to be payable, even though not yet matured. Theoretically it is not correct, for it is not the real amount of liabilities of the enterprise at that time. If the former method were used by native banks, the amounts of assets and liabilities would be nearer to the reality. In fact, the accountants of many native banks think that it is only a vain pursuit without any utility, but they are forced to do so on account of the collection of income-tax.[13]

At the end of each Chinese fiscal period, the amounts of accrued interests are to be added up and recorded first in the "Chuan Chang Liu Shui" as a receipt of the accrued interest payable account, and a payment of the interest paid. These two entries will be posted to the corresponding accounts in the "Ti Chang".[14][15] (See Example 15)

Example 15.

暫記存欠

要摘

應付未付利息
六月三十日收一萬元

利息帳

六月三十日付 應付未付息 一萬元

轉帳流水

六月三十日
收應付未付利息一萬元
付付出利息一萬元

When the interests are to be paid at maturity, the reverse entries are made in the "Chuan Chang Liu Shui", as a receipt of the interests paid account, and a payment of the accrued interest payable account, and reported in the corresponding accounts.[13 23] (See Example 16)

Example 16.

利息帳

八月十日
收一萬元 應付未付息

轉帳流水

八月十日
收付出利息一萬元
付應付未付利息一萬元

暫記存欠

應付未付利息

摘要

八月十日

付一萬元

The other accrued accounts are similar to this, so they will not be explained for brevity's sake.

(e) *Other kinds of deposits*—There are a few native banks whose organization is similar to that of modern banks; so three or four other sorts of deposits are operated, such as special current deposits, deposits at call, deposit receipts, and saving deposits. The forms and procedure are just the same as in modern banks and may be found in any book on bank accounting system. Hitherto, in the overwhelming majority of native banks, these kinds of deposits do not exist, even in larger ones.[1][2] Therefore, they will be omitted in this essay.

(f) *The rate of interest on deposits* — The deposits are loans contracted by the native bank, that is to say a liability of the enterprise. It is evident that the debtor should pay interest for the money borrowed; thus the depositors may get interest from the native bank. The rate of interest varies according to the duration of the deposit. In most native banks of Peking and Tientsin, the rate of interest on fixed deposits is from 4 or 5 to 8 or 9°/₀₀ per month, or from 6 to 10% per year, for the native bank can use the money freely within the period. The rate of interest on current deposits is lower, because the money is repayable at any time and cannot be utilized freely: they are allowed from 2 or 3 to 5 or 6°/$_{oo}$ per month, or from 3 to 6% per year. With regard to the deposits of other banks, the rate of interest is only 3 or 4% per year.[1][5] In fact the rate of interest allowed is lower in larger native banks, and higher in smaller ones in order to compete with the former.

(g) *Keeping specimens of seals or signatures* — There was no unified method of keeping specimens of seals or stamps and signatures in former times. No specified forms of cards was used, and the size of papers on which the customers stamped or signed was not regulated. The customer might choose any kind and any size of paper for stamping or signing on it, and gave it to the native bank stating that it was an evidence for withdrawals. But gradually this was reformed, on account of mishaps which occurred. A special book is prepared for this purpose; it is classified according to the items of accounts, and numbers are assigned in accordance with the order of accounts in the "Ti Chang". Recently, a number of native banks prepared books similar to those used by modern banks.[12][23]

2. **Loans**—The money absorbed from the market is distributed to those who are in need of it. In its broader sense the word: loan, includes the discount of bills; in the narrower sense it means loans proper, excluding discount. The discount is profitable, but the Chinese bills which can be discounted are very few, especially in Peking and Tientsin. In order that all the money of the enterprise should be well utilized, both ordinary loans and discount are practiced.[5]

Two kinds of advantages can be derived from the loans: one is for the society, and the other for the enterprise itself. The native banks may supply capital to entrepreneurs who are competent, but lack money to carry on business; then productive enterprises may be launched. This is a first advantage for the society. Furthermore, enterprises in temporary difficulties may be refloated by borrowing money from the native banks, and those doing well may be enlarged and developed. This is a second advantage for the society. The safety of the investment should also be taken into consideration: the business and financial conditions of the enterprise which needs money are to be investigated when the loan is asked for, and the bank may give advice to place them on a sound basis. This may be deemed as a third advantage for the society.[5] [36]

The discount of bills utilizes only a part of the working fund of the native bank; the loans enable the native bank to utilize it at full. Thus the monetary operations of the native bank are enlarged; other enterprises are developed by borrowing money; the people is enriched, and the business of the native bank is prosperous on account of the increase of deposits and loans. This is the advantage for the native bank itself.[5]

(a) *Fiduciary or unsecured Loan* (信用放款) — When money is borrowed from the native bank without any security or guarantor, but only based on the credit of the borrower, it is called a "fiduciary" or "unsecured loan". Generally, the credit is the fundamental condition of any transaction in native banks. They make a tremendous amount of such loans, which are much more restricted in modern banks. This is a peculiar feature of the business of native banks.[1] [13] [14] [15]

The borrowers of fiduciary loans are mostly business concerns, and in part individual persons who are well known to the enterprise. Such loans are divided in two kinds according to the time of reimbursement, namely fixed loan and call loan.[5]

(1) Fixed Loan—It is a fiduciary loan, with a fixed time for reimbursement; at the end of the fixed period, the borrower is bound to reimburse the sum lent together with the interest at the agreed rate. The periods granted by native banks are usually three months, six months and one year. The rate ot interest on fixed loans is much higher than that on deposits; this difference is the main source of profits in regular native banks. Many Chinese business concerns are maintained by these loans both in Peking and Tientsin,

because it is very difficult to borrow money from modern banks without any security.[15][34]

The evidence is the "Chê Tze" (摺子) which can be prepared either by the bank or by the customer. Generally business concerns of high standing are allowed to prepare it themselves; on the cover of the "Chê Tze" (摺查), the inscription "X X Yin Hao Chieh K'uan Chê" (某某銀號借款摺) is written, which means: "Chê Tze" of loans borrowed from X native bank. But the "Chê Tze" for ordinary concerns is prepared by the bank; the inscription is: "Yin Hao Fang K'uan Chê" (銀號放款摺),[15][34] "Chê Tze" of loans granted by X Native Bank.

Loans should be recorded in the "Hsien Chin Liu Shui" as a payment to the borrower when the money is lent, and reported on the "Ti Chang". In the fixed loans accounts, a new account is opened for the borrower, and the conditions, such as period, rate of interest, and evidence of the loan, are to be mentioned under the title of the account.[13] (See Example 17)

Example 17.

			現 金 流 水				定 期 放 款
		四 月 一 日			新 記		
		付 新 記 五 萬 元 <small>定期放款三個月月息一分</small>			一 日 四 月 付 五 萬 元 <small>鈔</small>	摘 要 <small>定期三月</small> <small>利息一分</small> <small>立有存扎</small>	

If the borrower receives a cheque or "Poh Tiao", an entry should be made in the "Chuan Chang Liu Shui", and posted to the borrower's account in the fixed loans accounts of the "Ti Chang", as payment of the amount lent. Another entry should be made in the "Chuan Chang Liu Shui" as a receipt of the amount of the loan from the other native bank or modern bank on which the "Poh Tiao" or cheque is drawn.[15][16] (See Example 18)

Example 18.

收德豐銀號五萬元　新記

付新記五萬元　定期放款定期三個月月息一分待豐票

四月十日

轉帳流水

四月一日付五萬元　新記　要摘　德豐票

定期放款

四月一日收五萬元　新記

德豐銀號　要摘

本埠同業存欠

When the period terminates and the borrower reimburses the loan with interest in cash, the accountant of the enterprise has to record the receipt in the "Hsien Chin Liu Shui" and post the sum of the loan to the borrower's account in the higher column, and transfer the interest of the loan to the interest account (See Example 19). But if the borrower brings a cheque or "Poh Tiao", the entry is recorded in the "Chuan Chang Liu Shui" as a receipt of the loan reimbursed, and a payment of the same amount to other native or modern bank for collection. Every entry made in the "Liu

Shui Chang", should be entered in the corresponding account of the "Ti Chang".[13] (See Example 19)

Example 19

(2)   Call Loans (活期放款)—There is no fixed period for reimbursement. They may be also called overdrafts on current account. As we have mentioned formerly when dealing with current deposits, the maximum amount of overdraft is agreed to at the opening of the current deposit account.[1][11] The native bank retains the right to demand reimbursement from the customer, but it should give a notice in advance.[10] Usually it is limited to one year, that is to say up to the end of each Chinese fiscal year. The borrower may reimburse both overdraft and interest at any time. The period may be prolonged when necessary.[1][33]

The customer may overdraw any sum of money within the maximum limit at any time. Each entry of overdraft in cash is made in the "Hsien Chin Liu Shui" as payment of the amount to the customer and is reported accordingly to the customer's account (See Example 20). It may also be recorded in the "Chuan Chang Liu Shui", as payment of the sum overdrawn and receipt of the same amount from the other native or modern bank, if a "Poh Tiao" or cheque is given. These entries have to be posted in the corresponding account of the "Ti Chang".[12] (See Example 21)

Example 20.

Example 21.

When the customer reimburses, the entries of amounts reimbursed or deposited, are made in the "Hsien Chin Liu Shui", if they are paid in cash, and are reported to the customer's current deposits account and interest account respectively (See Example 22).

If they are paid by a cheque or "Poh Tiao", these entries are made in the "Chuan Chang Liu Shui" with an additional entry of payment to another native or modern bank which acts for collection.[13][14] (See Example 23)

Example 22.

Example 23.

本埠同業存欠

摘要	德豐銀號	六月二日付 惠記 八千元

(b) *Loans on securities or Secured Loans* (抵押放款)—In general, this sort of loans were not much practiced by the Tientsin and Peking native banks in the past, because securities were required when the credit standing of a borrower was not well-known. Generally, the native bank is quite unwilling to lend to persons who lack a good credit. As time goes on, the credit has decreased in inverse proportion to the development of the civilization. As business complicates, fiduciary loans secured on the personal credit of the borrower alone provide no longer a sufficient guarantee in many respects. Consequently, the native bankers are obliged to demand collateral securities for the increasing number of loans and advances, in order to keep themselves on the safe side.[18] [20]

When the money is lent, the borrower should pledge a certain security, the value of which exceeds the amount borrowed. If the borrower cannot reimburse the debt, the native bank may sell the security by auction to repay the loan and its interest. The surplus, if any, should be returned to the debtor. The native bank is bound to return the security when the borrower reimburses.[23]

The securities pledged by borrowers to native banks are mostly bonds and shares; title-deeds of real estate come next; but the pledge of goods is limited to the native banks which have warehouses. The period of reimbursement may or may not be limited, at the native bank's option.[18]

When a security, such as warehouse receipt, negotiable securities, bonds. etc. is given in pledge, the native bank only delivers a receipt to the borrower. Usually, in native banks, the borrowers are the ordinary customers or depositors; so the amount lent can be recorded in the "Chê Tze" of current deposits (往來存款摺) with a mention of the loan on security, the period and rate of interest;[14] otherwise a special document or "Chê Tze" is delivered to the borrower.

The records written in either the "Hsien Chin Liu Shui" or the "Chuan Chang Liu Shui", and the "Ti Chang" are just the same as for unsecured loans. In most native banks there is no subsidiary book for recording the securities held, but in a few newly organized native banks subsidiary books are kept.[12] This kind of subsidiary books has been explained in the previous chapter.

For the completion of the whole record, the particulars of the securities are written in the borrower's account when there is no subsidiary book for the securities. Under the title of the account, the kind and value of securities pledged, the period for reimbursement, the rate of interest on the loan, and the name of the guarantor, as well as the number of the "Chê Tze" given to the borrower, are recorded.[12][21] (See Example 24)

Example 24.

Another kind of secured loans which should be taken into consideration are the "overdrafts on current account secured". It means that the current depositor may sign a contract with the enterprise, whereby he is allowed to overdraw up to a maximum limit, warranted by a certain amount of securities which are given in pledge. This is more advantageous for the borrower who can withdraw any sum of money at any time, and reimburse at his convenience. According to the usage of the native banks, the interest on overdraft is calculated from the date when money has been actually paid; then the borrower suffers no loss from interest payable.[5][17]

The native bank may, in case of urgent necessity, experience some difficulty in getting back the money lent, even though it retains the right of demanding reimbursement at any time. Frequently, when the date of reimbursement occurs, the native bank is unable to realize the security at once. Therefore the enterprises are very cautious before allowing overdrafts, even when they are secured.[17][17]

The records for this transaction are similar to those for overdraft on Current account. The securities pledged are entered similarly in the subsidiary book of secured loans. The only difference is that a brief note for particulars should be written in the customer's account.[13][17]   (See Example 25)

Example 25.

往來存款

豐盛號

摘要 存款週息二厘
欠款月息一分二
棉紗五百件作抵

付 鈔 五千元

(c) *Loans with a surety*(人保放款)—It is a kind of loan where the borrower is warranted by a third party who is familiar with the native bank. The guarantor or surety is entirely responsible for reimbursement when the borrower is insolvent. The contract should be signed or stamped by all the three parties. The amount lent, the period for reimbursement, the rate of interest and other conditions are mentioned in the contract, which is the evidence of the loan. The borrower may at any time withdraw any sum of money within the amount fixed and he is bound to reimburse both principal and interest on demand of the native bank. This may be considered as another kind of fiduciary loan, but it is based upon the credit of the third party.[17][17]

All the entries made in either the "Hsien Chin Liu Shui" or the "Chuan Chang Liu Shui", and in the accounts of the "Ti Chang" are identical, except that the name of the guarantor should be mentioned in the column of particulars.[18][18]　(See Example 26)

Example 26.

(d) *Debit account with modern banks*—This item may refer either to overdrafts of modern banks or to deposits made with them by native banks. The former is similar to overdrafts in current account; in other words, the modern bank may draw money up to the maximum limit in excess of its deposits. The records for this transaction are the same as the entries made in the accounts for overdrafts in current account.[18] [19]

The recording of deposits of the enterprise in a modern bank is simpler than for other kinds of deposits. When the money is deposited in a modern bank, an entry of cash payment to the bank with the note "deposited in local bank" (存放本埠同業) is recorded in the "Hsien Chin Liu Shui", and posted to the modern bank's account in the "Ti Chang" (See Example 27). If a cheque is paid, an entry should be made in the "Chuan Chang Liu Shui" as paying the amount to the modern bank, and it is transferred to the modern bank's account. Besides, another entry is written in both the "Chuan Chang Liu Shui" and the "Ti Chang" as a receipt for the other modern or native bank from which the cheque is to be collected.[18] (See Example 28)

Example 27.

Example 28.

When money is withdrawn from the modern bank, the opposite entries are recorded, as receiving the amount from the modern bank, in either the "Hsien Chin Liu Shui" or the "Chuan Chang Liu Shui" and the "Ti Chang".[18] (See Example 29)

Example 29.

收大中銀行二千元 支312　付大通銀行二千元 大中支

五月二日

轉帳流水

收二千元 支312號　大中銀行

存放本埠同業

付二千元 大中支　大通銀行

存放本埠同業

    (e) *Discount of bills* — In the Tientsin and Peking native banks, the operation of discounting bills is unimportant, though it is very active in modern banks. Formerly they discounted a kind of bills, called "Ch'ih Ch'i Yen Tiao" (遲卯鹽條), which were issued by the "Lu Kang Kung Shu" (蘆綱公署) in Tientsin. At certain times the "Lu Kang Kung Shu" had to deliver the amount of salt-tax collected to the Government, but in fact it was not yet levied in full and bills were issued for the purpose of getting advances by discount. When the taxes had been completely collected, the bills were redeemed.[19] At present, this kind of bills is no more issued.

    Frequently the native banks hesitate to accept time-bills for discount, but they like to discount bills with guarantors. They fear that the bill may be dishonoured at maturity and they are unwilling to bear the loss, notwithstanding that some discount receivable can be earned. This is the reason why this business is rarely operated in native banks. But the bills guaranteed by modern banks are in a better position.[20] [23]

A custom has sprung up in native banks that bills presented for discount should be guaranteed by a third party, unless the native bank is acquainted with the drawer. So it can avoid to take a bill which has been lost by the rightful payee and which might be declared null later on. Usually only the bills of customers are accepted for discount.[20]

The records are just the same as those for current accounts. They are posted to the customer's current account in the "Ti Chang". The unmatured bills are not mentioned in either the "Liu Shui Chang" or the "Ti Chang", but only in the subsidiary records. When payment is received, the amount is transferred to the "Ti Chang" by way of entries in the "Liu Shui Chang". The rate of discount is not fixed in each native bank; it is only determined at the time of discount, according to the credit of the customer.[20] [26]

(f) *Suspense Debits or Sundry Advances* — (暫記欠款) All the amounts paid out, that will be reimbursed afterwards but have no suitable account for recording, are entered temporarily in the lower columns of the suspense account. This way of proceeding is used commonly for earnest money paid out, such as earnest money on rent, on telephone, on electric meter, on water-meter, etc. The earnest money can be taken back when the object of the warranty ceases, but there is no interest received.[18]

At the time of payment of the earnest money, the amount is recorded in the lower column, either of the "Hsien Chin Liu Shui" if paid in cash, or of the "Chuan Chang Liu Shui" if paid by a cheque or "Poh Tiao". This entry is posted to the suspense account (See Example 30). When an additional rent has to be paid, another similar entry is made either in the "Hsien Chin Liu Shui" or in the "Chuan Chang Liu Shui", but a few words should be noted as "Complement for the year X X" (補某某年). The same entry is transferred to the "Ti Chang" accordingly.[18] (See Example 31)

Example 30.

現金流水

	一月一日 付房租押租五百元

暫記存欠　房租押租

摘要	一月一日付 五百元 鈔

Example 31.

現金流水

	三月一日 付房租押租五十元 補廿九年

暫記存欠　房租押租

摘要	一月一日付 五百元	三月一日付 五十元 由舊帳更來 補廿九年 鈔

Furthermore, the accrued interests receivable, accrued remittances receivable, and other accrued amounts receivable are also recorded in the suspense account. All these transactions are of the same nature; therefore one of them will be a sufficient illustration of the whole.[10]

At the end of each fiscal period, in order to show the real assets owned by the enterprise, the interest receivable and not yet collected should be entered in the suspense account. Before posting, it is recorded in the "Chuan Chang Liu Shui" as a receipt of "interest received", and a payment of "accrued interest receivable". The entry made in the higher column is reported similarly to the interest account.[13] (See Example 32)

Example 32.

暂记存欠

应收未收利息 摘要

六月
三十日 付八千元

When the receipt is already due, two opposite entries appear in the "Chuan Chang Liu Shui": the amount of interest received is recorded in the higher column, and the same amount of accrued interest receivable is shown in the lower column.[13] (See Example 33)

Example 33.

转帐流水

收应收未收利息八千元 十二月三十日

付收入利息八千元

(g) *Rate of interest on loans*—The rate of interest on loans is higher than on deposits. It varies in accordance not only with the kind of loan, but also with the credit of the borrower and the period for reimbursement. As a general rule, the rate for longer periods is usually from 6 to $10°/_{00}$ per month, and for shorter periods from 10 to $12°/_{00}$ or more.[27][28] For unsecured loans with a fixed period and for overdrafts on current accounts, it is between 10 and $12°/_{00}$; the lowest rate allowed is over $6°/_{00}$. Though the rate on loans is higher than on deposits, the difference is less than 1% p.a. The rate of interest for loans against securities is still higher: it is usually $12°/_{00}$.[1][21]

The rate of discount is higher than the interest on loans; it varies from $12°/_{00}$ p.a. to 20% p.a. It is higher when the bill has to run for a longer period and lower for the shorter term bills, on account of the risk involved.[22]

Notes of the Chapter

1—天津之銀號　王子建. 趙履謙合著（法商經濟研究室）P. 33—P. 35

2—Binyuan Chu: Banking Practice　　　　　P. 210—P. P. 211

3—Personal interviews with Mr. H. Y. Lu (陸效揚君), and Mr. P. H. Hsü (徐本河君) of Tientsin Native Bankers' Association　　　　　Dec. 25th 1940

4—Personal interview with Mr. H.P. Ch'ung(种容浦君), Manager of Ch'ing Fêng Native Bank in Tientsin Oct. 19th 1940

5—Personal interviews with Nr. C.P. Wei (魏景彭君), Manager; and Mr. C. C. Wan (宛濟川君) of Teh Hung Native Bank; and Mr. C. M. Ma (馬長民君) Feb. 16th 1941

6—Personal interviews with the same persons as 3. March 19th 1941

7—(書 名 同 1.)　　　　　　　　　P. 39—P. 40

8—Personal interview with Mr. C. P. Wei (魏景彭君) of Tah Chung Bank in Tientsin　　　　Aug. 21st 1940

9—(書 名 同 1.)　　　　　　　　　P. 42

10—Personal interview with Mr. C. C. Han (韓智齋君), Manager of Teh Fêng Native Bank　　　April 13th 1941

11—Personal interviews with Mr. S. S. Shang (尚絞珊君) of Peking Native Bankers' Association, and Mr. Y. T. Kuei (桂月汀君) in Peking　　Sept. 7th 1940

12—Personal interview with Mr. M. T. Wang (王慕唐君),
Manager of Chi Tai Native Bank in Peking　　Sept. 9th 1940

13—Personal interview with Mr. F. C. Sun (孫芳忱君),
Chief-Accountant of Teh Fêng Native Bank in
Tientsin　　March 31st 1941

14—Personal interviews with same persons as 3.　March 9th 1941

15—Personal interview with Mr. P. S. Chang (張寶善君),
Chief-Accountant of Hsin Shêng Native Bank in
Tientsin　　April 4th 1941

16—(書 名 同 1,)　　P. 23—P. 25

17—Personal interviews with Mr. F. C. Sun (孫芳忱君),
Chief-Accountant of Tientsin Teh Fêng Native
Bank; and Mr. J. C. Pien (邊榮璋君), Manager
of Peking　　April 14th 1941

18—Personal interview with Mr. S. S. Chang (張秀山君).
Sub-Manager of Teh Hung Native Bank　　March 5th 1941

19—Personal interviews with Mr. S. C. Chiao (焦世卿君),
Chairman of Tientsin Native Bankers' Association,
and Manager of Hsin Shêng Native Bank; and Mr.
P. S. Shang (張寶善君), Chief-Accountant　　April 4th 1941

20—Personal interviews with Mr. C. P. Wei (魏景彭君),
Manager of Teh Hung Native Bank; and Mr. F. C.
Sun (孫芳忱君), Chief-Accountant of Teh Fêng
Native, Bank　　March 22nd 1941

21—北京銀錢業　　劉奇新著　　(東方大學論文)　P. 24—P. 28

22—(書 名 同 1.)　　P. 27—P. 29

23—Yung Pao of Tientsin (天津庸報經濟版)　　March 26th 1941

24—Yung Pao of Tientsin (天津庸報經濟版)　　April 20th 1941

25—Personal interviews with same persons as 3.　March 30th 1941

26—Personal interviews with Mr. C. C. Han (韓智齋君),
Manager of Teh Fêng Native Bank; and Mr. C. F.
Wang (王春楚君)　　March 26th 1941

27—中國錢莊概要　　潘子豪著　　(華通書局)　　P. 82

28—Speech of Mr. C. C. Han (韓智齋君口述), Manager
of Teh Fêng Native Bank, recorded by Mr. J. C.
Pien (邊榮璋君筆記)

CHAPTER IV

TYPES OF BUSINESS OPERATED & THE ENTRY OF

TRANSACTIONS *(Continued)*

I. Accounts With Other Native Banks.

The inter-relations among native banks are very important: they can transfer any sum of money between themselves. It frequently occurs that the money in hand of a native bank is insufficient for its payments. Consequently the business of a native bank is maintained by transfers from other native as well as modern banks. There is a certain limit to these relations both in Tientsin and Peking, and the limit is not the same for all native banks within the same locality. The credit is based on personal relations, that is to say it depends largely on the mutual friendship of the managers, or proprietors. The relationship is more intimate when the two parties belong to the same group. As a matter of fact, the case of two native banks of different groups being closely related is very rare. Two special terms used for these relations are "K'ao Chia" (靠家) and "Ch'uan Huan Chia" (川換家).[1]

"K'ao Chia" means that a native bank relies upon another to assist it financially. The other native bank is called "K'ao Chia". If the money of a native bank is working at full, great profits can be made; thus, the native banks or modern banks invest all money in hand for greater profit. In case of urgent need, the business will be unable to meet its obligations if there is no way for accommodation. At that time, the "K'ao Chia" steps in and assists to tide over the financial difficulty; so the credit is maintained. This is the reason why the native banks are associated, and occupy a prominent position in economic circles. Since the establishment of the Republic, the credit base of native banks has been shaken on account of the bankruptcy of a few of them, for instance the "Chih Ch'êng" (志成) and "Shen Tê" (盛德) native banks in October 1927 (民國十六年十月); at the same time the "Yü Shêng" (裕生), "I Hsing", (義興) "Tai Ch'ang" (泰昌) and "Fu Shêng Hsiang" (蚨生祥) native banks were on the verge of bankruptcy. From that time on, the accommodation of money among native banks has been limited; the relation of "K'ao Chia" is not so close now as formerly. The accommodation of money is accomplished by a "Poh Mar" without transferring cash.[1]

"Ch'uan Huan" means a business transaction between native banks; thus, the "Ch'uan Huan Chia" are the native banks which have intercommunication in business.[1] The instruments used for transferring accounts among native banks are not the same in Tientsin and Peking. In Tientsin, it is called "Poh Mar" (撥碼), which amounts to a request for transfer,[3] but cannot be converted into cash.[5 6] It is common that a certain number of native banks make an agreement whereby the others are obliged to receive the "Poh Mar" drawn by one of them, and such orders can be transferred among them. This relationship is called "Ch'uan Huan".[1] These "Poh Mar" were originated in the last few years of the Ch'ing dynasty, but their nature varied at different times. The senior native bankers say that formerly all the disbursements and receipts were effected in cash (過現);[4] but it was troublesome to determine the quality and quantity of the silver which was the exchange medium used at that time; when a shortage in the amount of silver was discovered, disputes often arose; then a few native bankers arranged to set-off every night the smaller sums of money and to pay in cash only the difference. Gradually larger amounts were also substituted by "Poh Mar". At the present time the "Poh Mar" are used instead of cash by native banks, and sometimes also by modern banks. It is not taken into consideration whether the provision is sufficient or not. Thus, orders without provision often affect the credit of a native bank and involve the whole money market in trouble.[1 3]

It is evident that the amount received in "Poh Mar" will not usually be equal to that of "Poh Mar" issued by the same native bank; so the balance is settled in the next morning by a cheque or "foreign paper" (番紙),[6] which is an order issued on the comprador's office of a foreign bank.[7] Formerly, the process of clearing was done by off-setting the mutual claims in the Native Bankers' Association. Now the payment of clearing balances is carried out in the books of the comprador's offices of the three prominent foreign exchange banks, viz. the Hongkong and Shanghai Banking Corporation, the National City Bank of New York, and the Yokohama Specie Bank.[8] A time of clearing has been fixed by the Native Bankers Association in November 1927: All "Poh Mar" received before noon should be settled before 1.00 p.m., and notice be given to the native bank by which the "Poh Mar" are sent; for all orders received after 2.00 p.m. a notice should be given at 6.00 p.m.

The "Poh Mar" is based upon credit, for usually there is no deposit with other native banks, especially in those of the Tientsin group. According to the custom of Tientsin, when a native bank goes bankrupt, the "Poh Mar" should be paid first. But in the case of the bankruptcy of "Chih Chêng Yin Hao" (志成銀號) in 1927, the "Poh Mar" were not reimbursed in full. The Native Banker's Association ruled that "Poh Mar" should be issued against deposits in other native banks, but hitherto this rule has not yet been put into execution. The reciprocal issue of "Poh Mar" between two native banks is called "Fei K'ung Mar" (飛空碼). The advantage of this credit system is to facilitate the circulation of money, but it is very dangerous when the credit of a native bank is defective, and the whole money market may be put out of gear. An essay has been written by the former chairman of the Tientsin Native Bankers' Association, stating the defects of the "Poh Mar" and advising that cheques should be used in the place of "Poh Mar". Unfortunately the native bankers stuck to old customs; they were afraid of the obstacles which might occur and the suggestion has not yet been adopted. From our point of view, this system should be abolished, in order to maintain the original influence of the native banks in the money market, and to enable them to compete with other new money organizations in the long run. The abolition is not a question of argumentation, but of time.[7] [8]

Moreover, modern banks may refuse to accept irregular "Poh Mar"; but, as a matter of fact, both parties will be affected, and it will be detrimental to business if a modern bank refuses to accept a "Poh Mar" sent by a native bank. After mature consideration, they generally accept. A "Poh Mar" cannot be converted into cash, as it has been explained before; therefore, the modern bank must request another native bank to collect on his behalf. These transfers induce closer relations between native and modern banks. It is frequent that native banks do not pay immediately, or pay only a part, and keep the rest for their own use. This gives a bad impression to the modern bankers.[9]

The instrument for transfer between native banks in Peking is still simpler than in Tientsin. In former times the transfer was made orally "Tui Hua" (對話). In each native bank, the shroff had the power to demand any sum for transfer, but the transfers of cash were strictly limited. At that time, all the transfers were settled in the "Lu Fang" (爐房) in "Chu Po Shih" (珠寶市). Due to the stability of credit during that period, this method was carried on for many years.

When the telephone was introduced in China, the mode of transfer was by telephone. It was more convenient and quicker, but abuses were still easier. Now this is still used between Peking native banks. The clearing balance of transfers by "Tui Hua" is settled by a cheque on a modern bank in the next morning.[10] [11] [12] The method by "Tui Hua" is still worse than the "Poh Mar"; it should be reformed urgently.

From the above explanations we may see that the modern banks are very closely connected with native banks. Many years ago, the relationship between modern and native banks was nearly that of "K'ao Chia"; but now it has been relaxed for the purpose of safety. Anyhow, the modern banks still intercommunicate closely with native banks.[9]

There is another custom in the case of opening a new native bank. At the time of opening, the manager has to request the acquainted native bankers for assistance, and the other native bankers deposit large sums of money in order to show the good credit of the new enterprise. This is called "Chuang Ts'ang" (莊倉). On the next day, the newly opened native bank should retransfer a large amount to the native banks of "Chuang Ts'ang" for acknowledging the friendship and showing the abundance of its capital. But these deposits will be withdrawn very soon. After this procedure the relation of "Chuan Huan" between the two parties is created. The number of "Chuan Huan Chia" varies according to the capital, business conditions and ability of the manager.[1 14]

With reference to the records and accounts, there is nothing peculiar for recording the transfer made by "Tui Hua". But, in the accounts of Tientsin native banks, the name of the other native bank from which the "Poh Mar" is received has to be noted besides the entry.

When money is received from another native bank, it should be recorded in the "Hsien Chin Liu Shui" and posted to the account with other native banks. Both these entries are entered in the higher columns, and the word "received" (收) is added on the top of each entry. The cash payment is recorded just in the opposite columns in both the "Hsien Chin Liu Shui" and the "Ti Chang".[13 5] (See Example 34)

Example 34.

現金流水

		二月一日	
		收啟泰銀號鈔五千元	付穎生銀號二千元

本埠同業存欠

啟泰銀號

摘要	
二月一日收鈔二千元	

本埠同業存欠

穎生銀號

摘要	
二月一日付鈔二千元	

But if a "Poh Mar" or cheque is received, it is recorded in the higher column of the "Chuan Chang Liu Shui" as receiving the amount, and another entry is made as paying the same amount to a third native bank to which the instrument is committed for collection. Both these entries are recorded in the higher or lower columns of the corresponding accounts in the "Accounts with other native banks" of the "Ti Chang" (See Example 35). It is usual that there are more than two "Poh Mar" for the same transaction; all these orders should be entered in the same "Chuan Chang Liu Shui", as receiving each amount in succession, and paying the total amount to another native bank, if it is requested by the enterprise to collect the different "Poh Mar" or cheques. The receiving entries are reported to the other native bank's account in the "Ti Chang", and in the third native bank account, the total amount is reported as paid. All the orders should be mentioned separately.[18][15] (See Example 36)

Example 35.

Example 36.

轉帳流水

二月七日

收啓泰銀號二千元　大中支2072號

收啓泰銀號二千元　新生條

收啓泰銀號五百元　德豐條

收啓泰銀號一千五百元　慶豐條

付德恆銀號五千元　條四只

本埠同業存欠

啓泰銀號　要摘

二月七日收二千元　大中支2072號

收一千元　新生條

收五百元　德豐條

收一千五百元　慶豐條

本埠同業存欠

德恆銀號　要摘

二月七日付五千元　條四只

When the enterprise makes deposits in other native banks, the payment in cash is recorded in the lower column of the "Hsien

Chin Liu Shui", and is to be posted to the other native bank's account. If any sum is withdrawn, the oppsite columns are used for recording the receipt of the enterprise and the payment by the other native bank in both the "Hsien Chin Liu Shui" and Account with other native banks."[13][14] (See Example 37)

Example 37.

If the payment is represented by a "Poh Mar" or a cheque, it is recorded in the lower column of the "Chuan Chang Liu Shui", and another entry for collection is written in the higher column. These two entries are posted to their corresponding accounts in the "Ti Chang". Mention should be made of the name of the native bank where the money is deposited or to which the collection of the "Poh Mar" is committed. The withdrawals by "Poh Mar" or "cheque" are recorded in the opposite columns of the "Chuan Chang Liu Shui" and the "Ti Chang".[13][14] (See Example 38)

Example 38.

轉帳流水

四月二日

收德恆五萬元（新生）　　付新生五萬元（德恆界）

收新生二千五百元（裕記條/新生）　　付裕記二千五百元（新生）

存放本埠同業

新生銀號　　要摘

四月二日收二千五百元　　四月二日付五萬元（德恆界）

德恆銀號　　要摘

四月二日收五萬元（新生）

存放本埠同業

裕記銀號　　要摘

四月二日付二千五百元（新生）

The method and entries which are used for recording the transactions with other native banks of outside localities, are juse the same as those within the same district, except that neither the

"Tui Hua" nor the "Poh Mar" can be used for accommodation of money."

II. Remittances (匯兌)

It was the main business of native banks in the P'iao Hao period as illustrated in the first chapter; but gradually the modern banks took their place. Before the enforcement of fiat money system, exchange was very profitable to the native banks, but this kind of business ceased after the establishment of exchange control by the Government. In Peking, remittance business lost all its importance when the National Capital was removed to Nanking; there were only remittances between Tientsin and Peking, and even now they are not active in native banks.[4][44]

But Tientsin is the commercial center of North China, where all the exports and imports are concentrated or distributed. As a money market it is closely connected with Shanghai, the chief exporting center of China, and on the other hand it is the original market of export and the terminal market of import for North China. So this business is more prosperous in Tientsin than in Peking, especially the transactions of exchange between Tientsin and Shanghai.[1]

Before 1935, all the exchange between Shanghai and Tientsin was done by the Brokers' Union, called in Chinese "Kung Chi P'ao Ho Ch'u" (公記跑合處), which was organized by the native bankers and had a membership of about twenty brokers. At that time, the exchange in Shanghai taels (申匯) was dealt by native banks as agents; but it was paid or received in the Brokers' Union; even the banks had to go there for settlement of exchange. The parties to an exchange transaction were called "Shou Chiao Chia" (收交家), the buyer being the "Shou Chia" (收家), and the seller the "Chiao Chia" (交家).[6] Every morning at about ten o'clock, each broker of this union or exchange market telephoned to the native and modern banks with which he had some connection, to inquire about their requirements or offers of Shanghai exchange. When they met, if the purchases were equal to the sales, they usually maintained the rate of the previous day, if the purchases were in excess of sales, the rate was raised; if the reverse, it dropped. The idea in raising or lowering the rate was to influence purchases or sales so that both sides might be even.[ʾ] It sometimes happened that even by manipulating the rate, purchases and sales could be not matched for the day, and in that case, there was no official rate. This was called "Men Hang Shih" (閙行市). In this occurrence the buyers and sellers had to negotiate privately betwteen themselves. The rate agreed by them was called "An Hang Shih" (暗行市).[16] Such a situation was decidedly unsatisfactory and harmful to business interests, for remittances of all kinds had to be halted for the remaining part of the day, if there was no rate for Shanghai exchange.[ʾ] This method was applied for the twenty years preceding 1935 (民國二十四年). Since then, the control of currencies was enforced by the Government; this business was transferred to the three National banks, and the union disappeared.[16]

After the Lu Kou Ch'iao incident (蘆溝橋事變), the three national banks lost their controlling power, and the native banks became active in exchange again. But the newly established Federal Reserve Bank assumed the control of exchange, and it is possible that the native banks will again be deprived of the business in the near future.[6]

Remittances inland from Tientsin are mostly handled directly by the native banks. They have often branches in other districts for collection or delivery. The native banks which operate only in re-mittances are not many. They are usually organized on a very small scale, with only one or two persons to take charge of the whole business. The amount of business varies in accordence with the seasonal fluctuations. This is a peculiar phenomenon.[16]

In addition to domestic exchange, there was also formerly exchange with Japan, because of the importance of commercial transactions between Tientsin and Japan. Many branches of native banks were opened in Osaka and Kobe, dealing in foreign exchanges.

But after the Incidents, the conditions have changed considerably.[16] In the last years, this business was operated by the Japanese Banks and the Federal Reserve Bank.

The methods used for remittance are called, "Tien Hui" (電匯), "Hsin Hui" (信匯), "P'iao Hui" (票匯) and "Tiao-Hui" (條匯). The "Tien Hui" is similar to the telegraphic transfers of modern banks. At present, F. R. B. notes are received in Tientsin and they are paid in "Hui Hua" (匯劃) in Shanghai. This is usually called Shanghai exchange (申匯). The second method is called "Hsin Hui" (信匯), viz. the mail transfer universally used in this country. The remitter tells the name and address of the payee to the native bank, which sends by post a letter to a native bank of another district. On receiving the letter, this other native bank notifies the payee who can withdraw money on presenting the receipt sent by the remitter. This method is mostly used by the native banks of the "Si group" (西帮) and "Peking group" (京帮). The "P'iao Hui" is the most usual form: the bill is delivered to the remitter, who sends it directly to the payee, and the money will be paid on representing the bill, but the payee must have a guarantor. This kind of bill is usually a time-bill payable after one or two days, or up to five or seven days after sight. It is called bill of exchange in modern banks. The "Tiao Hui" method is similar to the postal order: it is written by the native bank for the amount to be paid, then is cut vertically into two pieces from the middle. The native bank and the remitter take each one of these pieces. When the two parts can be connected without any doubt, the money may be paid. So it is called "Tui Tiao" (對條) (Refer to p. 40-41). This method is not much used in large cities, but only in the smaller towns, on account of the simplicity of procedure.[4][16][17]

For recording the bills received or sent, a few special words are used in the "Shou Chiao Hui K'uan Chang" (收交匯款帳). The words "Chi Ch'i" (即期) are used for sight-bills, and the word "Ch'i" (期) following the date of payment for a time-bill. If the amount should be paid, the word "Chiao" (交) is added after the abbreviation of the place of the drawee; for instance, when a sight bill is payable at Tientsin, the transaction should be written "Chi Ch'i Tsin Chiao" (即期津交) (See Example 39). Suppose that a bill is committed to a native bank for collection, the entry is recorded with the word "Shou" (收) after mention of the place of the payee (See Example 40). The red stamp "Li Chi" (理訖) is stamped on the entry when the bill has been paid or received. When a letter is sent to the native bank for information of receipt or payment, a red word "Pao" (報) is stamped on the top. The red word "Fu" (疫) means that the letter is sent in answer to an inquiry. It is obvious that a bill sent by a modern bank is always a bill of exchange, but a bill sent by a native bank is usually a "Hui Hsin" (匯信). From the place written in the entry it may be known whether the native bank is drawee or drawer; for instance, the entry of "payable in Tientsin" (津交) means that the native hank in Tientsin is the drawee; if the entry is "payable in Peking" (京交), the native bank in Peking is the drawer.[18][17] (See Example 41)

Example 39.

Example 40.

北京積生銀號
收交匯款帳

四月十六日

即期津收寬記三千元

四月二十一日　期津收德豐銀號二千元

Example 41.

收交匯款帳

啓泰銀號　要摘

四月十日

即期京交鎮山堂八千元

四月十五日　期京交劉光甲二千元

收交匯款帳

啓泰銀號

四月十二日

即期京收薈經堂一千元

四月十七日　期京收泰記四千五百元

When the amount of a remittance is paid, it is recorded in the "Hsien Chin Liu Shui" if paid in cash, or in the "Chuan Chang Liu Shui" if paid in "Po Tiao" or cheque. The entry either in the

"Hsien Chin Liu Shui" or the "Chuan Chang Liu Shui" is to be reported in the account with other native banks in the "Ti Chang". [17] The remittance charges received aro posted into the Commissions Account as a receipt through the "Liu Shui Chang". (See Example 42)

Example 42.

現金流水

外埠費同存欠

積生銀號	要摘
四月十六日 寬記 三千元	

| 收積生銀號三千元 | 四月十六日 寬記 |

轉帳流水

北京積生銀號 收交匯款帳

| 四月十六日 | 收手續費三元 匯水 |
| | 付松茂堂三元 手續費 |

| 即期津收寬記 三千元 | 四月十六日 |

松茂堂 付三元（手續費） 摘要

往來存欵

收三元（松茂堂） 四月十六日

手續費

III. Warehousing

Warehousing business by native banks started only in the earlier years in the Republic. Due to the development of warehouses of modern banks, this business has been much affected. There are, however, a few warehouses of native banks still existing, because the regulations are not so complex and strict as in modern banks warehouses, and the working time is longer, which it is more convenient for the merchants who still follow the old Chinese business-custom. The Peking native banks doing warehousing business are very scarce, but in Tientsin, there are more than twenty native banks' warehouses. The actual number cannot be investigated exactly, not only because the names of the warehouses are different from the original names of native banks, but also because the native bankers are not willing to disclose their names in order to avoid the interference of the controlling authorities.[15]

In general, the warehouse belongs to the native bank; so all the salaries, wages and expenses are paid by the enterprise. The charges are collected by the native bank and there is no cash transaction dealt in the warehouse itself. The staff consist of a Principal (主任), a few accountants (司帳) and godown secretaries (司庫). There is no limit for working time and no holidays even on Sundays.

This is convenient for the customers, but from the view point of the health of the staff, it should be reformed later on.[15]

It sometimes happens that the goods stored in a native bank's warehouse is transferred to a modern bank warehouse, because of lack of space or other reasons. The kinds of goods in the native bank's godown are cotton, wine, oil, rice, flour and so on. Before the restrictions on commodities, cotton was much stored; but nowadays the cotton yarns take its place.[15 18]

The time-unit for calculating the warehouse charges is commonly one month, but the charges on cotton should be calculated weekly. The charges for hazardous goods like cotton, wine, oil, etc. are higher than for other kinds. With regard to long-term customers, half of a year is fixed as a period. As the goods are stored in the godown, no charge is paid in advance. The ordinary bailors pay the charges for the goods taken from the godown at the time of withdrawal. All charges are calculated, except for the goods still in the godown for account of merchants of outside localities, at the end of each month. A bill of warehouse charges (棧租計算帳單) should be given to the bailor at the time of payment.[15]

The insurance premium is added in the warehouse charges. But for the native banks all the goods stored in the godown are insured for a lump sum by one or more insurance companies. It is unnecessary to make a detailed statement the various kinds of goods in the warehouse, but notice should be given to the insurance company when the total value increases or decreases.[15 19]

Before storing, the bailor has to negotiate with the native bank. When everything is settled, the enterprise issues a receipt order for the warehouseman. In the meantime, the bailor has to transport his goods to the godown, and the godown-keeper receive the goods according to the particulars mentioned in the order. Then the native bank gives to the bailor either a warehouse receipt or a "Chê Tze" for goods stored (存貨摺), which is the evidence of goods stored in the godown. Usually for the longer period customers, the "Chê Tze" are used. The accountant must enter this operation in the "Huo Wu Liu Shui Chang" (貨物流水帳) as receiving such amount of goods, and report it in the "Shang Hao Ts'un Huo Chang" (商號存貨帳) if the bailor is a business concern (See Example 43). This entry has to be reported to the "K'o Hao Ts'un Huo Chang" (客號存貨帳) if the bailor is a private person.[15] (See Example 44)

Example 43.

第一　貨物流水帳　天津新生銀號　中華民國三十年一月立　號

三月一日

收東廣號棉紗一百件

收胡魁德米五袋

第二　商號存貨帳　天津新生銀號　中華民國三十年一月立　號

東廣號　第五十六圖捌

一月一日　移存棉紗五十件　由舊帳第一冊移來

三月一日　收棉紗一百件　存181百件

Example 44.

第二　客號存貨帳　天津新生銀號　中華民國三十年一月立　號

胡魁德　棧單第七十五號

一月一日　收米五袋

— 135 —

When a part of the goods is taken off by a bailor, the quantity is recorded as a payment in the lower columns of both the "Huo Wu Liu Shui Chang" (货物流水帐) and the "Ts'un Huo Chang" (存货帐). In either the "Shang Hao Ts'un Huo Chang" (商號存貨帳) or the "K'o Hao Ts'un Huo Chang" (客號存貨帳) a separate account is opened for each bailor. The date and particulars are written in the same way as in other accounts of the native banks.[15] (See Exaple 45)

Example 45.

货物流水帐

三月二日
付協成公司棉紗二十件
付白方立麵十袋

商號存貨帳
協成公司　第三十二號指
三月二日　付棉紗二十件

客號存貨帳
白方立　印五十一號摺
三月二日　付麵十袋

The balance of each kind of goods stored and withdrawn is written in "Su Chou Figures" (Refer to notes of Chapter II) on the top of the higher column with the word "Ts'un" (存) as long as there remains a balance stored. At the end of each period, the amounts of various sorts of goods in the godown should be balanced separately, and written by order after the last entry of that period. On the top of those balances, the two words "Chieh Ts'un" (結存) are added in order to show that these are the balances.[15] (See Example 46)

Example 46.

The insurance premium is paid according to the contract, so there is only one book prepared for the amounts paid or received. The receipts are recorded in the higher columns, and the disbursements are recorded in the lower columns. These entries are posted through either the "Hsien Chin Liu Shui" or the "Chuan Chang Liu Shui".[15] (See Example 47)

Example 47.

現金流水
一月四日
付太平保險公司一千五百元

保險留底
太平保險公司
一月一日付三千元
一月四日付一千五百元

The warehouse fees (棧租), insurance premiums (保險) and carriers expenses (槓力), when received, are entered in either the "Chuan Chang Liu Shui" or the "Hsien Chin Liu Shui". In the "Ti Chang", a book is prepared for all warehouse charges, which is called the "Ts'ang K'u Fei" (倉庫費) and in which three separated accounts are opened for above three different charges. These entries are posted through the "Liu Shui Chang".[15] (See Example 48)

Example 48.

現金流水
四月二日
棧租 收宏記一百四十元
保險 收宏記二十元
槓力 收宏記十元

倉庫費
棧租
批 宏記
收一百四十元

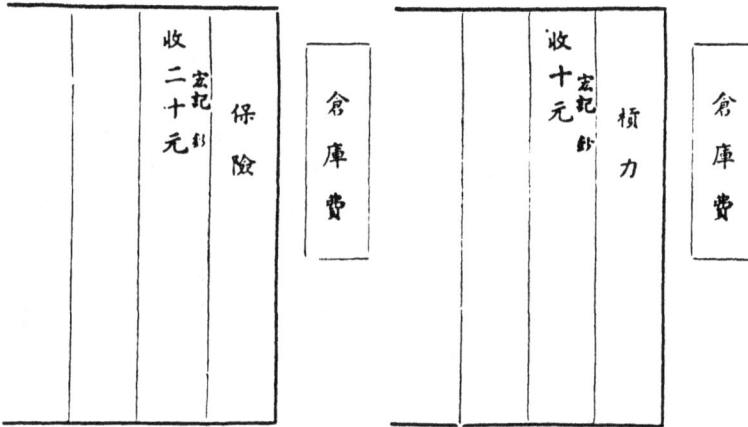

IV. Speculative Transactions

This kind of business was operated by various native banks in Tientsin and Peking, in the different periods; but it was not and still is not so active as in Shanghai which is the central money and exchange market of China. Owing to the frugal and conservative character of the people of North China, the native banks dealing in speculative operations were not very prosperous, especially in Peking.[6][16][18]

An exchange was created by Mr. Wang Kuai Yuan (王奎元) in Peking during the early years of the Republic.[20] From that time speculative transactions increased, but still they were less than in Tientsin. Only a few native banks dealt in negotiable securities, different metallic currencies, silver and gold bullion etc.[21] At present, owing to the restrictions enforced by the authorities to curtail the profiteers' dealings, this business is still not active.

Tientsin is different from Peking. Formerly Russian Rubles (羌帖), and silver dollars were bought and sold by native banks; but gradually, on account of the economic variations, transactions of gold bullion (足金), Shanghai standard gold (標金), Japanese Yen (老頭票) and a few kinds of securities took their place in the activities of Tientsin native banks. In 1919 (民國八年), the Japanese Yen replaced Russian rubles, because of the devaluation or depreciation of the latter currency. The market of Japanese Yen was very active after 1929 (民國十八年), but there was an interval later on. In November 1935 (民國二十四年十一月), when the currency control system was enforced by the government, the Japanese Yen in China became more stable. Gold bullion was also an important object of speculative transactions. A market was organized by native bankers and Japanese merchants in Jung Hsin Company (祭興公司) in the Japanese concession. Doney & Co. came up later on, and combined with the former market to operate the "Tientsin Shang Yeh Ching Chi So" (天津商業經濟所). In March 1936 (民國二十五年), Jung Hsin Co. retired from this business there remained only Doney & Co. Meanwhile the Shanghai standard gold bullion was also operated, with agents in the Shanghai market. The securities were negotiated by a small number of native banks according to the fluctuations of the Shanghai market."

The most active speculative business during last year (1940—民國二十九年) was in paints, Wu Fu Cloths (五福布), rice, flour, and other cereals. Most native banks made profits before the fifth month of the Chinese calender. But after the Chinese festival of the fifth month (五月節) the price of nearly every commodity dropped considerably; a large number of native banks were affected and the figures of their loss were tremendous. But in the present year (民國三十年), speculation has shifted to the Shanghai exchange, which is so called "Shen Hui" (申匯) in Chinese. Due to the deflation of prices, the money of the merchants flocked to the native banks. They neither bought goods nor lent to business concerns, but remitted to Shanghai, because with the rate of exchange prevailing in March, the remitter of Tientsin could make about three thousand dollars' profit for each ten thousand dollars. So the money market in Tientsin was very tightened."

At end of April 1941, on account of the money being so tight in Tientsin, the bnsiness turned to speculation. It is estimated that the profit and loss of all business concerns were about two or three hundred thousand dollars daily. The merchants crowded from dawn to night in the cotton market of Doney & Company. The four strongholds of speculation are "Ta Fu" (大孚), "Chi Ho" (致和), "Ch'iu Chang" (久章) and "Ch'ien Ho" (僉和) native banks, to which more than sixty smaller native banks are to be added. The transactions of the first day amounted to about three thousand seven hundred units of cotton. Under these special conditions, the profits or losses result from large differences.[14]

On the whole, this is not a regular business of native banks, and it is also under the strict supervision of the public authorities, so the native banks which deal mainly in speculative operations have to keep them secret. The records of these transactions cannot be shown openly in the accounts, but they are recorded in a different way. When any amount is paid for purchase of goods, it is recorded either in the "Hsien Chin Liu Shui" or the "Chuan Chang Liu Shui" as usual. But in the "Ti Chang" there is no stock account; there is only a personal account opened under the name of "Chi" (記). The amount of purchase is posted in this account through the "Liu Shui Chang" [18][15] (See Example 49)

Example 49.

現金流水

二月二日

付利記三萬五千元

利記

往來存款

二月付 二日

三萬五千元

要撥

When the goods are sold, the amount received is recorded in the higher column of either the "Hsien Chin Liu Shui" if received in cash, or the "Chuan Chang Liu Shui" for a cheque or "Poh Mar". Then it is posted accordingly to the account of the assumed person in the "Ti Chang"[18] (See Example 50). The difference of the two amounts is either a profit or a loss. If the amount received is more than paid, the profit is deemed to be the interest received, which will be transferred to the higher column of the interest account through the "Chuan Chang Liu Shui"[18][25] (See Example 51)

Example 50.

收利記四萬二千元　　二月十五日　　現金流水

二月十五日收四萬二千元　　利記　　往來存款　　要摘

Example 51.

往來存款

利 記 摘要

二月十五日收四萬二千元 鈔 付七千元 利息

轉帳流水

收收入利息七千元 付利記收入利息七千元 二月十五日

利息帳

收七千元 利記 二月十五日

When there is a loss in the transaction, the difference is recorded in the lower column of the "Chuan Chang Liu Shui" and reported to the "Ti Chang" by paying the amount of the loss. This balance is deemed to be a bad debt (See Example 52). But there is another way to close this book by writing off the amount of the loss: the balance outstanding in the fictitious personal account is left open until the end of the business year.[18]

Example 52.

往來存款

利記　要摘

十二月十日　付　三萬一千元
十二月廿一日　收　二萬八千元
十二月三十日　收　三千元

轉帳流水

十二月三十日
收利記三千元
付呆帳三千元　利記

呆帳

十二月三十日
付三千元　利記

V. Other Business Transactions (其他營業)

Formerly there were a few other kinds of business operated by Tientsin and Peking native banks. Money exchange was very important on account of the circulation of silver and metallic money. When inconvertible money was put into circulation, this business lost its importance. Another kind was to issue notes for the modern banks as agents. Owing to the establishment of the "Fapi" (法幣) system, and the monopoly of note issue granted to the three national banks, this business was no more possible. A few native banks dealt also in purchases of "Kuan Chin" (關金) (Customs gold units) from the national banks on behalf of merchants. They were used for paying duties on imported goods.[23][26]

At the present time, trust business is sometimes done by Tientsin and Peking native banks, but on a very small scale. This business has been seriously affected by the increased importance of modern banks and stock exchanges. Only small amounts of securities and bonds are purchased or sold for the customers.[20] At the same time, a native bank may pay or receive money on its customers' account. The procedure of recording is just the same as for general transactions. The payments and disbursements are recorded in either the "Hsien Chin Liu Shui" or the "Chuan Chang Liu Shui" according that the amount is paid or received in cash or cheques or "Poh Mar". Each entry should be reported to the corresponding account in the "Ti Chang" (See Example 53). The commission received is entered in the "Liu Shui Chang" and posted to the commission account.[17] (See Example 54)

Example 53.

現金流水

五月八日　付嵐記（代買上海股票）一萬七千元

往來存款

嵐記　摘要

五月八日付（代買上海股票帳）一萬七千元

Example 54.

轉帳流水

收手續費（嵐記）八十五元

五月八日　付嵐記（手續費）八十五元

往來存款

嵐記　摘要

五月八日付（手續費）八十五元

Notes of the Chapter

1—The speech of Mr. C. C. Han (韓智齋君), Manager
   of Teh Feng Native Bank in Tientsin; recorded
   by Mr. Y. C. Pien (邊榮璋君記錄)

2—北京銀錢業　　劉奇新著　　（北京東方大學論文）　P. 19

3—天津之銀號　　王子建，趙履謙合著　（法商經濟研究室）P. 7

4—Personal interviews with Mr. C. P. Wei (魏景彭君),
   Manager; and Mr. C. C. Wan (宛游川君) of
   Tientsin Teh Hung Native Bank; and Mr. C.
   M. Ma (馬長民君)　　　　　　　　　　　Feb. 16th 1941

5—中國錢莊概要　　潘子豪著　　（華通書局）　　P. 67—P. 77

6—銀 行 會 計　　顧 準著　　（商務印書館）　　P. 92, P.114—
   　　　　　　　　　　　　　　　　　　　　　　　P. 115

7—(書 名 同 3.)　　　　　　　　　　　　　　P. 18

8—Personal interviews with Mr. C. C. Han (韓智齋君),
   Manager of Teh Fêng Native Bank; Mr. F. C.
   Sun (孫芳忱君), Chief-Accountant　　　March 3rd 1941

9—(書 名 同 2.)   P. 22—P. 23

10—楊著中國金融論　楊蔭溥著　（黎明書店）　 P. 279

11—(書 名 同 6.)   P. 19

12—Personal interviews with Mr. H. Y. Lu (陸效揚君),
and Mr. P. H. Hsü (徐本河君) of Tientsin Native Bankers' Association   March 9th 1941

13—Personal interview with Mr. F. C. Sun (孫芳忱君),
Chief-Accountant of Teh Fêng Native Bank   March 31st 1941

14—Personal interview with Mr. H. S. Chang (張秀山
君), Sub-manager of Teh Hung Native Bank in
Tientsin   March 26th 1941

15—Personal interviews with same persons as 12.   March 19th 1941

16—(書 名 同 6.)   P. 137

17—(書 名 同 5.)   P. 75—P. 73

18—Personal interviews with Mr. F. C. Sun (孫芳忱君),
Chief-Accountant of Teh Fêng Native Bank
in Tientsin; and Mr. Y. C. Pien (邊策琛君),
Manager of Peking   April 14th 1914

19—(書 名 同 3.)   P. 20—P. 22

20—Personal interview with Mr. F. C. Sun (孫芳忱君),
Chief-Accountant of Tientsin Teh Fêng Native
Bank   May 4th 1941

21—(書 名 同 3.)   P. 30—P. 33

22—(書 名 同 5.)   P. 92

23—Personal interviews with the same persons as 12.   March 19th 1941

24—Personal interview with Mr. M. T. Wang (王慕店君),
Manager of Chi Tai Native Bank in Peking   Sept. 9th 1940

25—Personal interviews with the same persons as 12.   Dec. 25th 1940

26—Personal interviews with the same persons as 12.   March 30th 1941

27—Personal interview with Mr. H. P. Ch'ung (种磬
浦君), Manager of Ching Fêng Native Bank   Oct. 19th 1940

CHAPTER V.

DETERMINATION OF NET INCOME & CLOSING OF BOOKS

I. The Methods of Keeping Current-Accounts and Calculating Interest.

In native banks, the dates for settling up all accounts are customarily fixed at each of the three Chinese festivals (三節), which are the fifth day in the fifth month (五月初五) (or Dragon-boat Festival), the fifteenth day of eighth month (mid-autumn festival) (八月十五) and the last day of the Chinese calendar year (臘月三十). These festivals are called "Tuan Wu Chieh" (端午節), "Pa Yueh Chieh" (八月節) and "Nien Ti" (年底) respectively. Of these the end of the Chinese calendar year is the most important one. In regard to the time of settlement between the proprietors and the management, usually the end of the third year is the first term and the end of the fifth year is the final term: this is expressed by native bankers in the following sentence "San Nien I Hsiao Chang, Wu Nien I Ta Chang" (三年一小帳,五年一大帳).[1][2][11][14] At the arrival of the final term, everything may be changed in the enterprise, even the contract.

The first two festivals are less important than the third one: only the interests received and paid are calculated; but at the end of the Chinese year every account should be cleared up.

1. **Calculation of Interest** — Formerly, the method of calculating interest was kept secret by native banks; only the manager, the chief accountant and a few important employees knew how they were calculated. It was unfair for the customers, because either the amount or the number of days were reckoned below or over the actual figures. For instance, the interest on an overdraft or a loan which not exceeding seven days, was reckoned as for one

half of a month, or twenty days were reckoned as one month. It might also happen that interest was charged in addition to the amount which was due; when the customer discovered the fact and asked for explanations, the native banker granted a deduction. But as time went on, customers became more careful for the protection of their interests, and new methods were adopted by the majority of bankers; thus most of these abuses have ceased.[3][5]

The interests of native banks can be classified into interest received on loans, and interests paid for deposits; it must also be borne in mind that interests on both loans and deposits may vary according that the period of reimbursement is fixed or undetermined. Though the rates of interest are different, the methods of calculation are the same. The interests may be calculated annually, monthly or daily. Most native banks use the method of simple interest.[3][6]

(a) The *interest* payable or receivable *annually*, is called "Chou Hsi" (週息): three hundred and sixty-five days are reckoned as one year. This method is very simple for a fixed loan or deposit, the amount of which remains constant: it is sufficient to apply the ordinary formula "$I = P \times i \times t$". But in current-accounts where many different amounts are received or paid at various intervals, the number of days from one balance to another different balance should be calculated separately.[5][6][7]

In order to simplify form of accounts, the balance of each day is written beside the last entry in "Su Chow figures" (蘇州碼). The products of the number of days by the amount of each balance are added up and multiplied by the rate of interest. The total is divided by 365 days, and the interest is found. At the end of each period, all the accountants gather for calculating interest. One of them calls out all the amounts of each balance and one or more accountants add up the figures by using an abacus (算盤). When the results of all the calculators coincide, the amount is taken as correct. The calling figures is called "Ch'ang Shou" (唱數) by native bankers.[3][6][7]

Two kinds of temporary records are usually adopted to

facilitate the calculation of interest: one is the interest calculating book which has been mentioned in Chapter II, the other is a list or a rough paper on which the amount of each balance is written, together with the number of days, and the product. The latter is called by native bankers, "Ta Tan Tze" (打趴子); its nature is similar to that of the former. In a number of native banks the interests were formerly calculated directly from the "Ti Chang". In a few native banks, the form of the "Ti Chang" has been amended on the model of modern banks, which enables to find the product of each balance at the bottom of each column; this method is more convenient and progressive. [56] (Refer to Chapter II)

Let us now take a simple example: A native bank's deposits in another native bank are:

Example 55.

Jan.	13	Paid	$10,000.00
Feb.	19	,,	30,000.00
April	25	,,	31,000.00
July	28	,,	35,000.00
Oct.	12	,,	39,000.00
Nov.	29	,,	42,000.00
		Total	$177,000.00

rate of interest: 5%

The method of calculating interest is as follows:

Jan.	13	Paid	$10,000.00	36 days	Product $	360,000.00
Feb.	19	,,	30,000.00	66 ,,	,,	1,980,000.00
April	25	,,	31,000.00	93 ,,	,,	2,883,000.00
July	28	,,	35,000.00	74 ,,	,,	2,590,000.00
Oct.	12	,,	39,000.00	47 ,,	,.	1,833,000.00
Nov.	29	,,	42,000.00	31 ,,	,,	1,302,000.00
Total Paid			177,000.00		Total	10,948,000.00

(Total amount) $10,948,000.00 × (interest rate) 5% ÷ 365 (days)=

$1499.73 (interest)

In the native bank's account, this operation is written in the following manner:

Example 56.

(b) The *monthly interest* is common for loans or overdrafts, and the rate is evidently higher. Thirty days are customarily counted as one month, and half a month contains fifteen days. Even when the number of days of a balance is actually less than thirty or fifteen days, each balance is calculated as for one month or half a month, until the whole amount is cleared up.[1 9 10 11] The following example, shows how the monthly interests are calculated;

Example 57.

A. The Current account of Chi Tai native bank

Feb.	11		Paid	$4572.08
	19		,,	546.27
	21	Received $5000.00		
	26		,,	650.00
	29		,,	4957.00
March	18	,, 1000.00		
	20		,,	119.00
	21		,,	1415.00
	25		,,	2250.00
	28	,, 3000.00		
	30	,, 4680.74		
May	9		,,	314.07
	18		,,	57.49

May	21			Paid	2000.00
	23			,,	4400.00
	27	Received	2854.97		
June	11			,,	1520.00
	20			,,	256.00
	25	,,	750.00		
	28	,,	7000.00		
	30	Balance (Dr.)	$1228.80		

B. The method of calculating interest-interest rate 1.2% (Monthly)

Feb.	11			Paid $4572.08	
	21	Received $4572.08		half month interest	$27.42
	19			Paid 546.27	
	21	,,	427.92		
March	18	,,	118.35	one month interest	1.42
Feb.	26			Paid 650.00	
March	18	,,	650.00	one month interest	7.80
Feb.	29			Paid $4957.00	
March	18	,,	$ 231.65	one month interest	$ 2.78
	28	,,	3000.00	,, ,, ,,	36.00
	30	,,	1725.35	,, ,, ,,	25.70
	20			Paid 119.00	
	30	,,	119.00	half month interest	0.71
	21			Paid 2250.00	
	30	,,	1421.39		
May	27	,,	828.61	two months interest	19.89
	9			Paid 314.07	
	27	,,	314.07	one month interest	3.77
	18			Paid 57.49	
	27	,,	57.49	half month interest	0.34
	21			Paid 2000.00	
	27	,,	1654.80		
June	25	,,	345.20	one month interest	4.14
May	23			Paid 4400.00	
June	25	,,	404.80	one month interest	4.86

June	28	Received	3995.20	1½ month interest 71.91
	11			Paid 1520.00
	28	,,	1520.00	one month interest 18.24
	20			Paid 256.00
	28	,,	256.00	half month interest 1.54
	Balance (Dr.)		1,288.80	

Total interest $230.02

(c) The name for *daily interest* in native banks is "Ch'ai Hsi" (拆息); it is no more used at present in either Tientsin or Peking native banks, but it is still very common in Shanghai. The rate of interest in Shanghai is quoted twice a day, once in the morning and once at noon by the Shanghai Native Bankers' Association and the highest rate fixed is 7°/$_{oo}$. In Tientsin, a few years ago, the interests on short-term loans were calculated daily, and the rate of interest was determined by dividing the monthly rate by the number of days in a month, thirty. The rate was customarily expressed in terms of so many cents per thousand dollars, such as "daily interest 40cts." meaning forty cents being paid for each thousand dollars a day.[7][13]

2. **Handling Current Accounts**—Considering that the main business of native banks consists in deposits and loans, one will easily realize that the current accounts, which contain a whole picture of the native bank's current transactions, are of the utmost importance. Each transaction, either for deposit or for loan, is recorded in the "Hsien Chin Liu Shui" or the "Chuan Chang Liu Shui" according that the amount is paid or received in cash or in other bills. All these entries should be posted to the corresponding accounts in the "Ti Chang". The different rates of interest and the procedure of recording the above transactions have been illustrated in the third chapter. Concerning the records of interests, we find a special account called "Interest Account" mentioned in the second chapter. Both interests received and paid are posted in this account through the "Chuan Chang Liu Shui". If the interest is received, it is recorded in the "Chuan Chang Liu Shui" as a receipt of the

native bank and a payment of the debtor, and the two entries appear in the corresponding accounts of the "Ti Chang" (See Example 58). When the interest should be paid, the opposite entries of receipt by the payee and paying the interest appear in both the "Chuan Chang Liu Shui" and "Ti Chang".[3][0][13] (See Example 59)

Example 58.

轉帳流水

收收入利息三千五百元（延記）　四月十五日　付延記三千五百元（活期放款息）

活期存款

延記　四月十五日 付三千五百元（息）　摘要 定期三月月息一分二 立有存扎

利息帳

收三千五百元（延記）　四月十五日

Example 59.

往來存款

贏 古 堂　週息五厘

六月廿日收三百八十元　息

將帳流水

六月三十日

收贏古堂三百八十元　往來存款息

付付出利息三百八十元　贏古堂

利 息 帳

六月三十日

付三百八十元　贏古堂

The above transactions are those dealt with customers, other native banks, or any other parties. There is another case concerning the records of advances to staff members. No special book is prepared for recording the "Chia Chou" (加籌) which has been mentioned in the first chapter. The manager and important employees are often allowed to draw "I Hsin I Chou" (一薪一籌); these overdrafts are usually entered in the suspense account through either the "Hsien Chin Liu Shui" or the "Chuan Chang Liu Shui". No interest has to be paid on the "Chia Chou" by the borrower; so these entries never appear in the interest account. The deposits of the employees and the proprietors are recorded with the same procedure as other deposits accounts. So there is nothing peculiar, except that the rates of interest allowed are specially high.[14][15]

II. The Summarization of Profit and Loss

The policy of most native banks is to keep their books on the "cash basis", that is to say, to consider as income earned only that which has been received in cash, and correspondingly, only the expenses actually paid in cash constitute charges to current income. The terms of accrued income and deferred income are rarely found in these enterprises and, as a consequence, very few adjusting book entries are necessary at the close of each financial period.[4][6]

However, the financial condition in the whole year should be indicated clearly at the close of the fiscal period. The informations contained in "Ti Chang" are usually scattered over a large number of individual accounts. In order to obtain a concise view of the results of the business, all the informations have to be summarized. The statement prepared in native banks for summarizing the temporary proprietorship accounts and indicating the net results as to profits or losses is usually called now-a-days the Profit and Loss Account; but it is sometimes given a different name according to the opinion of the chief accountant.[4]

At an earlier period, there was no such statement as an intermediary for showing the total expenses and income. Gradually a special book was introduced for recording all temporary propreietorship items; but it was combined with two or more kinds of items, such as interest, commission, expenses, etc. All the expenditures and incomes were entered in this account. The amounts were often balanced at end of each month before recording, so that in the last day of the considered period only a total sum showing the net profit or loss was recorded.[4][6]

Later on, this was reformed, all the items of either profits or losses were recorded in this statement[4] which was named by using a few lucky words.[6] It was sometimes treated as a personal account, or in some native banks it was merely a temporary statement. In "Chu Po Shih" (珠寶市) Peking, the names commonly used by most native banks were "Ying Yü" (盈餘), "Chi Yü" (積餘), "Sê" (色) and some others. "Sê" meant the profit and loss on silver taels, due to the differences of fineness in silver bars or Yuan Pao (元寶); it contained two sets of items, the first one, "Ch'u Sê" (出色), being the expenditures and the second, "Ju Sê" (入色) the income.[3][16]

While this statement was treated as a personal account which was named "Yü Chin Tang" (餘金堂), or "Te Li Tang" (得利堂), or a supposed name of a person, the receipts and disbursements were recorded in the book. A note was written clearly beside each entry showing to which kind it referred.[16]

However, the enterprises kept formerly a book corresponding to the Profit and Loss Account in the double entry book-keeping. This statement became more unified only in the last twenty years. A few more conservative native bankers are still using their old method by transferring all items of profits and losses directly to the final account without the profit and loss statement.[17]

Before we proceed further to the Profit and Loss statement, the items of temporary proprietorship, which contain expenses and income, and their records should be explained first.

The items of income include the commissions, interests, remittance charges, warehouse charges, rents, income on investment and others. The comissions received include all the commissions for selling and buying gold and silver bars, securities, bonds, etc., and oftentimes the remittance charges received are also classified as commission. The income from interests is the main source of profit for the native bank, and is usually much in excess of others. The warehouse charges are limited to native banks which have godowns. At any rate, when any kind of income is received, the entry should be recorded in the "Liu Shui" and then posted to the "Ti Chang". As for other entries posted, the red word "posted" (過) is stamped on the top of the two identical entries entered in the "Liu Shui" and the "Ti Chang".[10][18] (See Example 60)

Example 60.

現金流水		
十一月二十日	收手續費三百元 （啟記）	收收入利息五百元 （明光號）

手續費	十一月二十日	收啟記三百元

利息	十一月二十日	收明光號五百元

The items of expenditure are various, they include all the
expenses disbursed for the purpose of carrying on business with a
profit, such as: commissions paid, interests paid, administrative
expenses, salaries, rent, taxes, insurance premium, printing and
stationery charges, remittance charges, writing off of preliminary
expenses, of repairs and maintenance, of cost of furniture and
fixtures, bad debts and other expenses paid.[9]

Under the title of commissions the charges paid to other
native banks or business firms for services rendered in buying or
selling negotiable securities, gold and silver bullion etc. are recorded.
It is evident that the interests paid are very important. All these
entries are recorded in the "Liu Shui" as expenditures paid and as
a receipt for the other party; every entry has to be reported
accordingly to the "Ti Chang".[18] (See Example 61)

Example 61.

The administrative expenses of a native bank represent the amounts paid for telephone, telegraph, stationery, postage, printing, electric light, water, diet, salaries, rent, taxes, entertainment charges, and miscellaneous expenses. As the disbursements are comparatively small and regular, a special "Liu Shui", which is called "Ying Yeh Kai Chih Liu Shui" (營業開支流水) and a "Fu Shih, Tsa Fei" (膳食,雜費) account in the "Ti Chang" are separately opened by many native banks (Refer to Chapter II). Therefore, the sundry entries may not appear in the ordinary "Liu Shui" before the close of each month. When any payment is made, it should be posted to the lower column of "Fu Shih, Tsa Fei" through the "Ying Yeh Kai Chih Liu Shui".[9] (See Example 62)

Example 62.

民國三十年一月一日立
營業開支流水
第一冊

二月二十九日

付郵電費五毛（郵票）

付福食七十元八毛（米一袋）

郵電費

二月廿九日付五毛（郵票）

福食
雜費

福食

二月廿九日付七十元八毛（米一袋）

福食
雜費

The item of preliminary expenses, exists only in newly established native banks. An informal account of preliminary expenses, called "Kai Pan Fei" (開辦費), is prepared at the beginning, and the capital invested is recorded first: receiving such amount of capital, or such amount borrowed from another native or modern bank. After the business has commenced, it should be posted to a formal Preliminary Expenses Account in the "Ti Chang" through the "Chuan Chang Liu Shui" (See Example 63). It is the custom of the enterprises that this amount should be written off within three years, but the yearly proportion depends on the amount of net profit.[19]

Example 63.

開辦費

十月八日 收新生一萬元 資本金

十月十日 付酬應費二百五十元

付登記費二百元

The amounts paid for furniture and fixtures, repairs and maintenance etc. should also be written off at end of each business year in the same manner as preliminary expenses. But the item of bad debts is somewhat different; for it may be partly or fully recovered later on. Therefore, the native bankers often write off the amount of bad debts at the close of each period; and if any sum is reimbursed in the next period, it will be deemed as an income. The account of bad debts is frequently kept open until there is no possibility for collection. The procedure of writing off is called "Tiao Chang" (挑帳). This entry is recorded in the "Chuan Chang Liu Shui" paid by bad debts, and received from the debtor; then it is reported to the corresponding accounts of the "Ti Chang"[6][8] (See Example 64). But this is not the practice of every native bank; the amount of bad debts is sometimes written off directly in the final statement according to the old accounting method of native banks.

Example 64.

転帳流水

收廣記五千元 拋出
十二月三十日
付呆帳五千元

定期放款

廣記
十二月三十日收五千元 拋

呆帳

十二月三十日
付廣記五千元

The transfer of the temporary proprietorship items—expenses and income—to the vested proprietorship accounts constitutes the work of closing. The Profit and Loss Account is used as a summary

— 165 —

through which the net result can be transferred to the vested proprietorship accounts by means of the "Wan Chin Chang" (萬金帳)[5] [13] [20] (Refer to Chapter II). Apparently the Profit and Loss Account constitutes a part of the method or medium of closing.

The transfer of the above mentioned entries is made first in the "Chuan Chang Liu Shui" and posted from there to the "Ti Chang", like all other entries. The current sections of the various expense and income accounts are then ruled off and the "Ti Chang" is said to be "closed"; the words "Ping" (平) or "Ch'u Ch'ing" (除清) are written on the top of the last entry of each book. In the Profit and Loss Account, all the items of expenditure are charged against those of income.[8] [16]

In relation to the procedure of transferring, the items of expenditure are recorded in the higher columns and those of income in the lower columns of the "Chuan Chang Liu Shui"; but an opposite entry for transferring to the Profit and Loss Account should be made next to the original entry. The balance of the two sets of entries is the net profit or loss, and this net profit or loss is recorded also in the "Chuan Chang Liu Shui" by receiving the net profit which is called "Chun I Chin" (純益金), "Ku Lee Chang" (股利帳), etc., and paying the same amount for the Profit and Loss Account. This statement is also closed after the transfer. The entries of profits and losses in the "Chuan Chang Liu Shui" will be briefly illustrated below.[16]

"Chuan Chang Liu Shui"

12th Month, 30th day.

Received Profit and Loss		$2,000.00	
	Paid	Commission Received	$20,000.00
Received Profit and Loss		$50,000.00	
	Paid	Interest Income	$50,000.00
Received Interest Paid		$10,000.00	
	Paid	Profit and Loss	$10,000.00

Received Administrative Expenses $ 5,000.00
           Paid   Profit and Loss $ 5,000.00
Received Salaries $5,000.00
           Paid   Profit and Loss $ 5,000.00
Received Preliminary Expenses Written off $400.00
           Paid   Profit and Loss $ 400.00
Received Repairs & Maintenance Written off $400.00
           Paid   Profit and Loss $ 400.00
Received Furniture & Fixtures Written off $300.00
           Paid   Profit and Loss $ 300.00
Received "Chun I Chin" (Net Profit) $39,000.00
           Paid   Profit and Loss $39,000.00

The following example is the form of "Chuan Chang Liu Shui" for Profit and Loss in Chinese.

Example 65.

收純益金三萬九千元 付盈餘三萬九千元	收攤提營業用器具三百元 付盈餘三百元	收攤提裝修費四百元 付盈餘四百元	收攤提開辦費四百元 付盈餘四百元	收全人酬勞五千元 付盈餘五千元	收營業開支五千元 付盈餘五千元	收付出利息一萬元 付盈餘一萬元	收盈餘五萬元 付收入利息五萬元	收盈餘二萬元 付手續費二萬元	十二月三十日	轉帳流水

It must be clearly understood that the above entries are not records of transactions but merely transfers. The purpose of these entries is obviously to close the various accounts of expenses and income and effect a summarization in the "Ying Yü" account. Thus, the words "Received" or "Paid" preceding each entry imply no other meaning than "recording on the upper part of the account" or "recording on the lower part of the account." [10]

In posting the closing entries of the "Chuan Chang Liu Shui" to the Profit and Loss Account in the "Ti Chang", usually only the group totals as indicated by the entry will appear. The directions of the entries appearing in the two sections of Profit and Loss Account are identical to those of the "Chuan Chang Liu Shui". In other words, an entry of higher column of "Chuan Chang Liu Shui" will be posted correspondingly in higher column of Profit and Loss Account. The Profit and Loss Account of "Ti Chang" for the illustration will appear as follows when completely posted: [10]

Profit and Loss

12th Month, 30th day.

Received Commission	$20,000,000	
,, Interest Income	50,000,000	
Paid Interest Paid		$10,000.00
,, Administrative Expenses		5,000.00
,, Salaries		5,000.00
,, Preliminary Expenses Written off		400.00
,, Repairs and Maintenance Written off		400.00
,, Furniture and Fixtures Written off		300.00
,, "Chun I Chin"		39,000.00
Received "Chun I Chin"	$39,000.00	
(Balanced)		

To show the original feature, the facsimile of Profit and Loss Account in Chinese is given below:

Example 66.

	民國廿九年十二月卅日立 盈餘

收純益金三萬九千元 付純益金三萬九千元 付攤提營業用器具三百元 付攤提裝修費四百元 付攤提開辦費四百元 付仝人酬勞五千元 付營業開支五千元 付付出利息一萬元 收收入利息五萬元 收手續費二萬元 十二月三十日

It should be kept clearly in mind that the Profit and Loss Account is only a summary account and should never be used for current entry, for the process of closing the books is merely a method or device by which the transactions for the fiscal year are summarized and the net result determined. The net result, whether a profit or loss, belongs to the proprietors and the management; and must ultimately be shown in the "Wan Chin Chang".[19] It is a custom of the native bankers to write off large sums for depreciation of buildings, furniture and fixtures, and preliminary expenses, when the net profit is large. If the net profit of the year is small, only a small amount is written off, in order not to make the business conditions of the enterprise to appear worse.[6]

After the net profit has been determined, it should be shared among the proprietors and the management in proportion to the ratio mentioned in the contract. If there is a small remainder, it is transferred to a surplus or reserve account which is called "Ying Yü Kun Ts'un" (盈餘滾存) through the "Chuan Chang Liu Shui", received by "Ying Yü Kun Ts'un" and paid by Profit and Loss Account.[10][31] (See Example 67)

Example 67.

純益金

十二月三十日
付盈餘滾存一千元

轉帳流水

十二月三十日
收盈餘滾存（純益金）一千元
付純益金（盈餘滾存）一千元

盈餘滾存

十二月三十日
收純益金（二十九年度）一千元

All the temporary proprietorship accounts for the current period are closed up when the items of expense and income are transferred to the Profit & Loss Account by means of the "Chuan Chang Liu Shui" (See Example 68). But the open balances shown in the "Ti Chang" constitute either assets, liabilities, or vested proprietorship which will be shown in the final statement.[27]

Example 68.

III. The Preparation of Final Statement

The method of accounting used in Chinese business fields, especially in native banks, for the presentation of the financial condition of a business is known as the "Four Pillars Method" (四柱法). It is so called because of the four groups into which the items of accounts are divided namely "Balances Carried Down" (舊管), "New Receipts" (新收), "Amounts Paid Out" (開除) and "Balances in Hand" (實在).[5 33 33] These four pillars will be illustrated in turn.

(1) **Balances Carried Down** — It contains the credit balances of accounts which are carried down for the next financial period. They are chiefly the capital, the "Hu Pên" and reserves which are owed to the proprietor or proprietors and various kinds of deposits. The capital and "Hu Pên" are the liabilities of the enterprise toward the proprietor or proprietors. The reserves are the profits undivided which are also liabilities of the native bank.[3 33 34]

As to the deposits, they can be classified into fixed deposits, modern banks deposits, deposits of other native banks, current deposits (called "Chê Chiao Ts'un K'uan" — 摺交存款) and temporary deposits. The temporary deposits contain the dividends due to proprietors reported for the previous years, balances carried from previous years, interests unpaid which are also liabilities of the enterprise. Thus, the whole amount of this group is a liability of the native bank.[7 34]

(2) **New Receipts** — In the second group there are the items of gains on the income accounts. They are the accounts of the sales and other gains such as interest received, commissions received, etc.. Consequently, the accounts under this group are the gains of the enterprise.[5 33 34]

(3) **Balances Paid Out** — In the accounts of this group, we find all the amounts paid for expense purposes by the enterprise, recorded as administrative expenses, interest paid, and other

expenditures. Generally this group shows the loss of the native bank.[23][24]

(4) **Balances in Hand** — All the assets of the native bank are included in this group, such as cash in hand and in other native banks, loans to debtors, etc.[4][22][24]

The respective position of the above mentioned four groups is shown in the following formula:[22]

"BALANCES CARRIED DOWN + NEW RECEIPTS — AMOUNTS PAID OUT=BALANCE IN HAND"

The norminal accounts are closed when the profit or loss is determined, but the "Ti Chang" accounts still show the assets, liabilities and proprietorship; so the formula is changed into:[22]

"BALANCES CARRIED DOWN+NEW RECEIPTS=BALANCE IN HAND"

The above mentioned method and formulas are applied generally in subsidiary records, especially in the final statement.

It is the custom of native banks to close the accounts at the end of every month, to find the net profit or loss during the month as an information to the management. At the end of each Chinese business year, there will be a final closing of accounts in order to find the net profit or loss during the year. When the net profit or loss is found, it is possible to determine whether there are profits to be shared to the proprietor or proprietors and the management; and whether there is a bonus to the staff or not.[24][25]

The approximate form and order of the "Monthly Report" which is compiled at the end of each month, to show the business and financial condition of the enterprise (See Chapter II) is shown herebelow:

Monthly Report

From ··········· Month ··········· day to ··········· Month ··········· day in year of Republic of China

Balances Carried Down (舊管)

Capital

Received ⋯⋯⋯⋯⋯⋯⋯⋯ Tang (堂) ⋯⋯⋯⋯⋯⋯ dollars

" ⋯⋯⋯⋯⋯⋯⋯⋯ " ⋯⋯⋯⋯⋯⋯⋯ "

Total Receipt ⋯⋯⋯⋯⋯⋯⋯⋯⋯⋯⋯ dollars

Fixed Deposits

Received ⋯⋯⋯⋯⋯⋯⋯⋯ Tang ⋯⋯⋯⋯⋯⋯⋯⋯⋯⋯⋯⋯⋯ dollars

" ⋯⋯⋯⋯⋯⋯⋯ Hao (號) ⋯⋯⋯⋯⋯⋯⋯⋯⋯⋯⋯⋯ "

" ⋯⋯⋯⋯⋯⋯⋯ Chün (君) ⋯⋯⋯⋯⋯⋯⋯⋯⋯⋯⋯⋯ "

" ⋯⋯⋯⋯⋯⋯⋯⋯ ⋯⋯⋯⋯⋯⋯⋯⋯⋯⋯⋯⋯⋯ "

Total Receipt ⋯⋯⋯⋯⋯⋯⋯⋯⋯⋯⋯ dollars

Modern Banks' Deposits

Received ⋯⋯⋯⋯⋯⋯⋯⋯ Bank ⋯⋯⋯⋯⋯⋯⋯⋯⋯⋯⋯⋯⋯⋯⋯ dollars

" ⋯⋯⋯⋯⋯⋯⋯⋯ " ⋯⋯⋯⋯⋯⋯⋯⋯⋯⋯⋯⋯⋯⋯ "

" ⋯⋯⋯⋯⋯⋯⋯⋯ " ⋯⋯⋯⋯⋯⋯⋯⋯⋯⋯⋯⋯⋯⋯ "

Total Receipt ⋯⋯⋯⋯⋯⋯⋯⋯⋯⋯⋯ dollars

Other Native Banks' Deposits

Received ⋯⋯⋯⋯⋯⋯⋯ Native Bank ⋯⋯⋯⋯⋯⋯ dollars

Total Receipt ⋯⋯⋯⋯⋯⋯⋯⋯⋯⋯⋯ dollars

Current Deposits (摺交存款)

Received ⋯⋯⋯⋯⋯⋯⋯ Hao (號) ⋯⋯⋯⋯⋯⋯⋯⋯⋯⋯⋯ dollars

" ⋯⋯⋯⋯⋯⋯⋯ Company ⋯⋯⋯⋯⋯⋯⋯⋯⋯⋯ "

" ⋯⋯⋯⋯⋯⋯⋯ Foreign firm ⋯⋯⋯⋯⋯⋯⋯⋯ "

Total Receipt ⋯⋯⋯⋯⋯⋯⋯⋯⋯⋯⋯ dollars

Temporary Deposits

Received ⋯⋯⋯⋯⋯⋯⋯⋯ Tang ⋯⋯⋯⋯⋯⋯⋯⋯⋯⋯⋯⋯⋯ dollars

(The dividend of the proprietors reported for the previous years)

Received ⋯⋯⋯⋯⋯⋯⋯⋯ Tang ⋯⋯⋯⋯⋯⋯⋯⋯⋯⋯⋯⋯ dollars

(Balances carried from previous years)

" Interest Unpaid ⋯⋯⋯⋯⋯⋯⋯⋯⋯⋯⋯⋯⋯ dollars

"New Receipts" (新收)

Received Profit of ⋯⋯⋯⋯⋯⋯⋯ ⋯⋯⋯⋯⋯⋯⋯⋯⋯ dollars

" " " ⋯⋯⋯⋯⋯⋯⋯ ⋯⋯⋯⋯⋯⋯⋯⋯⋯ "

" " " ⋯⋯⋯⋯⋯⋯⋯ ⋯⋯⋯⋯⋯⋯⋯⋯⋯ "

Total Receipt ⋯⋯⋯⋯⋯⋯⋯⋯⋯⋯⋯ dollars

"Balances Carried Down" ⎫
"New Receipt" ⎰ Grand Total Receipt ················· dollars

"Amounts Paid Out" (開除)

Paid Interests ·· dollars
  ,, Miscellaneous Expenditures ······················ ,,
  ,, Daily Expenses ····································· ,,
  ,, Rent ·· ,,
           Total Disbursement ················· dollars

"New Balance in Hand" (實在)
Fixed Loans

Paid ··············· Tang ················· dollars
  ,, ················· Hao ··············· ,,
         Total Disbursement ····························· dollars

Loans to Modern Banks

Paid ··············· Bank ··············· dollars
  ,, ··············· ,, ··············· ,,
         Total Disbursement ····························· dollars

Loans to Other Native Banks

Paid ··············· Native Banks··············· dollars
  ,, ··············· ,, ,, ··············· ,,
         Total Disbursement ····························· dollars

Current Loans (摺交欠款)

Paid ··············· Hao or Firm ··············· dollars
  ,, ··············· ,, ,, ,, ··············· ,,
         Total Disbursement ····························· dollars

Temporary Loans

Piad ································· ····················· dollas
  ,, Earnest Money on ································· ,,
  ,, Accrued Interest Receivable ················· ,,
         Total Disbursement ····························· dollars

Cash on Hand

Paid Bank Notes ························· dollars
         Total Disbursement ····························· dollars

CHAPTER V

"Amounts Paid Out"
"New Balance in Hand" } Grand Total Disbursement ·········· dollars

Clearing up

"New Receipts"

Profit of ···················   ························· dollars

  „ „ ···················   ·························· „

  „ „ ···················   ·························· „

      Total Profit ····························· dollars

"Amounts Paid Out"

Interest Payable Written off ······························· dollar

Miscellaneous Expenditures Written off ······················· „

Daily Expenses Written off ······························· „

      Total Amounts Paid Out·············dollars

All should be cleared up

    Under (仰蒙)

The Profits bestowed by Heaven···········dollars (New Receipts —

Amounts Paid Out

    Future Wealth (裕後)   = Net Profit)

    Like stream never stops flowings.

(Refer to Appendix II)

The "Annual Report" is the final statement of the enterprise at the end of each business year; it ascertains the general financial position of the enterprise. The "Four Pillars Method" is similarly applied in this statement, but each item shows the amount for the whole year.[15]

The first pillar, "Balances Carried Down" is used to denote sums owing to persons who have given credit to the enterprise, and which are represented by credit balances on personal accounts. This is a liability of the native bank. The second one, "New Receipts" includes the sums earned by the enterprise. If the total of the third group, "Amounts Paid Out" which comprises all the expenditures and loss of the enterprise during the concerned period is deducted from the total of "New Receipts", the remainder will be the excess of assets over liabilities, which is the proprietor's interest in the native bank. With regard to the last pillar, "Balance in hand," we may find any property owned by the enterprise. It is represented by debit balances on real accounts and personal accounts.[29]

From the above explanations, we may conclude that this statement serves just the same purpose as the Balance Sheet used in double entry book-keeping by any commercial banks.

The form and arrangement of items are similar to those of the "Monthly Report" as mentioned previously. But it should be remembered that this statement is generally used to show the financial condition of the enterprise to the proprietor or proprietors; so the amount of profit or loss which is shared either by the proprietor and or by the manager, according to the proportions mentioned in the contract, should be mentioned clearly in addition.[35] This additional part is entered between the amount of net profit and a few lucky words, as:

....

The Profits bestowed by Heaven..............dollars

........Tang, Share of Proprietor ....Feng (份) (%) being......dollars

Mr......., Share of the management...... Feng (%)   ,, ...   ,,

Surplus Reserve Fund.........Feng (%)   ,, ...   ,,

    Total amount shared...........dollars

IV. The Appropriation of Earned Surplus and Its Relation to the Proprietors' Interest

It is apparent that the capital is the fundamental instrument for starting the enterprise. As has been said previously, the contract should be concluded first, and both the contents of the contract and the amounts of capital and "Hu Pên" are copied into the proprietorship account called "Wan Chin Chang" (萬金帳), in which the net profit or loss of each business period will be entered from time to time. Meanwhile, another capital account used only for recording the amount of capital is opened in which the amount of capital is posted through either the "Hsien Chin Liu Shui" (See Example 69) or the "Chuan Chang Liu Shui".[4 10 10] (See Example 70)

Example 69.

| 現金流水 | 一月一日 | 收資本金五萬元 經山堂 | 收資本金五萬元 普經堂 |

| 資本金 | 一月一日 | 收五萬元 經山堂 | 收五萬元 普經堂 |

Example 70.

| 轉帳流水 | 一月一日 大中支 | 收資本金五萬元 經山堂 大中支 | 收資本金五萬元 普經堂 大中支 | 付大中銀行十萬元 支二只 |

| 資本金 | 一月一日 大中支 | 收五萬元 經山堂 大中支 | 收五萬元 普經堂 大中支 |

Concerning to the "Hu Pên", the procedures for recording is similar to that for fixed deposits; the amount deposited is posted through the "Liu Shui".[10][11][10] (See Example 71) (Refer to Chapter II)

Example 71.

When all the capital and "Hu Pen" have been received by the native bank, the business operations can be commenced. Usually the net profit of a newly opened enterprise is not disposed of during the first two years. It is a custom that the net profit or loss is shared between the proprietor or proprietors and the manager at the end of the third fiscal year. A part of the earned surplus is commonly kept for reserve fund, and another smaller part is distributed to the staff as a bonus, as it has been said in the first chapter.[18] All the records appear in the "Wan Chin Chang" and are posted through the "Chuan Chang Liu Shui".

The reserve fund is called "Hou Ch'êng" (厚成), or "Ts'ai Shêng Ku" (財神股), or "Kung Chi" (公積) by native bankers. It is an accumulation of net profits, after all expenses, including reserves or provisions have been provided for. The object of such a reserve is to conserve the resources of the enterprise for the purpose of:—

(1) Providing extra working capital, or
(2) Increasing the financial stability of the concern.[27]

The proportion of the reserve to the total net profit is usually agreed by the proprietor or proprietors and the manager at the end of the business period. Ordinarily, its amount is ten per cent of the total surplus in native banks. But in the enterprise, the manager is always treated partly as a proprietor and is entitled to a fixed proportion of the surplus. When the reserve is deducted from the net profit which is owned by both proprietor and the manager, the latter is part-owner of the surplus in the reserve. Therefore he may take back his part of surplus kept as reserve, when he leaves the enterprise.[10]

At the end of each business period, the surplus is recorded in the "Chuan Chang Liu Shui" as a receipt of the amount of net profit, and payment of the same to the proprietor and the manager, or to reserve. Meanwhile, the amount placed in reserve should be received by the Reserve Fund account: on account of the simplicity of the records. Furthermore, the year in which the reserve fund is appropriated has to be mentioned by a side-note in the entry.[10] (See Example 72)

Example 72.

厚成	民國二十九年	十二月 三十日收一萬元 廿九年提出		轉帳流水		十二月三十日	收純益金十萬元	付鍾山堂五萬元	付著經堂五萬元	收厚成一萬元 廿九年提出	付厚成一萬元

Notes of the Chapter

1—Personal interview with Mr. C. P. Wei （魏景彭君）
of Tah Chuang Bank in Tientsin   Aug. 21st 1940

2—Personal interviews with Mr. S.S. Shang （尚殺珊
君）, of Peking Native Bankers' Association;
and Mr. Y. T. Kuei （桂月汀君) in Peking   Sept. 7th 1940

3—Personal interviews with Mr. H. Y. Lu（陸效揚君),
and Mr. P. H. Hsü （徐本河君) of Tientsin Native Bankers' Association   March 9th 1941

4—Personal interviews with Mr. C. C. Han（韓智齋君),
Manager of Teh Fêng Native Bank; and Mr. C.
F. Wang （王春埜君), in Tientsin   March 26th 1941

5—Personal interviews with Mr. H. P. Ch'ung （种罄
浦君), Manager of Ching Fêng Native Bank;
and Mr. C. P. Wei (魏景彭君), Manager of Teh
Hung Native Bank in Tientsin   Oct. 10th 1940

6—Personal interview with Mr. H. S. Chang （張秀山
君), Sub-manager of Teh Hung Native Bank   March 5th 1941

7—錢 業 珍 寶   徐本河君抄本

8—Personal interviews with same persons as 3　　March 30th 1941

9—Personal interviews with Mr. C. P. Wei（魏景彭君），
　　Manager; and Mr. C. C. Wan（宛濟川君）of
　　Teh Hung Native Bank; and Mr. C. M. Ma（馬
　　長民君）in Tientsin　　　　　　　　　　Feb. 16th 1941

10—Personal interview with Mr. F. C. Sun（孫芳忱君），
　　Chief-Accountant of Teh Fêng Native Bank in
　　Tientsin　　　　　　　　　　　　　　March 5th 1941

11—Personal interviews with same persons as 3　　March 19th 1941

12—Personal interview with Mr. P.H. Hsü（徐本河君），
　　of Tientsin Native Bankers' Association　　May 10th 1941

13—Personal interviews with same persons as 3　　Feb. 26th 1941

14—Personal interviews with same persons as 3　　March 26th 1941

15—天津之銀號　　王子建,趙履謙合著　（法商經濟研究室）P. 52

16—Personal interviews with Mr. C. P. Wei（魏景彭君），
　　Manager of Teh Hung Native Bank; and Mr.
　　F. C. Sun（孫芳忱君），Chief-Accountant of Teh
　　Fêng Native Bank　　　　　　　　　March 22nd 1941

17—Personal interviews with same persons as 3　　March 31st 1941

18—Personal interviews with Mr. F. C. Sun（孫芳忱君），
　　Chief-Accountant of Teh Fêng Native Bank
　　in Tientsin; and Mr. J. C. Pien（邊榮璋君），
　　Manager in Peking　　　　　　　　　April 14th 1914

19—Personal interviews with Mr. C. C. Han（韓智齋
　　君），Manager; and Mr. F. C. Sun（孫芳忱君），
　　Chief-Accountant of Teh Fêng Native Bank　　March 29th 1941

20—Personal interviews with Mr. T. H. Yü（余天休君），
　　Mr. Y. T. Kuei（桂月汀君），and Mr. S. S. Shang
　　（尚毅珊君）in Peking　　　　　　　　Sept. 11th 1941

21—Paton: Accountant's Handbook　　　　P. 277

22—Yeh Shu Yuan: The Method of Accounting used
　　in Chinese Business Field　　　　　　P. 7—P. 8

23—Personal interview with Mr. M. T. Wang（王慕唐君），
　　Manager of Chi Tai Native Bank in Peking　　Sept. 9th 1940

24—（書 名 同 15.）　　　　　　　　　　附錄 P.19—P. 23

25—徐本河君抄本

26—Pitman: Book-keeping Simplified　　　P. 51—52

27—(The same book as 26)　　　　　　　P. 211

CHAPTER VI.

CONCLUSION

I. The Reasons for Existence and Depression

Before the Ch'ing dynasty, the term "bank" (銀行) was unknown. But the "Fei Chüan" (飛券) and "Ch'ao Yin" (鈔引), of the Tang dynasty (唐朝), were similar to modern bills of exchangef and the "Chiao Tze" (交子) and "Hui Tze" (會子), of the Sung dynasty (宋朝), were similar to modern bank-notes. At the end of the Ming dynasty (明朝) or the beginning of the Ch'ing dynasty at least, if not earlier, financial institutions under the name of "Tui Huan Chuang" (兌換莊), "Chien Chuang" (錢莊), "Yin Hao" (銀號), "Lu Fang" (爐房), and "Hui Tui Chuang" (匯兌莊) or "P'iao Hao" (票號), were to be found in the chief commercial cities.[1] Later on, most of them were transformed into one kind of financial institutions, which were called "Native Banks" in recent years (Refer to Chapter 1). Thus, the primitive financial institutions of China originated several hundred years ago. But, during the last hundred years, the social and economical conditions have changed tremendously under the influence of Western civilization, the organization of the markets became more intricated, and these financial institutions were insufficient to meet the various needs; so the modern banks came up instead. It may be asked, due to the overwhelming power of the modern banks, how it was possible for so many native banks to maintain their existence in the last decades. If we examine the facts, a few reasons can be found.[2]

1. Reasons for Existence — The establishment of modern banks in China, dates back to about forty-five years. Since then, the total number of modern banks has been approximately four hundred; but there are only three-sevenths of this number left at present.[3] In Tientsin, there are no more than forty modern banks, including branches. Tientsin is the leading commercial city in North China, and the amount of money circulated in the money market is very large. Apparently the capital supplied by these modern banks is inadequate for circulation. On the other hand, the population either in Tientsin or in Peking has increased largely in recent years. People coming from the villages around these two cities usually carry with them their entire fortune; thus, the financial resources of North China are concentrating in Peking and Tientsin, the business opportunities have consequently developed in these two places and the money market is very active. In fact, the modern banks of to-day are not yet strong enough to regulate the supply and demand of money; and the activity of the money market partly depends upon the native banks as accessory organisms. It is necessary therefore that native banks be maintained. This observation refers to the quantitative point of view.[2]

Why do not the modern banks try to extend their operations, in order to replace the native banks? This is a question of quality: hitherto the business operated by modern banks cannot meet the full demand of the entire money market. There are some functions of native banks upon which the modern banks rely. A modern bank is a purely capitalistic financial institution; the peculiar features of its business operation are technically twofold:

(1) With the advent of Capitalism, nearly every branch of production was developed, and merchandise was circulated in large quantities. So, modern banking operations should be large and involve huge sums of money.

(2) Due to the extent of banking operations, the bank which grants credits does so more on consideration of the securities pledged than of personal relationship.[3]

Moreover, under the present business conditions in China, it still holds true, as in the former period, that huge amounts of money are not often needed by general business firms. On the other hand, the traditional custom in business still attaches much importance to personal connections. Modern banks and general business concerns cannot cooperate in this line, and the native banks, which are the product of the former feudal society, still exist and continue to develop. According to the custom of most markets in China, the native banks serve as intermediaries for business firms to borrow money from modern banks. This is not only because the modern banks are unwilling to operate in trifling business, but also because the native banks provide a better and more reliable security, which is an essential requirement of modern banks.

If we enter into details, a few characteristic features of native banks should be considered. The first one is the establishment of a credit system, which may be ascertained from the following actual facts.[2]

(1) If we refer to the statistical data given in Chapter I, we find that there is only one native bank with a capitalism of four hundred thousand dollars in Tientsin, and one with a capitalization of two hundred thousand dollars in Peking. Commonly, the amount of capital is about 50,000 to 100,000 dollars; but the turnover depends generally on the standing and connections of the managers and proprietors; in other words, it is guaranteed by the credit.

(2) The inter-relations among native banks include "K'ao Chia" (揩家) and "Ch'uan Huan Chia" (川換家) (Refer to Chapter IV). The former represents the financial accommodation and assistance among themselves, and in the latter case, the "Poh Mar" which is drawn by one of them should be accepted by any of those "Ch'uan Huan Chia". This is also based upon credit.

(3) The loans of native banks, whether for a fixed period or on current account are mostly unsecured; and the loans against securities are scarce, as stated in the third chapter. The absorption of money by native banks relies upon credit; therefore the money lent to their customers also depends on their credit.

The above explanations show clearly that a native bank may operate the enterprise on a large scale with only a small amount of capital, and that native banks may help mutually. On the other hand, due to the simple procedure of loans without securities, the transactions are more easily concluded. Unfortunately the credit of the native banks in Tientsin and Peking has been depressed. Although it has recovered in part recently, it cannot be expected that their former power will be restored.

Furthermore, the procedure of native banking operations is adapted to the customs of Chinese business fields. This is another reason for their existence. The amount of loans granted by native banks varies according to the businessmen's option, and there is no certain limit; if the business firm is trustworthy, the securities are of less importance. There is no regulation for working hours, and any transaction may be dealt at any time from morning to night. All these points are convenient for the business concerns, and are the main force for the maintenance of native banks.[1]

Moreover, there are specific advantages in organization and management of native banks, that were adequate to the former circumstances of their existence:

(1) The manager of a native bank possesses an almost dictatorial power to control the personnel. If the manager is a man of honesty and ability, he may use his power to fit for any special circumstance, without any confusion resulting therefrom. The efficiency is naturally higher.

(2) The native bank is organized on a small scale, but the working hours are rather long; thus the clerks employed are very thrifty. There are usually not more than fifty persons, even in a larger native bank. Also, due to the low remuneration of the employees and economy in expenditures, more profits can be earned much more easily. Whether such practice is proper is another question which will be discussed later on. But from the viewpoint of the native bank, it is certainly a peculiar characteristic.

CONCLUSION

Finally, there are a few kinds of business transactions in both the Tientsin the and Peking money markets which are not handled by modern banks. Although they are not general transactions, yet they yield large profits on which the native banks may rely for existence. Those peculiar transactions are: Shanghai Exchange, Purchase and Sale of merchandise, of notes, of gold and silver bullion, as well as of Japanese Yen.[3]

Before the enactment of the fiat money system, all the native banks dealt in Shanghai exchange, especially in Tientsin. In the last two years, these transactions were more active, though there has been an interruption three years ago.[4] The purchase and sale of merchandise such as cloth, paint, corn, etc., are at present extensive and speculative transactions of the native banks. A kind of cloth which is called "Tah Wu Fu" (大五福) is a risky piece of business, in which a few native banks may be enriched or bankrupted.[5] The transactions in old notes purchased and sold against Federal Reserve Bank notes are operated secretly in very large quantities every day, although they are not permitted officially. Transactions in gold and silver bullion were more active a few years ago, for the gold and silver market was formed by gold and silver shops (金店) and native banks at an earlier period. The native banks were formerly operating in purchases and sales of Japanese Yen, and a market for this purpose was annexed to the Native Bankers' Association; even now, they are still dealt with actively in native banks. The above transactions are not only operated by the native banks for their own account; they also often act on behalf of their customers for the purpose of getting commissions.[2] (Refer to Chapter IV)

On the whole, the existence of the Tientsin and Peking native banks up to now is not due to chance. The main reason is that the native bank is a remnant of the old Chinese business society. Its origin is due to practical needs of the commercial circles; and it will maintain its existence as long as the services rendered still prove useful to its customers.

2. **Reasons for Depression** — In the recent years, the depression of native banks is a common phenomenon nearly everywhere. From nine or ten years ago, the rural economy was almost ruined; the credit system was completely destroyed, and the market of native goods was inactive. All kinds of business were receding and many business concerns became insolvent. Native banks were in the same condition and suffered from depression, because they were closely connected with the native commercial market. It was possible for those of better financial standing to restrict their business activity, but the unsound ones were, crushed without any remedy and became bankrupt at last. There were many bankrupt native banks in the whole country, even in small cities or villages. At such a critical stage, how could the native banks in Peking and Tientsin get rid of it? Fortunately most of these native banks were more conservative and had sounder bases, and they were also willing to assist each other. Therefore they still exist at present; but their business cannot avoid the shake up, and has fallen into decay. The reasons are detailed as follows:

a. *The influence of general depression in business fields.*—As stated above, the financial chaos in villages reduced the purchasing power of the farmers and provoked a sudden fall of commodity prices. In comparison with their former inventories, business firms suffered heavy losses. On the other hand, the farmers could not reimburse their debts. These two facts caused the bankruptcy of many business concerns. The deposits in native banks consequently diminished, and a large part of their loans could not be reimbursed; evidently this is the main cause for the downfall of many native banks.[1] [10]

Meanwhile, Tientsin is a sea port, and Peking is a densely populated city, where the business was very active formerly; but now, owing to the governmental control of export and import, and of foreign exchange, the circulation of merchandise is almost idle. Therefore the circulation of money is frozen, which forces many native banks to reduce their business or to liquidate.[6]

b. *The influence of bankruptcy of credit* — In native banks the credit is the most important point, as it has been explained previously, and the securities are less significant for loans. But, at present, in time of poverty of the social economy and tightened money market, it is very difficult for the native banks to maintain their original position. When a business firm which is debtor to a native bank declares itself bankrupt, the native bank cannot make up the losses, because most of its loans are unsecured. Usually this risk does not only counterbalance the profits of the enterprise, but also impairs its capital, and sometimes even the private fortune of the proprietors is seized as well.[3]

Moreover, the inter-relation among native banks is maintained only by credit; but, in the present extraordinary circumstances, the whole economic system is restricting the relations of credit; therefore it is very hard to maintain the credit of native banks. We have seen that the methods of transfer used by Tientsin and Peking native banks are "Poh Mar" and "Tui Hua", which both are based upon credit. If the credit system collapses, the circulation of currency will be influenced immediately, the whole money market will be in a chaotic condition. The native bankers are cautious in granting unsecured loans, in order to prevent this accident; but their business is thereby limited and reduced.[7]

c. *The influence of changes in modern banks policies* — Heretofore, the relation between modern and native banks was very close; ordinarily a native bank got the acknowledgement of one or two modern banks as "K'ao Chia" (靠家), for the purpose of getting more money for loans. From the side of the modern banks, they did not like to deal in loans for small amounts; but they could grant loans to business firms through native banks. This relation has been interrupted by the collapse of the credit system, and the confidence in native banks is shaken. As a consequence, modern banks have adopted a restrictive policy in granting loans to native banks; and the latter have to reduce their business because of exhaustion of their money sources.[3]

Besides, the operations of modern banks become more

difficult due to the same reasons. Gradually they abandon their former business schemes. Many of them establish branches in the same places to absorb deposits and deal with small loans. In the meantime, the working time is prolonged in order to adapt to the general business traditions. As far as we can guess, although it is impossible for modern banks to take out the entire business of the native banks, a part of it at least has been shifted to them.[6]

d. *The influence of speculation* — There are many native banks which deal mainly in speculative transactions, especially in Tientsin. During this period of chaos in social economy, their success or failure may confuse the whole money market and affect indirectly the native banks dealing in regular transactions. An obvious example at the present time is the remittance of huge sums of money to Shanghai, which tightens the whole Tientsin and Peking money market.[7] (Refer to Chapter IV)

The above unfavourable factors are external. In fact, there are also a few internal causes, such as the trend to concentration of capital, the increasing extension of business, the difficulties of nvestigating credit of business concerns, the decline of organization of native banks, and so on, which may cause a depression.[8]

II. The Tendency Towards Reformation

In the last two years, the number of Tientsin and Peking native banks has increased, and they are tending to reform themselves in applying the scientific method of organization and accounting system of modern commercial banks. The causes of this tendency are similar both in Tientsin and Peking.

Firstly, on account of the competition of modern banks and the evolution of civilization, most native banks have realized that they are behind the times and facing a great danger. They are alive to it and try to restore their original prosperity.

The levy of income-tax is the main cause of improvement of accounting system of the enterprises. The old method of accounting cannot show the financial condition accurately and clearly, and it is

CONCLUSION

different for each native bank, even in regard to the classification of accounts. Now they are forced to apply partly the methods of accounting used in modern banks, or planned by an auditor. This is a great change in their hundred years'history. At present, the classification of accounts used by most native banks in either Peking or Tientsin has been reformed on the model of that of modern banks, through the forms of accounts remain the same. This is convenient not only for the assessment of income tax, but also for the commercial banks which are inter-related with these native banks. A few kinds of subsidiary books are kept instead of the rough notes used formerly. They provide stable and minute records. Concerning the form of accounts, there is not much change. Only those in the "Ti Chang" become more complicated, but the form of the "Liu Shui", which comprises both the "Hsien Chin Liu Shui" and the "Chuan Chang Liu Shui", is still as usual.[7 9]

A few native banks have changed their accounting system and made it completely identical to that of modern banks. The Cash Journal Method and Voucher system are applied: vouchers, day-books, general ledger, subsidiary books, daily report, monthly report, balance-sheet, etc. are used, as well as cheques. It is certainly much more complex than the old accounting system, and the accountants often feel some trouble in recording, for most of them have learnt the simple old method for many years during the time of apprenticeship. Another difficulty arises from the custom of writing by hand with a Chinese brush pen. If they are ordered to write with pen and ink, it will take a long time of practice at the beginning, not only because the writing instrument is quite different, but also because they have to write horizontally and no more vertically.[8 10]

The vouchers, which the accountants of native banks dislike most, are indeed not quite convenient for the transactions of the enterprise; for there are too many detailed and constantly repeated transactions, especially the receiving and paying of "Poh Mar". The firm will be crowded with apprentices and customers at all times, if each transaction should be recorded in the voucher first, which will take much time for recording. A funny instance has occurred in a Peking native bank where the voucher system is applied: the accountants record all the transactions in "Liu Shui" by the old method, but they should copy them in the vouchers at the very night. That forms a twofold procedure which is found nowhere else, either in modern banks or in other native banks. That is because the accountants are not accustomed to write with pen and ink as speedily as with brush pen, and the voucher system takes more time than the "Liu Shui". This will be discussed in detail in the following section.

Some accountants of native banks have worked previously in modern banks and are so acquainted with new methods; but a part of the old method of accounting still remains.

Cheques are now more extensively used by native banks, but many transfers among native banks are still made by means of "Poh Mar" in Tientsin and "Tui Hua" in Peking. It has been suggested by a few well known native bankers to adopt cheques instead; but due to business conservatism, this suggestion has not yet been put into execution. In fact, there is a tendency in a few Peking native banks to use cheques in the place of "Tui Hua"; but in Tientsin, the reform of the "Poh Mar" will not be easily effected.

As regards internal organization, almost every native bank, either in Peking or in Tientsin, has effected some changes in its system to make it similar to that of modern banks, especially the same terms are used to designate the employees (Refer to Chapter I). There is one native bank in Tientsin, called "Chi Ming Hsin Chi" (啓明新記), which is organized as a Company (Refer to Appendix V). This is certainly a new trend.[8]

Most of these reforms are influenced by the develoment of modern banks, because the inter-relations between modern and native banks become closer and closer, and the transactions between them have increased considerably. In order to fit the new circumstances, the native banks underwent important changes.

Another cause of the stimulation of the native banks towards reformation is the depression of modern banks after the incident of 1937. From that time on, the extent of their banking operations has been seriously restricted, especially during the blockade of the British and French concessions; the native banks took the chance and rose up. Their organization and accounting system were improved for the purpose of competing with modern banks. But, in fact, their old customs are still existing, and are a hindrance to progress.[10]

III. The Suggested Points for Reformation

1. Necessity of Reformation

The native bank is the product of the former feudal society. The economic situation of our country in the last century was moving towards capitalism, under the stimulant of imperialism; but up to now the inland commercial markets and a part of the commerce in port-cities are still in the stage of former feudalism. This circumstance is quite suitable for the business of native banks; so, if we consider the economic organization as a whole, the life of native banks will not be ended in the near future. But due to the present depression of the social economy, and to lack of knowledge in business administration and operation, it is beyond the capacity of the native banks to meet the extraordinary circumstances. They are in imminent danger of chaos and annihilation, whereby the commercial and money markets will be seriously affected and become more confused and depressed.[11]

The effects of the depression are threefold: (1) on business circles: — the money of native banks is often lent to business concerns that are very closely connected with them. The dullness of the business conditions affects the operations of the native banks; on the other hand, the depression of the latter deprives the business concerns of the support which is necessary for recovery and development. For the sake of safety, the native banks, after suffering losses, adopt the policy of restricting advances to business concerns; the circulation of money is more difficult and, due to the lack of liquid resources, the number of bankrupt business firms increases.[1] (2) on modern banks: — they usually rely upon native banks to grant loans indirectly to business firms; but, as the position of native banks is shaken, they often consider over and over again before granting loans to the native banks, because they are afraid of loss in case of insolvency. This causes not only a restriction of the circulating capital of native banks, but also a loss of profit for modern banks. (3) on native banks:—the main businesses of native banks consists of deposits and loans, and most of their loans are based on the credit of the borrower. To-day, the credit of business concerns deteriorates more and more, and the native banks are unwilling to make advances; but the scope of business operations of these enterprises is thereby restricted. In order to prevent the lingering of money in hands, the native banks indulge into speculation with these consequent disturbances in the money market, and greatly increased risks for the enterprise itself.[1]

From the above points, we may understand that it is urgent to save the native banks from the crisis not only for the sake of the enterprises-themselves, but to safeguard the economic order of the whole society. The only way to salvation is reformation of the enterprises; but, before going into the particulars of such reformation, the advantages and disadvantages of the present system should be considered.

A. *Advantages*—They refer either to the methods of transacting business or to the methods of accounting. Under the first heading we may note the following four points:

(1) Approach of merchants—Generally, the merchants like to deal with native banks, because their staff is acquainted with the customs of the market.[1]

(2) Loans mostly unsecured — When a merchant borrows money from a modern bank, a pledge is required, and sometimes the signature or seal of a surety is needed as a guarantee. If money is borrowed from a native bank, a security is not always necessary,

for the bank is familiar with the credit of the merchant; loans to honest and reliable merchants or business firms are usually advanced without any security.[12]

(3) No minimum amount fixed—The industrial and commercial enterprises of our country are still very young; the amounts needed by merchants are generally small. The loans of native banks are granted even for quite small amounts, in order to adapt to the economic conditions.

(4) Convenience of time — The working hours of modern banks are regulated and there is a rest on each Sunday. In native banks, except the few days of the three Chinese festivals, there is no holiday, like Sunday, etc., and the working hours are from morning till night. The transactions can be dealt at any time which is suitable to the Chineses business customs.[12]

On the other hand, there are a few points of advantage in the present method of accounting of the native banks.

(5) Simplicity of theory — The gist of the accounting method is cash receipts and disbursements, which is easily understood.[13 14 15]

(6) Simplicity of method — The recording and posting in native banks' accounting are very simple: all the receipts are recorded as received, and every disbursement is written as paid.

On account of the above two reasons, the method can be understood by the majority of persons who know handwriting and arithmetics; after a short time of training, the accounts can be recorded.

(7) Saving of Expenditures—The cost of books of accounts and Chinese stationery articles is low. The accountants are easily trained, and their salaries are lower.[13]

B. *Disadvantages*—They can be shown in two respects:—
(a) *In regard to business operations.*

(1) Small amount of capital—The native banks are organized in sole-proprietorship or partnership. In the former case, the capital of one person is limited and comparatively smaller than that of a

partnership. The capital, at most, does not exceed four hundred thousand dollars (Refer to Chapter I). This is very far from the capital investment of modern banks. The amount of capital of a native bank is usually too small to permit a full swing of business operations.[13]

(2) Limited scope of business—There are a few native banks which have branches in outside localities. As a rule, they rarely intercommunicated with other native banks of other districts; so the possibility of enlarging the business of the enterprise is apparently small.[15]

(3) Lack of technical knowledge—Although there are many employees who have sufficient knowledge and long experience, still a large part of the employees and apprentices are introduced on recommendation of well known persons, without having any knowledge and training. This is useless for the enterprise, and is just a waste of salaries. The experts are rather rare.[16]

(5) Transactions in negotiable securities and speculation— Due to their limited capital, restricted scope of business operated, lack of communication with the authorities, and absence of branches in other commercial cities, the purchase and sale of negotiable securities as well as other speculative transactions are not suitable for the native banks.

(b) *For accounting system.*

(1) Cash as the basis of entries—The native bank book-keeping, through single-entry in form, is double-entry in idea. All entries in the books of accounts are made in respect of cash, so that the "Hsien Chin Liu Shui" is in fact the principal book in which most of the transactions are first recorded. For instance, the payment of expenditures is merely recorded in the lower column of the "Hsien Chin Liu Shui", while in the expenditure account of "Ti Chang", the entry is posted also in the lower column as paying such amount. This is quite similar to the idea of the debit and credit of the double-entry book-keeping.[17]

CONCLUSION

(2) Negligence of impersonal records — Customarily the records for persons are given more importance than those for things, such as the reason for disbursements, the usage of the things purchased, etc. This is due to the old conception "Credit is more important than evidences", which cannot be uprooted.

(3) Lack of standardization of account books—The number of volumes for each account is variable; especially the interrelations of accounts are confused by the fact that the same volume may be used for several purposes, and a set of books may be applied for one purpose only.

(4) Tabular system not applicable—As we have seen, the Chinese books of account are divided into higher and lower vertical columns. But in double-entry book-keeping, the debit and credit sides are separated. For convenience sake, analysis columns are added sometimes on the debit or credit side of the account, in order to save the trouble of detailed posting and to introduce the method of control account. This is called in accounting "the tabular system". The method of Chinese hand-writing is vertically from top to bottom, and the payment and disbursement columns are in the same vertical column: being thus limited by the space of the account, it is not easy to have many columns.[17]

(5) Inconvenience of writing figures—In the Chinese method of writing, there is no decimal point to denote the unit of figures, so that the unit of each figure should be mentioned successively even in using "Su Chou Figures" (蘇州碼); one or two words should be used to note the digits of figures such as hundred or thousand, etc. This is a waste in procedure and time.

(6) Difficulty of audit—The purpose of audit is not only to check the accuracy of records, and the reliability of bills, tables, etc., but also to find the defects of the present accounting system, and to detect the defalcations of the accountants. But in native banks, it is a custom that no person other than the manager can audit any part of the accounts, even the proprietors; to the

manager, an audit means lack of confidence in his honesty and ability; usually it causes his resignation. This is certainly a hindrance to the development of the enterprises.[17]

(7) Inaccuracy of depreciation charges—Concerning the valuation of fixed assets and merchandise at the end of each business period, the depreciation of fixed assets is generally not made in accordance with good accounting practice. The value of fixed assets written off generally depends upon the amount of net profit of the enterprise. In the year of abundant profits, the rate of depreciation is comparatively high; it is common that the whole value is written off within two or three years, no matter whatever the amount is. On the contrary, if the surplus gained is less, or there is a loss, the depreciation is usually omitted or a small amount is written off. The value of the land and buildings, securities and merchandise, held by the native bank is usually so flexible that it permits manipulations of any kind, which are evidently detrimental to the business.[18]

(8) Inaccuracy concerning bad debts—There is no such item as reserve for bad debts in the native banks, accounting system; therefore a doubtful debt is usually not reckoned as a loss, and included in the Profit & Loss Account of the concerned period, unless the insolvency of the debtor be certain.[18]

(9) Lack of accrual bases—These are used to show the amounts receivable or payable, but not yet received or paid at the time of accounting period. In native banks these amounts are often neglected[18]

(10) No conservation of original evidences—As explained previously, the credit is considered as the most important point for the enterprise; so the original evidences are considered as supplementary notes and are of no significance. According to good accounting practice, each business transaction should be supported by a business paper. When there is such evidence, the responsibility of the accountant can be released; therefore, the original evidences have to be kept in order.[18]

(11) **Lack of internal check**—The method of recording is similar to single-entry book-keeping; therefore the records of payments and disbursements may easily be transposed, and mistakes are unavoidable.[20] Due to the confusion of the accounting system and to lack of technical knowledge, there is no internal check in the enterprises.

(12) No standard form of accounts—If we keep in mind that the forms of accounts and the methods of recording payments and disbursements are different in each native bank according to the opinion of its chief-accountant (Refer to Chapter II), the forms, whether simple or complex, are not uniform. On the contrary, in double-entry book-keeping the debit and credit sides are standardized and it is easy to understand them clearly.[13]

2. **Suggested Scheme of Reformation**.—The disadvantages of the present accounting system of the native banks show the points to be reformed and the remedies to be applied. We suggest here below a few important points for business organization and operation.

(a) *Enlargement of capital investment.*—The number of proprietors or the shares of capital should be increased, or the native banks should be organized as companies.[20]

(b) *Specialization of employees*—If each employee or accountant is responsible for only one particular kind of work, the work can be specialized, and every-thing will be in order. Thereby the mistakes in accounting may be reduced to a minimum.

(c) *Cooperation with other native banks of different localities.*—As stated previously, the branches in outside localities are very rare. Other banks have to cooperate, otherwise extension of business will be difficult.[30]

(d) *Establishment of night school*—From the night school, the employees without sufficient knowledge may learn the principles of commercial law, business morality, commercial mathematics and other subjects useful in business field.[16]

(e) *Improvement of the apprentice system.*—The apprentices should be engaged through examination, even those introduced by well known persons. They should be made to learn each part of the office routine successively, and their treatment should be bettered. Their remuneration should be increased according to the results of their work, in order to encourage them.

(f) *Prohibition of speculation.*—The prohibition of speculative transactions enacted by the authorities has not much effect; but the Native Bankers' Association may warn and show the risks involved. In the meantime, the proprietors should also know the danger and their responsibility, and restrict the managers in operating such business.

(g) *Holidays*—According to the Chinese business custom, there are no holidays, except the three Chinese festivals. It is the same in native banks, because native bankers think that, if one day is allowed for rest, the income of that day will be lost. But the energy of the employees is limited: it is better to have half a day rest on each Sunday—The morning is preferable; this will not affect seriously the business.[19]

(h) *Increased salaries*—With the present high cost of living, the remunerations ought to be raised in order to give to the employees a sufficient standard of living.

(i) *Improvement of offices.*—Although the offices of the enterprises do not need to be so grand as for modern banks, yet they should not be so small as now-a-days; the furniture should be cleaner and neater.[20]

(j) *Publishing business conditions*—It is necessary for the enterprises to publish every year their business conditions in the newspapers, like the modern banks which publish their Balance Sheets at end of each year. The confidence can be thereby increased in the public, and their business will undoubtedly be more prosperous.[20]

(k) *Special care of unsecured loans*—For the purpose of avoiding heavy losses, the credit, assets, and honesty of the borrower, the reputation of his business, as well as the use of the money borrowed, should be investigated minutely and well considered.[20]

(l) *Institution of savings and safe-keeping departments*—Savings-business is also a sort of deposits which encourages thrift and enhances the confidence of the customers. As for safe-keeping, it was the original business of the enterprises, which is now carried on by the modern banks. If the native banks want to restore their position on the money market, this business has to be expanded.

(m) *Amelioration of "Tui Hua" and "Poh Mar" system*—Transfer by Peking native banks are made chiefly by "Tui Hua", the defects of which are many as explained previously. The system has to be abolished completely, and may be substituted by cheques. The "Poh Mar" has good points, although there are some drawbacks. The form of the "Poh Mar" may be improved and made more formal: well printed, according to a uniform model regulated by the Native Bankers' Association, with series numbers noted on them. The special seal may still be used, for if it is lost, the person who finds it usually does not know who the drawer is. But an important reform should be made, namely the "Poh Mar" should be drawn only against deposits, or a certain fraction should be covered by a deposit, or there should be a limit for overdraft: these points should be fixed by the Native Bankers' Association, and every member native bank should be bound to obey. If so, the risk of loss caused by the bankruptcy of a drawer native bank would be diminished.

(n) *Abolition of "Yuan Tiao Ta"* (原條打)—This is too simple with no adequate protection against defects; so it should be abolished, and cheques should be used instead.

If we turn to the scheme for improving the accounting system, native banks should apply the new methods concerning the classification, organization and forms of accounts, as well as the regulations for recording; the original Chinese accounting system, when it is not contrary to the scientific method and accounting theory, may still be kept. A number of more important points are suggested in the following:

(a) *Organization of accounts*

(1) Classification of accounts—The classification of accounnts is not uniform in various native banks; this is inconvenient for other native bankers and the authorities. Although most native banks have adopted the same classification as modern banks, still it is necessary to make it more consonant and regular. This point might be regulated by the Native Bankers' Association with reference to the classification of accounts edited by the joint meeting of Chinese Modern Banker's Associations in 1924 (民國十三年).[21]

(2) Original evidences — According to the Law on Income-Tax, the person bound to pay the income-tax has to show all the evidences; if he fails to do so within a certain period, the authorites may fix the amount of tax according to their own valuation; and the payer cannot refuse to pay. So, to keep in good order the original evidences is important not only for recording accounts, but also for the assessment of income-tax.

(3) Voucher system—A few native banks have adopted the voucher systems in the place of "Liu Shui"; but, in fact, the "Liu Shui" has some favourable points, such as convenience for recording, saving of time, easy posting in the "Ti Chang", etc. While the voucher system is not quite suitable for the accounting of native banks, yet it is more progressive and complete; but, if the voucher is used, the Chinese brush and method of writing have to be abandoned; and also the transfers of other native banks are so frequent that making vouchers will waste too much time. From these general observations it seems that the "Liu Shui" system may still be retained after improving a few points which will be illustrated later on.[22]

(4) Signs for recording—There are many special seals for different purposes, that are not found, even equivalently, in the

accounting system of modern banks. This is an excellent point which should be retained with a few improvements. The red words: "Kuo" (過) for the entry posted, "Ping" (平) and "Ch'u Ch'ing" (除清) for the amounts balanced, "Pao" (報), "Fu" (覆) and "Li Ch'i" (理訖) for bills received or sent, and the blue words "Li Ch'i" (理訖) and "Tui Hui" (退回) for term bills, may be used as usual. The red word "Ch'ung" (冲) is used for cancelling an entry which is either wrongly recorded or entered twice. An opposite entry is made in order to balance an entry which is inaccurate: that means that an entry as paid for such amount is made, if an entry of the same amount received is not correct (See Example 73); but in fact, this opposite entry is unnecessary, if another seal "Wu Ju" (誤入) or "Wu Chi" (誤記), which means "recorded wrongly", is stamped on its top. It will show obviously that this entry is to be omitted. In addition, the seal or the special sign of the accountant who cancels this entry should be stamped beside it. (See Example 74)

Example 73

Example 74

The seal with the name or special sign of each accountant should be stamped on or below the entry which is made or posted by him. Thus, the person responsible for the entries made can be easily found, when some error is detected. (See Example 75)

Example 75.

(b) *Forms of accounts.*

(1) "Liu Shui Chang" A few necessary points, which are the series number of the pages, the folio and the seal of the accountant, should be taken into consideration for the reformation of "Liu Shui": they apply for any kind of "Liu Shui". The form of account—c printed in page 49, is more progressive. The first and last two shorter columns may be used for the representative word of the folio and the seal of the accountant, the upper longer column is for receipts, the lower, for payments. The series number of each page should be printed on the left or right side of each page. The folio of each account can be designated by a special representative word, such as very commonly used by Chinese: "天, 地, 元, 黃,……" or "子, 丑, 寅, 卯,………" or "甲, 乙, 丙, 丁, ………" or "乾, 坎, 艮, 震,………" and so on. The series number of pages may be written in "Su Chou Figures". (see Fig. XXXIX)

Fig. XXXIX. The Improved Form of "Liu Shui"

(2) "Ti Chang"—The form introduced in page 57 can be used as a basis: two shorter vertical columns are added at both the top and the bottom with the same purpose as illustrated for the "Liu Shui". (See Fig. XL)

Fig. XL. The Improved Form of "Ti Chang"

						特比⊗		現上∞	數 頁
						丂		丂	人手經
						六月十日		五月廿日	李宏宬
				六月二日付一千元	卅日付四百元	收五千元		收二千五百元	要 摘
									欠息一分二 月息九厘 逆支額一萬
甲十五				存	存		存	欠或存
				川	十		數 日
								額 積
								人手經
				現二∞	現三∞			數 頁

往來存款

(3) Subsidiary records—Due to the simplicity of business transactions, the books already used by native banks are sufficient to meet the various needs. Thus, there is no necessity to make any suggestion.

(4) Daily report—The "Shui P'ai" is similar in nature to the daily report used in modern banks, but the defect is that the records of the "Shui P'ai" will be rubbed out daily. In order to keep a permanent daily record, a special form may be printed on paper. Its disposition would be similar to that of "Shui P'ai", but the title, number and date should be written in the first vertical column, and the headings of horizontal divisions should be printed in the next one. A space for the seals of manager, sub-manager, chief-accountant, cashier, checker and recorder, may be reserved at the bottom of the page. The fixed items of accounts may be printed in advance in

each middle vertical column. The total amount of each item is recorded in "Su Chou Figures" in the upper or lower shorter column which is used for receipt or payment respectively.[23] (See Fig. XLI)

Fig XLI. The Form of Suggested Daily Report

合計													收項	中華民國　年　月　日	日記表　第　號
計													會計科目		
													付項		

經副理　　　　　會計主任　　　　　覆核員　　　　　記帳員

(5) Table of Cash in hand (庫存表)—In order to show clearly the amount of cash in hand, a table for showing the cash in hand might be printed, when necessary. The first vertical column should be used to record the title and date; in the following ones, the upper and lower division would be for the amounts received and paid, and the middle division for the particulars. The next four columns, would show respectively the cash in hand at the end of the previous day, the total receipts of the day, the total payments of the day, and the cash in hand at the end of the day. The total would be noted in the last vertical column. A space for the seals of the manager and other accountants would be kept below.[24] (See Fig. XLII)

Fig. XLII. The Suggested Form of Table for Cash In Hand

合計				今日庫存	今日共付	今日共收	昨日庫存	國幣 摘要 國幣	中華民國 年 月 日
									庫存表

經副理   會計主任   出納主任   覆核員   記帳員

(6) Monthly and Annual Reports—The original forms of monthly and annual reports can show clearly the business and financial conditions of the enterprise, but, due to the arrangement and form of the report, they are not quite convenient for consultation and comparison. They should therefore be improved. The Chinese names of each pillar in the "Four Pillars Method" which is applied by these reports, might be changed: "Balances Carried Down" which is called "Chiu Kuan" (舊管) might be changed into "Shang Chi Chieh Yü" (上期結餘); "New Receipts", "Hsin Shou" (新收), might be called "Pên Chi Shou Hsiang" (本期收項); "Amounts Paid Out", "Kai Ch'u" (開除) might be named "Pên Chi Fu Hsiang" (本期付項), and "Pên Chi Chieh Yü" (本期結餘) might be used in the place of "Balance in Hand", "Shih Tsai" (實在).[35]

A narrow stripe of paper might be used for monthly or annual reports. It should contain from top to bottom five divisions for the name of account, the "Shang Chi Chieh Yü" (上期結餘), the "Pên Chi Shou Hsiang" (本期收項), the "Pên Chi Fu Hsiang"

(本期付項) and the "Pén Chi Chieh Yü" (本期結餘). The second and fifth divisions should be subdivided in two parts; the upper one for receipts and the lower one for disbursements. On the right side of the table, the title and date should be printed, and space for the seals of the manager and accountants should be left at the bottom. (See Fig. XLIII)

Fig. XLIII. The Suggested Form of Monthly and Annual Report.

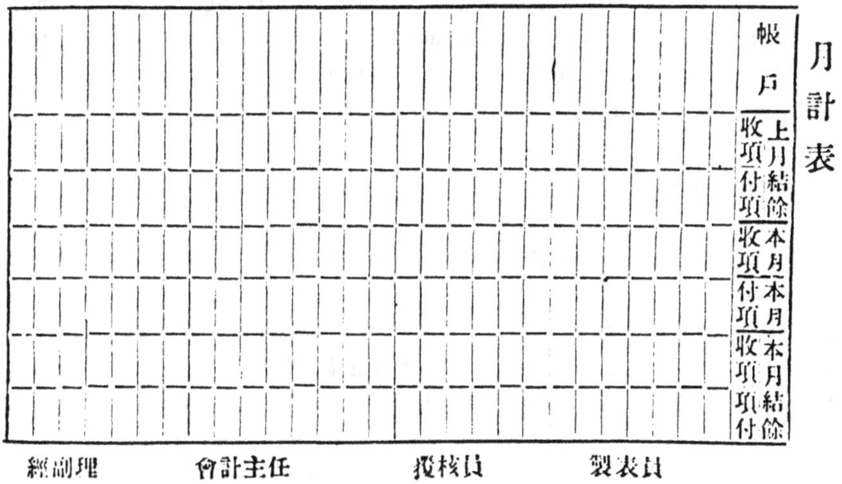

帳戶 / 收項付項 上月結餘 / 收項 本月 / 付項 本月 / 收項 本月結餘 / 付項

月計表

經副理　　　會計主任　　　覆核員　　　製表員

(c) *Accounting Theory*

(1) Methods of recording—In the "Hsien Chin Liu Shui", each entry is recorded once only, that is to say there is merely one entry for each payment or receipt. This may be called the common method. There is an old method called "Lung Men Shin" (龍門式): wherein each entry involves an opposite entry, which means that the same amount is recorded as being paid to or received from the treasury; it is called in Chinese "Ts'un K'u" (存庫). Both these entries of the same transaction are posted in the "Ti Chang" where a special account called "Cash in Hand" (庫存) is opened. Explanatory notes can be written next to the entry to make it quite clear. This is obviously a double-entry system, similar to the

cash-book and journals of the so-called Continental Method. The only difference is that the former entry is still made in the same direction in the account "Cash in hand". Most business firms have abandoned this method.

In our opinion the so-called common method may still be applied.[20] The "Four Pillars Method", which was originated in the Sung dynasty (宋朝),[24] can be applied satisfactorily by the enterprises for certain purposes, and has a few points of advantage; but, if the accounting system of modern banks is generally adopted by native banks, this method will be thrown off.

(2) Bad debts—It occurs frequently that sums lent cannot be reimbursed fully or in part and become doubtful debts. This loss cannot be imputed to the period when it becomes a bad debt, but it should be ascribed to the period in which the money has been lent. It is better to estimate the part which cannot be reimbursed in the future as the loss of that year. According to the "Draft of instructions for collecting income-tax from profit-making enterprises of the first category" (第一類營利事業所得稅徵收須知草案) a claim may be estimated as a loss, when one of the two following conditions is fulfilled: (1) if on account of the debtor being insolvent, or absconding, or being declared bankrupt, or for any other reason, a part or the whole of his debt cannot be reimbursed, or (2) if the debt is overdue for two years, and after demand of the creditor, the principal or interest cannot be refunded. The amount of bad debts cannot be computed freely in advance, but only according to law. However, according to good accounting principles, it is always considered advisable to anticipate for loss from doubtful accounts so that a Bad Debts Reserve can be set up either from the accumulated profits or by some other means.

(3) Depreciation of fixed assets—The depreciation of fixed assets is a loss of the enterprise, and its nature is identical to that of other expenditures. Therefore it should be invariably written off no matter whether the business results in a loss or a profit.

CONCLUSION

The amount of depreciation should be regular for each period; to increase or decrease it arbitrarily is not permitted. The methods regulated by Chinese Income-Tax Law are "Straight Line Method" and "Diminishing Value Method".[23]

(4) Accrual basis—At the time of closing accounts, the accrued receivable and payable accounts should be investigated, and posted as an asset or income and a loss or liability respectively. The purpose is to adjust the income or expenditure already earned or incurred, although there has been no actual payment in cash, and to include them in the profit and loss of the concerned period. Owing to the prepaid income and expenses, the same theory holds true. Income received in advance is a deferred liability which should be deducted from the total income; on the other hand, the prepaid expenses are a deferred asset that has to be carried to the next trading period. If they are so managed, the estimate of profit and loss and the statement of assets and liabilities within the period will be accurate.[37]

IV. Future Outlook

On the whole, the social economy of China to-day is in a period of transition: one part still remains in the stage of former feudalism, and the other part is marching speedily towards a capitalistic society. In this stage most native banks are benefited by extraordinary circumstances which will not be maintained in the long run. Therefore native bankers have to consider how to adapt themselves to a new environment, this is an urgent question to be solved at present. As a general principle, the native bankers should keep their old specific features, and maintain their previous inter-relation. On the other hand, they ought to discern what belongs to a departed past and contrive to make progresses. Otherwise, when the time passes on and the general circumstances change, their old organization and system will be extinguished by natural selection. Therefore, we expect the native bankers to rise up and unite together to reform resolutely.

CHAPTER VI

Notes of the Chapter.

1—Binyuan Chu: Banking Practice   P. 22—P. 23

2—天津之銀號 王子建, 趙履謙合著 (法商經濟研究室)   P. 63—P. 66

3—現代世界經濟史綱要 伍純武著 (商務印書館)   P.317—P.320

4—Yung Pao of Tientsin (天經庸報經濟版)   March 26th 1941

5—Yung Pao of Tientsin (天津庸報經濟版)   April 20th 1941

6—Personal interviews with Mr. H.Y. Liu (陸效揚君),
     and Mr. P.H. Hsü (徐本河君) of Tientsin Native
     Bankers' Association   March 9th 1914

7—Personal interviews with same persons as 6.   March 30th 1941

8—Personal interviews with sams persons as 6.   April 4th 1941

9—Personal interviews with Mr. C.P. Wei (魏景彭君),
     Manager of Teh Hung Native Bank; and Mr.
     F.C. Sun (孫芳忱君), Chief-Accountant of
     Teh Fèng Native Bank   March 22nd 1941

10—Personal interviews with same persons as 6.   April 12th 1941

11—(書名同 2.)   P. 71—P. 72

12—中國錢莊概要 潘子豪著 (華通書局)   P.243—P.245

13—會計雜誌 (徐永祚會計師事務所) 第三卷 第一期   P. 2—P. 3

14—(書名同 13.) 第三卷 第一期   P. 62

15—北京銀錢業 劉奇新著 (北京東方大學論文)   P. 40

16—(書名同 12.)   P.248

17—中國經濟問題 (中國經濟學社) (商務印書館)   P.215

18—所得稅原理及實務 潘序倫, 李文杰合著 (商務印書館) P.289

19—(書名同 12.)   P.249—P.253

20—(書名同 15.)   P. 41

21—銀行會計 顧準著 (商務印書館)   P. 15—P.17

22—(書名同 18.)   P.296

23—Personal interviews with Mr. C.P. Wei (魏景
     彭君), Manager; Mr. C.C. Wan (宛溎川君)
     of Teh Hung Native Bank in Tientsin   Feb. 16th 1941

24—(書名同 13.) 第三卷第一期   P. 22

25—(書名同 13.) 第三卷第一期   P. 26—P.27

26—(書名同 13.) 第三卷第四期   P. 84

27—(書名同 18.)   P. 298

APPENDIX I

The Form of Contract for the Establishment of a Native Bank

The undersigned proprietors Mr. ·············· and Mr. ··············· agree by common consent to contribute the joint capital for the organization enterprise of ····························· Native Bank as an unlimited liability. The address is ···························· The set of regulations is annexed as follows:

1. The name of the firm is ····················· Native Bank; the head office is established in ····························

2. The capital of the firm is ······················· dollars (national currency) and shall be entirely paid in one time. For the future development of business, it may be increased by the "Hu Pên". The amount of capital is presently as follows:

   Share of Mr. ·····················   ·················· dollars
   Share of Mr. ·····················   ·················· dollars

3. The firm engages Mr. ····································· as manager and Mr. ·································· as sub-manager: they shall help each other in the performance of their duties.

4. The manager of the firm shall be paid a monthly salary of ························· dollars, and is allowed to draw ····················· dollars a month. The sub-manager shall be paid a monthly salary of ··············· dollars and is allowed to draw ·············· dollars a month. Beyond these sums, they are not allowed to contract any floating debt or to draw in excess of their salaries. The advances drawn in account shall be deducted from the sums to which they are entitled at the time of distribution (of profits) at the end of three years.

5. Once a year, the firm closes its accounts and prepares a general annual report to be handed over to the proprietors for examination once every three years, there shall be a general settlement of accounts, and all the expenditures shall be deducted from the

profit bestowed by heaven. The profit shall be distributed in such proportion between the shares of capital and the shares of industry. In this distribution the proprietor shall have so much %; the share of the god of wealth (財神股) shall have so much as reserve. In the distribution of the shares of industry, the manager so many persons shall have so many shares, the sub-manager so many persons shall have so many shares.

6. The head office of the firm is presently located in ··················· Branches shall be established, at any time in prosperous commercial areas according to circumstances.

7. The proprietors and the employees of the firm cannot usurp the common name of the firm for their private affairs. Any use of the seal as a guarantee is forbidden.

8. The employees or the proprietors are not permitted to borrow money from the firm for the operation of their own businesses.

9. In case that the losses incurred in business by the firm should reach one half of the capital, a meeting of the proprietors must be held for deciding the continuation or stopping of the business; it is not permitted to conceal (such losses) for the purpose to make good the deficit.

10. The scope of the business of the firm includes:—remittances; buying and selling of foreign currencies of gold and silver, and various securities; deposits, unsecured loans, loans against security; but mortgages of immovables are not permitted.

11. Unsecured loans of the firm even to concerns of the highest standing, should not exceed three tenths of the capital of these concerns.

12. When the firm disposes of the reserve fund, it must be divided equally between the shares of capital and the shares of industry.

13. No employee of the firm is permitted to draw any money,

in excess of his monthly (regular) salary and advances. The manager and sub-manager are responsible for any intentional breach of the rules.

14. All the employees of the firm must be of good character and familiar with the business conditions. Moreover, they must have a reliable guarantor who is responsible for compensation (in case of unproper acts).

15. If any of the shown above articles is found not to be convenient in practice, it may be amended by the meeting of the proprietors.

Proprietor ··· Tang　(堂)　··············

Proprietor ··· Tang　(堂)　··············

··

··

Mediators

··

··

Manager　　···

Sub-manager ···

Drawn ·················· day ·················· month ·················· year of the Republic of China.

The Form of Annual Report and Monthly Report in Chinese

附錄二一　年總(月報同此)

中華民國○年○月○○日至○月○○日

管本項下

各股項下

○○堂　存洋○○　○　元
○○堂　存洋○○　○　元元
以上共存洋○　○　元

定期存款項下

○○堂　存洋○○　○　元元
○○號　存洋○○　○　元元
○○君　存洋○○　○　元元
○○○　存洋○○　○　元元
以上共存洋○　○　元元

銀行存款項下

○○○銀行　存洋○○　○　元元
○○○銀行　存洋○○　○　元元
以上共存洋○　○　元元

同業存款項下

○○○銀號　存洋○○　○　元元
○○○銀號　存洋○○　○　元元
以上共存洋○　○　元元（此係撥交存款）

活期存款項下

○○○號　存洋○○　○　元元
○○○公司　存洋○○　○　元元
○○○洋行　存洋○○　○　元元
以上共存洋○　○　元

暫時存款項下

○○○堂　存洋○○　○　元元（應年報告股東之得利）
○○堂　存洋○○　○　元元（應年得利滋存利）
出息未付　存洋○○　○　元

以上共存〇　〇　元

新存收
〇〇〇得利存洋〇　〇　元元
〇〇〇得利存洋〇　〇　元元
〇〇得利存洋〇　〇　元
以上共存洋〇　〇　元

新舊
收管總存洋〇　〇　元

房日雜出
利息欠洋〇〇〇〇　〇　元元元
用租欠洋〇〇〇〇　〇　元元
以上共欠洋〇　〇　元元

實存項下
定期放款堂
〇〇〇號欠洋〇　〇　元
以上共欠洋〇　〇　元

銀行欠款項下
〇〇〇銀行欠洋〇　〇　元
〇〇〇銀行欠洋〇　〇　元元
以上共欠洋〇　〇　元

同業欠款項下
〇〇〇銀號欠洋〇　〇　元元
〇〇〇銀號欠洋〇　〇　元元
以上共欠洋〇　〇　元

活期透支項下
（此係摺交欠款）
〇〇號欠洋〇　〇　元元
〇〇〇號欠洋〇　〇　元
以上共欠洋〇　〇　元

暫存欠款項下
〇〇〇電話欠洋〇　〇　元
押租欠洋〇　〇　元

進息未收欠洋 ○　○　无无
以上共欠洋 ○　○　无无

貸款

現欠洋 以上共欠洋 ○　○　无无

作除總共欠洋 ○　无

○○○○伏利洋 收 ○　○　无无无
○○○○伏利洋 ○　○　无无无
○○伏利洋 ○　○　无无无
以上共伏利 ○　○　无无

一一除出總洋 除 ○　○　无无无
一一除催項洋 ○　○　无无无
以上共日用洋 ○　○　无无无
以上共開除洋 ○　○　无无

天開嗣利洋仰一應投清 ○　○　无

（此洋應作成紫數由新收減開除所得）

源退流長

— 219 —

APPENDIX III

The Form of a Certificate of Loan

The maker of this certificate of loan presently borrows from ······················Native Bank························National Currency exactly. It has been agreed orally, that the interest will be calculated at the rate of ·······················, that the loan will come to maturity on ····························· and that at maturity the principal and interest shall be reimbursed integrally. If the borrower is in default, the guarantor shall pay in his place, without advancing any plea whatever for an extension of the period. Lest there be no evidence of an oral agreement, we make at the present certificate in proof thereof.

The Borrower····································.

The Guarantor ·································.

(Date) ···

附錄三　借據

立借據人

　銀號國幣　　　　　　　　　　今借到

言明按　息　　計息以　　　　為期到期本利整

如數歸還倘有延誤即由承還保人清償決不藉口延宕

恐口無憑立此為據

花印

中華民國　年　月　日

　　　　　　立借據人

　　　　承還保人

APPENDIX IV

The Form of a Certificate of Loan against Security

Certificate of Loan against Security.   No. ⋯⋯⋯⋯⋯⋯

    The Undersigned ⋯⋯⋯⋯⋯⋯⋯⋯ presently borrows $⋯⋯⋯⋯ National Currency exactly from ⋯⋯⋯⋯⋯⋯Native Bank with the following a security. The agreed interest is calculated at the rate of ⋯⋯⋯⋯⋯⋯ per thousand per month. The agreed period is fixed at ⋯⋯⋯⋯⋯⋯⋯ months, from ⋯⋯⋯⋯⋯⋯ to ⋯⋯⋯⋯⋯ (each Date). At maturity, the principal shall be reimbursed integrally together with interest. Both parties are willing to observe the conditions herebelow, and have made out the present certificate in proof thereof.

    1. If the value of the security falls down owing to a natural calamity or to any other cause, the borrower shall provide an additional security or remit cash, at least to the extent which will be sufficient to compensate the fall in value.

    2. If the borrower does not reimburse at maturity or does not provide an additional security or remit cash, in case the value of the security fall down when the period is running, it is a breach of contract. Your bank is entitled, without having to give a written notice, to sell the security in order to pay the principal and interest. If the proceeds are insufficient, the borrower bears a joint and several liability to make up immediately the balance. If the proceeds are in excess of the debt, (the bank) may use the surplus to pay other debts of the borrower.

    3. If the borrower is unable to perform the above clauses, the guarantor is willing to assume full responsibility for reimbursement and to give up the benefit of discussion (先訴抗辯權).

Security	

To ⋯⋯⋯⋯⋯⋯⋯⋯ Native Bank   Borrower { Name ⋯⋯⋯⋯⋯⋯
                                                     { Address ⋯⋯⋯⋯⋯⋯

                                           Guarantor { Name ⋯⋯⋯⋯⋯⋯
                                                     { Address ⋯⋯⋯⋯⋯⋯

(Date) ⋯⋯⋯⋯⋯⋯⋯⋯⋯⋯⋯⋯⋯⋯⋯⋯

附錄四　抵押放款借款據

抵押放款借款據

第　　　號

立借據人　　　今以左列抵押品向

銀號押借到國幣　　　整訂明由本年

月息　　厘計息定期　　個月由　　　日起至　　　日止到期本

月利一併如數清還所有左列條件均願遵守立此本

為據

一　抵押品如因天災及別項事故致低落價格以至少於借款時現金至借款所押之抵押品號借款人不能補足時須由借款人另行增加抵押品或交

二　抵押品如到期如不照約即行清償所有押借款項抵押品號亦任憑 銀號將抵押品變賣

三　以剩餘各款以本金償還倘借款人不足清償時仍須由借款人完全負責清償

抵押品	

借欵人姓名
　　　　住址
保証人姓名
　　　　住址

銀號
　台照

中華民國　　年　　月　　日

THE TABLE OF TIENTSIN NATIVE BANKS

as at end of April 30th 1941.

Name of Native Bank 字號	Group 幫派	Types of organization 組織	Capital 資本額	Hu Pên 護本額	Address of the business 營業所所在地	Date when business started 開業日期	Manager 總理人姓名	PROPRIETORS 出資人 Names 姓名	Occupation 經歷
I Sheng 義勝	Tientsin 津	Partnership 合夥	$ 80,000		Road No. 4 F.C. 法租界四號路 一三四號	2, 15, 1933	S. C. Chiao 焦世卿	C.K. Lu; C.C. Chao; etc. 陸沛恭, 趙仲橫, 等四人	Trade 商
I Ho 頤和	"	"	$100,000		Road No. 26 F.C. 法界租二十六號路 二十號	1929	S. J. Ni 倪絅廂	F.W. Wang, C.S. How, etc. 王撫武, 侯仲笙, 等四人	"
Yu Tah Hung 餘大亨	"	"	$150,000		Road No. 5 F.C. 法租界五號路		J. T. Wang 王孫洋	S.Y. Wang, Y.S. Chang 王晚岩, 張印孫, 等五人	"
Chung Ho 中和	"	"	$400,000		Road No. 6 F.C. 法界界六號路 一二〇號	4, 15, 1929	H. C. Liu 劉翰背	T.S. Wang, B.C. Liu, etc. 王嗣軒, 劉鈞周, 等八人	"
Tah ch'ang 大昌	"	Sole Proprietorship 獨資	$100,000		Road No. 5 F.C. 法租界五號路 三十三號	3, 8, 1935	E. T. Sun 孫潤岸	S R. Chi 吉佩如	"
Yuan Tai 元泰	"	Partnership 合夥	$100,000		Shou-Teh Building F.C. 法租界壽德大樓 九號	6, 16, 1931	W. Y. Mao 毛女元	N. M. Chao, Y.C. Mao 趙化民, 毛雅泉	"

Name of Native Bank 字號	Group 杜派	Types of organization 組織	Capital 資本額	Hu Pên 護本額	Address of the business 營業所所在地	Date when business started 開業日期	Manager 經理人姓名	PROPRIETORS 出資人 Names 姓名	Occupation 職業 Trade 商務
Duen Ch'ang 敦昌	Tientsin 津	Sole proprietorship 獨資	$ 50,000		Road No. 8 F.C. 法租界八號路一○九號	10, 1900	C. H. Fan 范鎮軒	H. Y. Feng 馮熙誼	Trade 商務
Tien Jui 天瑞	"	Partnership 合夥	$100,000		Road No. 5 F.C. 法租界五號路二十一號	1, 10, 1925	S. C. Liang 梁毅庭	C.C. Kuo, S.S. Chia etc. 郭斂臣, 賈紹三 等四人	"
Ch'ing I 慶益	"	"	$100,000		Road No. 30 F.C. 法租界三十號路三十一號	2, 16, 1934	H. S. Tso 左航係	M. L. Sun, Mrs. Chu, K. S. Ma etc. 孫參先 朱氏 馬桂山	"
Hua Feng 華豐	"	"	$100,000		Road No. 20 F.C. 法租界二十號路二十號	6, 12, 1935	S. T. Li 李少芋	C. Y. Wang, K. C. Li etc. 王季揚, 李閣臣 等四人	"
Yü Yuan 裕源	"	"	$ 50,000		Road No. 2 F.C. 法租界二號路六十一號	4, 18, 1929	C. T. Shen 沈健孚	N. C. Wang, M. S. Li etc. 王乃利, 劉銘三 等四人	"
Ch'ien Feng 謙豐	"	"	$100,000		Sze Teh Li, F.C. 法租界四德里四十一號	3, 7, 1934	H. M. Wang 王西銘	Y. W. Pian, C. Y. Kuo etc. 卞潤吾, 郭李纓 等三人	"
Chi Ch'ang 致昌	Shen-Chi 深冀	"	$100,000		Road No. 20 F.C. 法租界二十號路十八號	1918	H. C. Liu 劉錫成	C. K. Wang, S. C. Wang 王澤兌, 王穎謙	"
Teh Jen 稻仁	Tientsin 津	"	$100,C00		Road No. 30 F.C. 法租界三十號路和西里九號	3, 8, 1935	C. S. Ni 倪牧山	C. S. Chao, Y. C. Sun 甯仲三, 孫越陔	"

APPENDIX V—THE TABLE OF TIENTSIN NATIVE BANKS

Name of Native Bank 字號	Group 杈派	Types of organization 組織	Capital 資本額	Hu Pèn 護本額	Address of the business 營業所所在地	Date when business started 開業日期	Manager 經理人姓名	PROPRIETORS 出資人 Names 姓名	Occupation 職歷
Pao Sheng 寶生	Tientsin 津	Sole proprietorship 獨資	$40,000	$40,000	Asahi Road J. C. 日租界旭街	8, 1923	P. Chang 張琪	Y. F. Wai 魏汝楓	Trade 商
I Hsing Cheh 金興珍	"	Partnership 合夥	$150,000		Yang-Fu-Yin Road F.C. 法租界楊楊嗣路路	1875	P. C. Li 李賀設	S. N. Wang, S. P. Fan, T. F. Chin, ect. 王聖恩 范士禮 靳廷輔 等五人	"
Yao Yuan 耀遠	"	Sole proprietorship 獨資	$100,000		Road No. 5 F. C. 法租界五號路 四十一號	2, 5, 1935	Y. S. Wu 吳英三	S. T. Pan 潘少庭	"
Hsiang Sheng 祥生	"	Partnership 合夥	$100,000		Road No. 32 F. C. 法租界三十一號路 十七號	7, 24, 1933	C. H. Shang 桑叔涵	M. L. Sun, C. P. Li, C. P. Wanz 孫慕陸 李子潘 王子崚	"
Ho Feng 和豐	"	"	$160,000		Road No. 6 F. C. 法租界六號路 一百廿二號	1, 31, 1933	Y. F. Lu 盧公紡	S. L. Hwa, K. J. Liu, etc. 華欣如 劉金瑞 等十二人	"
Hung Yuan 宏源	"	"	$50,000	$50,000	Sze-Teh-Li F. C. 法租界四德里	5, 13, 1935	S. Y. Chi 齊上淵	Y. J. Chang, C. Y. Kuo 張㭪人 郭叔侯	"
Hung Chi 鴻記	Shansi 山西	Sole proprietorship 獨資	$80,000	$80,000	Road No. 6 F. C. 法租界六號路	1879	N. K. Tang 蒸慇貸	F. H. Chang 張鳳翔	Trade and Politics 商政
Tai Ho 泰和	Tientsin 津	"	$100,000		Road No. 1 F. C. 法租界一號路	5, 15, 1934	P. J. Wu 吳百榮	H. Ma 馬珩	Trade 商

APPENDIX V—THE TABLE OF TIENTSIN NATIVE BANKS

Name of Native Bank 字號	Group 幫派	Types of organization 組織	Capital 資本額	Hu Pên 護本額	Address of the business 營業所在地	Date when business started 開業日期	Manager 經理人姓名	PROPRIETORS 用資人 Names 姓名	Occupation 營業 經歷
Tien Hsing Hung 天興恆	Tientsin 津	Partnership 合夥	$20,000	$60,000	Ho-Pei-Ta-Chieh 河北大街	3, 17, 1931	C. Y. Chang 張振元	S. H. Kao, J. P. Shen 高誉恆, 沈瑞年	Trade 商
I Heng 義恆	"	"	$50,000		Shou-Teh-Building F. C. 法租界壽德大樓	1854	H. C. Tien 田協臣	P. N. Kuo, W. H. Yuan 郭柏年, 宛文軒	"
I Cheng Yu 義成裕	"	Sole proprietorship 獨資	$20,000		Pei Men Wai Ta Chieh 北門外大街	1911	H. P. Yang 楊湘伯	Y. T. Wang 王幼廷	"
Hung Kang Hsing 宏康	"	Partnership 合夥	$60,000		Shou-Teh-Building F. C. 法租界壽德大樓	2, 16, 1928	C. T. Tang 唐駿廷	Mrs. Chen, H. T. Chen etc. 陳處氏, 陳曇臣 等五人	"
Wan Hua 萬華	"	"	$40,000		Hai-Ta-Tao F. C. 法租界海大道誠安里	3, 4, 1931	K. W. Mong 孟殿文	C. S. Yin, C. C. Li, etc. 尹敬三, 李志清 等四人	"
Tung Teh 同德	Peking 京	Sole proprietorship 獨資	$50,000		Road No. 26 F. C. 法租界二十六號路	1926	C. N. Wu 吳襄儒	S. Y. Wei 魏筱潤	Trade 商
Hsiang Jui Hsing 祥瑞興	"	"	$20,000		Road No. 23 F. C. 法租界二十三號路	1911	L. M. Liu 劉良牧	C. W. Yang 楊兆五	"
Chü I 聚義	"	Partnership 合夥	$20,000		Road No. 2 B. C. 英租界二號路四宜里一號	1916	M. C. Tien 田啟人	S. P. Sun, Y. C. Kou 孫欣圃, 岣峻芝	"

APPENDIX V—THE TABLE OF TIENTSIN NATIVE BANKS

Name of Native Bank 字號	Group 杜派	Types of organization 組樣	Capital 資本額	Hu Pên 護本類	Address of the business 營業所所在地	Date when business started 開業日期	Manager 經理人姓名	Proprietors Names 姓名	Occupation 出資人 經歷
Dun Tai Yung Chang Chi 收泰永昌記	Peking 京	Sole Proprietorship 獨資	$100,000		Road No. 1 F. C. 法租界一號路五十一號	4, 11, 1932	Y. N. Chang 張逸廷	C. S. Ma 馬作臣	Trade 商
Chin Sheng 晉生	Tientsin 律	Partnership 合夥	$80,000		Road No. 30 F. C. 法租界三十號路	1, 9, 1933	Y. C. Li 李雲茲	I. T. Li 李揮庭, S. P. Hsu 許彼坡	"
Chian I 謙	"	"	$100,000		Road No. 23 F. C. 法租界二十三號路	5, 25, 1934	M. H. Li 李繁繩	S. S. Chia 買紹三; P. Y. Chia 買步雲	Trade & Banking 商, 錢
Fu Kang Jen 福康仁	"	"	$100,000		Sze Teh Li F. C. 法租界四德里	3, 19, 1934	K. Wang 王銳	S. C. Kuo 郭士, Y. T. Chang 張德儀, C. H. Pien 卞澤新	"
Jui Yuan Yung 瑞源永	"	Sole Proprietorship 獨資	$100,000		Road No. 8 F. C. 法租界八號路七十五號	3, 23, 1934	H. T. Wang 王心田	P. S. Chin 金品三	Trade 商
Chi Ming Hsin Chi 啟明新記	Shantung 東	Company 公司	$150,000		Road No. 23 F. C. 法租界二十三號路	3, 1, 1935	L. Y. Tu 杜樑閣	Company	"
Hsin Sheng 新生	Tientsin 律	Partnership 合夥	$200,000		Road No. 26 F. C. 法租界二十六號路	3, 1, 1937	T. C. Wang 王佐才 S. C. Chiao 焦世卿	C. C. Lu S. C. Liu etc. 魯際清, 劉晚辰等四人	Trade & Banking 商, 錢
Kwang Li 廣利	"	"	$200,000		Road No. 27 F. C. 法租界二十七號路	4, 7, 1937	Y. H. Tu 杜雲鍚	C. W. Yu 于繪文, C. P. Li 李金岱, Y. H. Tu 杜喬岱	"

Name of Native Bank 字號	Group 社派	Types of organization 組織	Capital 資本額	Hu Pên 護本額	Address of the business 營業所所在地	Date when business started 開業日期	Manager 經理人姓名	PROPRIETORS Names 姓名	Occupation 出資人 職歷
Chi Lu Chun Chi 裕豐劉記	Shen-Chi 深記	Sole Proprietorship 獨資	$ 50,000		Road No. 1 F. C. 法租界一號路四十五號	3, 1, 1934	K. H. Wei 魏廣宇	C. S. Chang 張仲三	Politics 政
Kwang Yü 廣裕	Tientsin 津	"	$ 100,000		Sze Tch Li F. C. 法租界四德里	7, 1937	L. C. Wei 魏朗清	Y. S. Sun 孫潤生	Trade 商
Jui Chang Hsiang 瑞昌祥	Shangtung 山東	"	$ 200,000		Rue de France F. C. 法租界中街五十一號	2, 8, 1938	P. C. Sa 沙秉琛	Ching-Shen-Tang Meng 欣帆室孟	Trade and Banking 商, 錢
Ta Hsin Yuan 大信源	Tientsin 津	Partnership 合夥	$ 150,000		Rue de France F. C. 法申街四十四號	2, 2, 1940	Y. H. Chang 張汪祥	C. T. Ma, M. C. Cheng etc. 馬俊庭, 鄭以枚等四人	"
I Sheng 益生	"	"	$ 100,000	$ 100,000	Road No. 8 F. C. 法租界八號路	3, 1, 1939	H. S. Chen 陳錫三	Y. S. Chang 張兩生	Trade 商
Ching Tung 慶通	"	"	$ 80,000		Sze-Teh Li F. C. 法租界四德里五十五號	3, 1937	H. F. Wen 溫學勤	C. C. Ho, H. F. Wen 何謺勤, 溫學勤	"
Chü Sheng 聚生	"	Sole Proprietorship 獨資	$ 20,000		Shou-Teh Building F. C. 法租界壽德大樓	1, 9, 1938	N. T. Sun 孫蔚亭	K. J. Chi 紀佩如	"
Heng Tai 恆泰	"	Partnership 合夥	$ 40,000		Yang-Fu-Yin Road F. C. 法租界楊福蔭路	9, 1927	A. T. Sun 孫安亭	P. C. Feng, H. T. Li 馮邦傑, 李照淳	"

Name of Native Bank 字號	Group 社派	Types of organization 組織	Capital Hu Pên 資本額	Address of the business 營業所所在地	Date when business started 開業日期	Manager 經理人姓名	PROPRIETORS 出資人 Names 姓名	Occupation 經歷
Chih Cheng 誠	Shen-Chi 深冀	Sole Proprietorship 獨資	$60,000	Road No. 2 B. C. 英租界二號路信誠里	1, 1937	M. S. Chen 陳鳴笙	D. F. Jung 榮端珠	Agriculture 農
Heng Yuan 恆源	Tientsin 津	”	$100,000	River Bank Road I. C. 義租界河沿路	10, 26, 1939	H. I. Tu 杜鴻儀	P. C. Feng 馮邦傑	Trade & Banking 商, 錢
Lao Heng Li 老恆利	Peking 京	”	$50,000	Fu Sze Road J. C. 日租界扶十街	3, 6, 1935	W. P. Chui 崔文波	Heng Li Gold Store 恆利金店	Trade 商
Ching Chü 慶潨	Shen-Chi 深冀	Partnership 合夥	$80,000	Road No. 23 F. C. 法租界二十三號路	1, 1922	S. T. Han 韓毓岵	C. P. Shian, C. S. Shian 冼澂波 談瀅生	”
Yu Min 裕民	Tientsin 津	”	$60,000	Road No. 23 F. C. 法租界二十三號路	3, 23, 1939	Y. S. Yang 楊穉孫	C. P. Li, Y. S. Yan, etc. 李竹波, 閻玉山等	”
I Tai 益泰	”	Sole Proprietorship 獨資	$20,000	Road No. 3 I. C. 義租界三馬路	7, 23, 1939	H. F. Wen 溫學舫	H. F. Wen 溫學舫	”
Tung Yü 同裕	Shen-Chi 深冀	”	$50,000	Road No. 32 F. C. 法租界三十二號路	3, 1935	Y. C. Lu 劉毓村	J. H. Chia 賈日新	”
Chih Hsing 孜興	”	Partnership 合夥	$60,000	Road No. 5 I. C. 義租界五號路	3, 23, 1938	H. T. Liu 劉向亭	K. C. Liu, P. K. Li, etc. 劉崗金, 劉秉國等五人	”

APPENDIX V —THE TABLE OF TIENTSIN NATIVE BANKS

Name of Native Bank 字號	Group 村派	Types of organization 組織	Capital 資本額	Hu Pen 認本額	Address of the business 營業所所在地	Date when business started 開業日期	Manager 經理人姓名	PROPRIETORS 出資人 Names 姓名	Occupation 範歷
Hui Chang 惠昌	Tientsin 津	Partnership 合夥	$100,000	$1,00,000	I-Sheng Building I. C. 英租界河沿路 義生大樓	4, 23, 1939	Y. L. Hóu 侯幼林	Y. S. Chang, H. N. Shiao, M. S. Ting, 章竹筌 蕭惠安 丁明山	Trade 商
Tien Yü 天裕	Shangtung 山東	"	$50,000		Yang Fu Yin Road F. C. 法租界楊福蔭路	6, 13, 1936	H. C. Chao 趙令卿	C. W. Chiao, C. T. Peng 趙賡吾, 彭柱天	"
Kwang Jui 廣瑞	Tientsin 津	Sole Proprietorship 獨資	$100,000		Yang Fu Yin Road F. C. 法租界楊福蔭路	3, 5, 1929	H. F. Li 李祥卿	N. K. Li 李恩巖	"
I Lung 益隆	"	Partnership 合夥	$100,000		14, Pei Ma Lu 北馬路一十四號	1, 1, 1939	W. C. Liu 劉文溪	Y. L. Fan, T. F. Chin etc. 范雅林, 靳廷輔等	"
Chian Ho 乾和	Shen-Chi 深冀	Sole Proprietorship 獨資	$40,000		Road No. 14 F. C. 法租界一十四號路	3, 19, 1919	L. K. Wang 王迪村	H. F. Ning 甯心荣	"
Yung Tsong Ho Tung Chi 永崇合通記	Peking 京	Partnership 合夥	$20,000		Road No. 27 F. C. 法租界二十七號路 一〇六號	6, 12, 1919	C. C. Liu 劉朝卿	S. C. Li, C. W. Yang 李曉岯 楊濟五	"
Shen Chang 誠昌	"	Sole Proprietorship 獨資	$60,000		Wen Hsing Li F. C. 法租界文興里	3, 1, 1939	Y. C. Liu 劉延鈞	T. J. Chang 張體仁	"
Hui Feng 惠豐	Shen-Chi 深冀	Partnership 合夥	$50,000		Shu Chioh J. C. 日租界旭街南口	5, 24, 1939	Y. C. Ts'ao 曹雅儕	N. H. Chin, Mrs. Chuei 金峋卿, 崔耀氏	"

APPENDIX V—THE TABLE OF TIENTSIN NATIVE BANKS

Name of Native Bank 字號	Group 幇派	Types of organization 組織	Capital 資本額	Hu Pên 護本額	Address of the business 營業所所在地	Date when business started 開業日期	Manager 經理人姓名	PROPRIETORS 出資人 Names 姓名	Occupation 經歷
Chian Sheng 謙豊	Shen-Chi 深幇	Partnership 合夥	$20,000		Road No. 40 F. C. 法租界四十號路	2, 1929	Y. L. Wang 王永廉	Y. S. Ho, C. C. Wang 何又叔, 王傑忱	Trade 商
I Hua 益華	"	Sole Proprietorship 獨資	$100,000		Road No. 2 B. C. 英租界二號路收以里	6, 27, 1939	H. N. Chia 賈緬侗	H. F. Chow 周希甫	"
I Feng 益豊	"	Partnership 合夥	$100,000		Road No. 6 F. C. 法租界六號路	4, 4, 1939	S. H. Li 李順興	S. S. Chi, Y. T. Di, S. C. Chang 邵伸石, 邸玉堂, 常小川	"
Pen Li Yung 本立永	"	Sole Proprietorship 獨資	$50,000		Road No. 3 I. C. 義租界三號路	10, 10, 1939	C. T. Liu 劉鑑班	C. C. Liu 劉炳臣	Banking 錢
Tung Sheng Hsiang 同生祥	"	"	$50,000		Road No. 32 F. C. 法租界三十二號路	2, 2, 1929	L. T. Chen 陳縂廷	S. H. Chia 賈鴻	Trade 商
Jung Chang Ho 榮昌和	"	"	$50,000		Road No. 4 F. C. 法租界四號路	2, 9, 1939	C. P. Chang 張作溥	N. F. Wang 王迺封	"
Tai Hsing 泰興	Peking 京	"	$50,000		Road No. 23 F. C. 法租界二十三號路	3, 1936	C. C. Chao 趙彩章	C. C. Chao 趙彩榮	Banking 錢
Hsin Chi 信記	Tientsin 津	"	$40,000		Hua Chung Road F. C. 法租界華中路三十五號	1, 1, 1921	M. H. Dai 戴茂祥	M. H. Dai 戴茂祥	Trade 商

APPENDIX V—THE TABLE OF TIENTSIN NATIVE BANKS

Name of Native Bank 字號	Group 社派	Types of organization 組織	Capital 資本額	Hu Pên 護本額	Address of the business 營業所所在地	Date when business started 開業日期	Manager 經理人姓名	Proprietors 出資人 Names 姓名	Occupation 經歷
Chen Hsing Chang 振興長	Tientsin 津	Sole Proprietorship 獨資	$30,000		Yang-Fu-Yin Road F.C. 法租界楊福蔭路	3, 9, 1933	Y. T. Yang 楊炆耀	Y. T. Yang 楊炆田	Trade 商
Yuan Shong 原生	Shen-Chi 深冀	"	$20,000		Road No. 3 I.C. 義租界三馬路廿七號	11, 12, 1939	C. N. Tu 杜盛年	C. S. Liu 劉乾生	"
Yu Chang 餘昌	Tientsin 津	"	$60,000		45, Kung Pei Ta Chieh 谷北大街四十五號	11, 1, 1939	C. M. Wei 魏長明	N. C. Sun 孫恩慶	"
Chin Chi Hsing 錦記興	Shen-Chi 深	Partnership 合夥	$80,000		Chiu Shan Road J.C. 日租界秋山街東口	5, 20, 1932	S. W. Ma 馬世五	C. F. Hsiao, T. C. Lu 蕭馥棠, 盧子楨	"
Chu Hua Chang 翠華昌	"	Sole Proprietorship 獨資	$60,000		Road No. 23 F.C. 法租界二十三號路	1, 25, 1937	K. C. Liu 劉國忱	C. H. Tung 仝潔才	"
Hung Hsing 宏興	"	Partnership 合夥	$20,000		5, West Road I.C. 義租界西馬路三十三號	3, 1937	M. P. Hu 胡梅波	Hung Yü Tang Li 怡元堂李 Chia Hsüan Tang Cheng 家萱堂鄭	Trade & Banking 商, 錢
Tung Ching Lung Sheng Chi 同慶隆盛記	"	"	$30,000		4, West Road I.C. 義租界西馬路北口四號	10, 28, 1935	M. L. Cheng 鄭翠林	Tung Ching Lung 邢台縣同慶隆祥布莊	Trade 商
Wei Chang Cheng Chi 維章成記	"	"	$56,000		Road No. 5 I.C. 義租界五馬路西口五十二號	11, 10, 1939	C. Li 李沿	C. T. Shen, C. K. Li 申任田, 李仁魁	Trade & Banking 商, 錢

APPENDIX V—THE TABLE OF TIENTSIN NATIVE BANKS

Name of Native Bank 字號	Group 紮派	Types of organization 組織	Capital Hu Pên 資本額 護本額	Address of the business 營業所所在地	Date when business started 開業日期	Manager 經理人姓名	Proprietors Names 出資人姓名	Occupation 經歷
Ching Feng 慶豐	Shen-Chi 深祭	Sole proprietorship 獨資	$100,000	Road No. 5 F. C. 法租界五號路三十一號	5, 14, 1937	C. M. Li 李治民	T. C. Chao 趙紫宸	Politics 政
Hsin Feng 信豐	Tientsin 津	Partnership 合夥	$40,000	West Road I. C. 義租界四馬路德生糧棧內	9, 7, 1939	Y. C. Shao 邵毓珽	Y. H. Chang, Y. C. Hsiao 張玉軒, 蕭毓珽	Trade & Banking 商, 錢
Yu Chang Hou 裕昌厚	Shansi 山西	"	$100,000	Road No. 3 I. C. 義租界三馬路三十一號	4, 4, 1939	C. P. Li 李竹坡	Y. H. Chang, L. H. Li, etc. 張玉軒, 李林森等五人	Trade 商
Liu Chu 六柒	Shen-Chi 深祭	"	$40,000	Road No. 14 F. C. 法租界十四號路四十二號	2, 1938	C. C. Chang 張北箴	C. P. Hsien, C. S. Hsien 冼啟波, 冼榮生	"
Teh Fêng 德豐	"	Sole proprietorship 獨資	$100,000	Road No. 20 F. C. 法租界二十號路	3, 29, 1939	C. C. Han 韓智修	H. F. Chon 陳秀峰	"
Hung Ching Yu 鴻慶裕	"	"	$20,000	Hsin I Li, B. C. 英租界信義里	2, 17, 1930	Y. T. Chou 周潤德	H. L. Tien 田掌熙	"
Tung Fu Chang Chi 同孚昌記	"	Partnership 合夥	$100,000	River Bank Road I. C. 義租界河沿路十六號	10, 1, 1939	C. Y. Li 李砷谷	J. C. Chi, C. C. Keh 齊任之, 戈璧匠	"
Chih Hua 志華	"	"	$40,000	Road No. 3 I. C. 義租界三馬路廿號	10, 14, 1939	F. J. Liu 劉芳幼	Y. N. Cheng, C. F. Kung 程際術, 孔錦舫	"

APPENDIX V—THE TABLE OF TIENTSIN NATIVE BANKS

Name of Native Bank 字號	Group 社派	Types of organization 組織	Capital 設本額	Hu Pên 護本額	Address of the business 營業所所在地	Date when business started 開業日期	Manager 經理人姓名	Proprietors Names 出資人 姓名	Occupation 經歷
Ho Sheng Ho 和生	Shen-Chi 深業	Partnership 合夥	$20,000		Chiu Shan Road J. C. 日租界秋山街	4, 15, 1939	H. H. Li 李星輝	Y. S. Chang, K. C. Wang 張鈺陞、王國鎮	Trade 商
Hsin Teh 信德	"	Sole Proprietorship 獨資	$20,000		Chiu Shan Road J. C. 日租界秋山街東首	10, 11, 1934	C. H. Yuan 袁崇樾	H. C. Tung 仝信樓	"
Ding Feng 鼎豐	Peking 京	Partnership 合夥	$50,000		25, Hsi Road I. C. 英租界西路馬路廿五號	5, 24, 1939	C. M. Lu 盧則淜	Y. S. Yian, F. W. Chang 閆玉山、張範五等四人	"
Chu Teh Chong Chi 聚德成記	Shen-Chi 深業	"	$40,000		Shou Chieh J. C. 日租界壽街二番地三號	1, 6, 1920	K. C. Wang 王國鎮	C. C. Wang, C. C. Tung 王成子、仝忠權	"
Chih Tung 志通	"	Sole Proprietorship 獨資	$60,000		Road No. 6 I. C. 英租界六馬路荆荆里	11, 14, 1939	Y. S. Chuei 崔阪生	C. S. Li 李阪升	"
Ho Sheng 和生	Tientsin 津	Partnership 合夥	$100,000		Kung Nan Ta Chieh 宮南大街廿九號	1, 20, 1939	T. W. Li 李庭武	Y. T. Yang, T. W. Li 楊雨亭、李庭武	Trade and Banking 商、錢
Teh-Cheng 德成	Shen-Chi 深業	"	$60,000		Road No. 5 I. C. 英租界五馬路後排四十九號	1, 5, 1939	S. C. Pan 賜守誠	S. F. Shao, S. T. Sun, S. C. Pan 邵馨甫、孫孝庭、賜守誠	Trade 商
I Cheng 義誠	"	"	$50,000		Yang Fu Yin Road F. C. 法租界楊編編路	3, 12, 1937	S. P. Chin 秦絜波	C. C. Hsin, S. P. Chin 辛伯誠、秦絜波	"

APPENDIX V—THE TABLE OF TIENTSIN NATIVE BANKS

Name of Native Bank 字號	Group 幫派	Types of organization 組織	Capital Hu Pèn 資本額	Address of the business 營業所任地	Date when business started 開業日期	Manager 經理人姓名	PROPRIETORS 出資人	
							Names 姓名	Occupation 經歷
Lung Hsin I Chi 隆信徐記	Shen-Chi 深繫	Partnership 合夥	$60,000	West Road I. C. 飛租界四馬路正和里一號	3, 11, 1939	J. P. Ch'ü 徐履謙	T. C. Kao, L. C. Ch'ü 高廷棨, 徐履謙	Trade 商
Fu Chu 茯聚	"	Sole proprietorship 獨資	$30,000	Road No. 20 F. C. 法租界二十號路	10, 20, 1938	T. T. Wang 王丹泟	C. C. Chang 張子泉	Agriculture 農
Song Seng 生生	"	Partnership 合夥	$24,000	Road No. 14 F. C. 法租界十四號路	1921	Y. S. Feng 馮殖三	W. C. Li, C. T. Hsing, Y. N. Chao, 李許廷, 邢竹庭, 趙益祖	Trade 商
Wan Hong 萬亨	"	Sole proprietorship 獨資	$50,000	Road No. 2 I. C. 飛租界二馬路十二號	3, 1, 1939	H. J. Liu 劉浩如	Y. F. Liu 劉承溥	"
Fu Tai Heng 福泰恆	"	Partnership 合夥	$30,000	Road No. 14 F. C. 法租界十四號路	12, 19, 1938	F. P. Kao 高芳圃	Y. S. Keng, C. S. Li 耿潤身, 李仲三	"
Tung Hsing 同興	Peking 京	"	$100,000	Road No. 1 F. C. 法租界一號路	9, 1930	C. W. Chang 常軸五	Company, Limited 有限公司	"
Chuen Ho 祥和	"	"	$100,000	Yang-Fu-Yin Road F.C. 法租界揚福蔭兩際路	4, 8, 1935	H. I. Chang 張鴻一	P. H. Chan, P. F. Chao 殷葆衡, 趙鵬飛	"
Fu Feng 福豐	Tientsin 津	Sole proprietorship 獨資	$80,000	Road No. 5 F. C. 法租界五號路	3, 16, 1938	H. C. Liu 劉新周	P. H. Wang 王伯蓀	"

Name of Native Bank 字號	Group 幫派	Types of organization 組織	Capital Hu Pên 資本額	Address of the business 營業所所在地	Date when business started 開業日期	Manager 經理人姓名	PROPRIETORS 出資人 Names 姓名	Occupation 經歷
Chih Yuan 致遠	Peking 京	Partnership 合夥	$60,000	Road No. 23 F.C. 法租界廿三號路	3, 5, 1936	M. W. Liu 劉明五	S. C. Shao 邵貴清, L. S. Chuei 崔誠秀	Trade & Agriculture 商農
Hsin Hua 信華	Shen-Chi 深冀	Sole Proprietorship 獨資	$30,000	Road No. 2 I.C. 義租界二號路二十三號	3, 23, 1939	I. C. Feng 封逸暄	D. H. Wang 王蹈	Trade 商
Shen Hsing 誠興	Peking 京	"	$20,000	Road No. 29 F.C. 法租界二十九號路 吉祥里	3, 1928	C. M. Hou 侯肇民	P. C. Li 李璞	"
Hui Yuan Yung 匯源永	Paoting 保定	"	$50,000	Road No. 25 F.C. 法租界二十五號路 忠厚里	1, 6, 1927	I. C. Chang 張一清	K. S. Han 韓兌生	"
Yu Hsing 裕興	Tientsin 津	Partnership 合夥	$20,000	Road No. 5 I.C. 義租界五號路	11, 18, 1939	S. C. Wang 王少洲	S. C. Tung 董餅之, S. T. Li 李聞榮	"
Jen Feng 仁豐	Peking 京	Sole proprietorship 獨資	$80,000	Yang-Fu-Yin Road F.C. 法租界楊嗣蔭總路	3, 4, 1926	C. F. Wang 王捷帆	C. F. Wang 王捷帆	Banking 錢
Fu Shun 福順	Shen-Chi 深冀	"	$60,000	Road No. 8 F.C. 法租界八號路七十九號	1, 1935	L. T. Tung 仝連光	S. C. Tung 仝臣	Trade 商
Tai Ho Chi 太和記	"	"	$60,000	Road No. 24 F.C. 法租界二十四路	1, 1933	C. K. Tung 仝紫光	W. Y. Tung 仝文遜	"

APPENDIX V—THE TABLE OF TIENTSIN NATIVE BANKS

Name of Native Bank 字號	Group 社派	Types of organization 組織	Capital Hu Pên 資本額 護本額	Address of the business 營業所所在地	Date when business started 開業日期	Manager 經理人姓名	Proprietors Names 出資人 姓名	Occupation 經歷 商
Tung Feng 桐豐	Tientsin 津	Sole Proprietorship 獨資	$40,000	Yang-Fu-Yin Road F.C 法租界楊桐陰路	4, 4, 1914	C. T. Sun 孫俊泫	C. T. Sun 孫俊泫	Trade 商
Chi Tai 啟泰	Peking 京	Partnership 合夥	$20,000	Road No. 2 I. C. 義租界二馬路十九號	3, 17, 1939	C. J. Kao 高清如	C. J. Kao, etc. 高清如 等	"
Tung Shan 同善	Shen-Chi 深	"	$50,000	Road No. 26 F. C. 法租界二十六號路	3, 1939	Y. T. Chao 趙毓孚	C. C. Chia, A. T. Wang, F. C. Tien 賈哲生 王愛棠 田紹衡	"
Yuan Chi 元吉	Paoting 保定	Sole Proprietorship 獨資	$50,000	Road No. 2 B. C. 比租界二號路	1932	H. C. Wang 王和庭	P. C. Kao 高芭泉	"
Yu Teh 裕德	Shen-Chi 深	Partnership 合夥	$40,000	Road No. 29 F. C. 法租界二十九號路	5, 23, 1938	M. H. Liu 劉孟吼	P. C. Han, C. T. Liu 韓蓬作 劉幹臣	"
Hsin Cheng 信波	Peking 京	Sole Proprietorship 獨資	$20,000	Yang-Fu-Yin Road F.C 法租界楊桐陰路	4, 19, 1937	D. C. Wu 吳慈卿	C. Y. Wang 王仲玉	"
Tien Feng Tai 天恩泰	Shen-Chi 深	"	$20,000	River Bank Road I. C. 義租界河沿馬路新記木行對過	11, 5, 1939	T. L. Ho 何德隆	H. Lu 祭 浩	"
Fu Chang 福昌	Peking 京	"	$50,000	Road No. 31 F. C. 法租界三十一號路	10, 11, 1938	S. W. Hsing 邢絵蔚	C. A. Chu 祝積盃	"

APPENDIX V —THE TABLE OF TIENTSIN NATIVE BANKS

Name of Native Bank 字號	Group 棧賑	Types of organization 組織	Capital Hu Pên 證本額	Address of the business 營業所所在地	Date when business started 開業日期	Manager 經理人姓名	PROPRIETORS Names 姓名	Occupation 營業
Tai Chi 大棅	Shen-Chi 深	Sole Proprietorship 獨資	$20,000	Shou-Teh Building F.C. 法租界壽德大樓	3, 15, 1939	C. F. Liu 劉子譯	C. S. Liu 劉乾生	Trade 商
Yuan I 元一	Tientsin 津	Partnership 合夥	$30,000	Road No. 25 F.C. 法界租二十五號路五號	2, 24, 1939	S. C. Wu 烏樹鈞	S. C. Wu, W. P. Li 烏樹鈞, 李維邦	"
Tung Hsing 東興	Shen-Chi 深	Sole Proprietorship 獨資	$50,000	South East Road I. C. 義租界東馬路十五號	1, 6, 1935	C. T. Chen 陳金堂	H. C. Lu 魯惠泉	"
Chia I Kung 甲乙公	"	"	$200,000	Chu Yuan Li F. C. 法租界存益里	2, 1934	J. C. Cheng 鄭萊琮	J. C. Chong 鄭萊琮	"
Shen Feng 慎豐	"	"	$60,000	Kuo Dien Chieh 鍋店街公津里五號	12, 15, 1939	C. C. Meng 孟宗周	C. M. Li 李子梅	"
Sheng Yuan 盛遠	"	"	$60,000	Pei Ma Lu 北馬路前代銀行後院	12, 27, 1939	C. C. Li 李振家	T. S. Wang 王棠生	Politics and Trade 政, 商
I Chu 魏棨	Peking 京	"	$30,000	Road No. 6 F. C. 法租界六號路益支坊	3, 18, 1937	H. P. Li 李疆坡	Peking I Chü 北京魏棨	Trade 商
Fu Chi 福記	Shen-Chi 深	"	$40,000	Road No. 27 F. C. 法租界二十七號路六十三號	10, 1932	C. C. Tien 田建設	F. T. Chuei 崔輔庭	"

APPENDIX V—THE TABLE OF TIENTSIN NATIVE BANKS

Name of Native Bank 字號	Group 紙派	Types of organization 組織	Capital 資本額	Hu Pèn 護本額	Address of the business 營業所所在地	Date when business started 開業日期	Manager 經理人姓名	PROPRIETORS 出資人 Names 姓名	Occupation 經歷
Chih Ta 志達	Shen-Chi 深記	Sole proprietorship 獨資	$20,000		Asahi Road J. C. 日租界旭街	3, 5, 1913	C. H. Li 李仙溪	H. C. Liu 劉煥卿	Trade 商
Pen Li Yuan 本立源	Paoting 保定	"	$50,000		I-Yu-Feng F. C. 法租界益友坊七號	1932	C. C. Li 李叔忠	P. S. Chiang 蔣彬生	"
Hung Chang 宏昌	Shen-Chi 深記	Partnership 合夥	$30,000		Road No. 17 B. C. 英租界十七號路內去義銀號內	12, 28, 1939	Y. T. Han 韓卿川	Y. C. Li, Y. F. Li 李鳴鎮、李永幸	"
Ping Ho 平和	"	Sole proprietorship 獨資	$40,000		Road No. 25 F. C. 法租界二十五號路北首十七號	1, 10, 1936	C. C. Li 李昌岐	C. C. Li 李昌岐	"
I Hsing 義興	"	"	$50,000		Ta Ma Lu 2nd S. A. 特二區大馬路七十一號	1, 7, 1940	Y. F. Lü 呂雅鳳	I. C. Liu 劉護卿	"
Hui Chi 滙記	Shansi 山西	"	$40,000		Road No. 29 F. C. 法租界二十九號路九十一號	1, 1, 1938	M. S. Wu 武明山	C. Y. Chiang 蔣菊岩	"
Chao Feng 肇豐	Shen-Chi 深記	"	$100,000		West Road No. 3 I. C. 義租界內西路北首三號	1, 7, 1940	C. H. Li 李咏修	H. Y. Li 李興遠	"
Teh Chang 德昌	"	Partnership 合夥	$20,000		Kuo Dien Chieh, Chin Jen Li 鍋店街近仁里七號	1, 16, 1940	Y. C. Li 李毓才	S. T. Ma, S. C. Li 馬三元、李普陸	"

APPENDIX V—THE TABLE OF TIENTSIN NATIVE BANKS

Name of Native Bank 字號	Group 社派	Types of organization 組織	Capital 資本額	Hu Pên 護本額	Address of the business 營業所所在地	Date when business started 開業日期	Manager 總理人姓名	PROPRIETORS Names 出資人姓名	Occupation 經歷
Tung Hua 同華	Shen-Chi 深裂	Sole Proprietorship 獨資	$60,000		River Bank Road I. C. 英界河沿許路十六號 大樓	2, 1940	F. N. Li 李毓恩	H. T. Li, etc. 李滌滋等六人	Trade 商
Yuan Hsing 源興	Tientsin 津	"	$80,000		Road No. 2 I. C. 英租界二馬路四十號	2, 13, 1940	P. N. Hsu 許鵬年	Yuan Sheng Steel Co. 源盛鋼鐵公司	"
Kwang Yuan 廣源	Shansi 山西	Partnership 合夥	$60,000		Road No. 13 B. C. 比租界十三號路 九號玄源後內	2, 15, 1938	S. C. Tsai 戚湘閣	F. Ch'ih, C. H. Yang, etc. 示咔 楊仲昆等五人	"
Yung Tai 永泰	Tientsin 津	"	$100,000		Road No. 3 I. C. 英租界三馬路十六號	3, 1, 1940	Y. C. Chang 張耀卿	C. S. Li, Y. S. Tu 李靜藻, 杜積山	"
Chao Feng 兆豐	"	"	$80,000		Road No. 5 I. C. 英租界五馬路西口 五十三號	2, 19, 1940	D. M. Chan 詹殿銘	C. C. Wang, L. F. Liu, C. C. Shao 王蕃介 劉鈺沛 蕃做清	"
I Kang Jung Chi 金陵榮記	Shen-Chi 深 ○	"	$50,000		East Road I. C. 英租界東馬路 五十二號	3, 4, 1940	C. C. Kung 扎振芝	M. H. Chen, H. M. Chi, F. W. Ma 陳念修 齊協民 馬輪五	"
Dun Hsiang 孜祥	Tientsin 津	"	$100,000		Siao Ma Lu I. C. 英租界陝院小馬路 四號	3, 23, 1940	C. C. Li 李子純	C. H. Li, I. T. Chang, etc. 李敏先, 張裂庭等四人	Trade & Banking 商, 錢
Hsin Ho 信和	"	"	$150,000		Road No. 6 I. C. 英租界六馬路 乙字四號	3, 5, 1940	P. C. Liu 劉渫航	H. C. Chen, S. S. Yan, etc. 陳匯秩, 閻諮山等四人	"

APPENDIX V—THE TABLE OF TIENTSIN NATIVE BANKS

Name of Native Bank 字號	Group 社派	Types of organization 組織	Capital 資本額	Hu Pên 護本額	Address of the business 營業所所在地	Date when business started 開業日期	Manager 經理人姓名	PROPRIETORS Names 出資人 姓名	Occupation 經歷
Fu Teh 福德	Tientsin 津	Partnership 合夥	$100,000		Road No. 5 I.C. 英租界五馬路三十八號	3, 4, 1940	P. S. Sun 孫保詐	C. C. Wen, 溫敬之 P. S. Sun 孫保詐	Trade & Banking 商，錢
Hung Hsin 洪信	Shen-Chi 深聚	Sole Proprietorship 獨資	$100,000		Road No. 3 I.C. 英租界三馬路東首八號	3, 14, 1940	P. T. Hsu 許楗之	C. P. Hung 洪靜波	Trade 商
Hong Hsian 恆祥	Tientsin 津	"	$100,000		East Road I.C. 英租界東馬路十三號	3, 23, 1940	I. J. Hua 華以牧	M. F. Wang 王夢符	"
Wei Feng 蔚豐	Paoting 保定	"	$200,000		Road No. 6 I.C. 英租界六馬路四號	2, 13, 1940	Y. N. Cheng 程蔭南	Y. N. Cheng 程蔭南	"
Chu Cheng 聚誠	Shantung 山東	Partnership 合夥	$50,000		West Road I.C. 英租界四馬路北省七號	3, 17, 1940	L. C. Feng 馮潤生	S. T. Chang, I. C. Tung, S. H. Ma 張叔逵 董霓華 馬樹軒	Trade & Banking 商，錢
Chu Lung 聚隆	Shen-Chi 深聚	Sole Proprietorship 獨資	$50,000		41, Ruh Chi Hutung Ho-Pei Ta Chieh 河北大街肉架胡同四十一號	3, 20, 1940	C. L. Chen 陳兆麟	C. L. Tang 唐之良	Trade 商
Ta Heng 大亨	"	Partnership 合夥	$50,000		West Road I.C. 英租界四馬路廿五號	1, 1940	Y. H. Lu 路蘊和	P. C. Fan, Y. Y. Chen, C. C. Ning 潘百川 陳衍祥 甯紹麒	"
Ho Hsing 和興	"	"	$60,000		Road No. 6 I.C. 英租界六馬路八號	3, 17, 1940	C. C. Li 李智忱	H. F. Wen, 溫香圃 C. C. Li 李智忱	Trade & Banking 商，錢

APPENDIX V—THE TABLE OF TIENTSIN NATIVE BANKS

Name of Native Bank 字號	Group 幇派	Types of organization 組織	Capital 資本額	Hu Pên 護本額	Address of the business 營業所所在地	Date when business started 開業日期	Manager 經理人姓名	PROPRIETORS 出資人 Names 姓名	Occupation 經歷
I Heng Chang 金恆昌	Paoting 保定	Sole proprietorship 獨資	$50,000		Road No. 6 F.C. 法租界六號路 益友坊四號	2, 15, 1933	C. C. Chi 齊子琛	J. C. Hwang 黃榮昌	Trade 商
Chi Shang 集商	Shansi 山西	"	$50,000		East Road I. C. 義租界其馬路 五十二號	2, 1938	S. C. Chin 秦修齋	K. C. Yang 楊國楨	"
Heng Yuan I 恆源金	Paoting 保定	"	$50,000		Road No. 6 F. C. 法租界六號路 益友坊	3, 1, 1927	C. C. Wang 王炯珍	K. L. Chiang 蔣貿琛	Politics 政
Ching Hsiang 慶祥	Tientsin 津	"	$50,000		Road No. 5 i. C. 義租界五馬路門口 五十二號	3, 11, 1940	H. C. Tan 譚鴻彩	Y. C. Chang 張玉慶	Trade 商
Teh Sheng 德生	"	Partnership 合夥	$120,000		Road No. 6 I. C. 義租界馬路六號 b字十三號	3, 21, 1940	T. S. Yang 楊道三	L. T. Liu, T. S. Yang, P. C. Kuo 劉伯冷三 郭伯平	Trade and Banking 商，錢
Tien Feng Ta Chi 天豐達記	"	"	$100,000		Road No. 5 I. C. 義租界五馬路 二十六號	3, 9, 1940	C. C. Li 李錦檣	S. N. Wang, P. L. Pong, C. T. Kao 王松伯 彭伯良 高敬棠	"
Teh Hsiang 悌祥	Shen-Chi 深集	"	$50,000		Leo Chan Ta Chieh F. C. 法租界太梁人街 大安里四十八號	1930	C. H. Chao 趙劭軒	S. S. Chang, C. T. Chao, C. Y. Chen 張多生 趙紹蓀 陳中普	Trade 商
K'wang Feng 廣豐	Tiontsin 津	Sole Proprietorship 獨資	$20,000		East Road I. C. 義租界其馬路 五十四號	6, 1939	H. C. Lu 盧惠忱	H. C. Lu 盧惠忱	"

APPENDIX V—THE TABLE OF TIENTSIN NATIVE BANKS

Name of Native Bank 字號	Group 系派	Types of organization 組織	Capital 資本額	Hu Pên 護本額	Address of the business 營業所所在地	Date when business started 開業日期	Manager 經理人姓名	PROPRIETORS Names 出資人 姓名	Occupation 經歷
Yu Tung 裕東	Shen-Chi 深系	Partnership 合夥	$60,000		Road No. 6 I. C. 發租界六馬路鮑家大樓B字十一號	4, 1940	T. H. Chen 陳棟溪	C. J. Chang, H. Y. Liu, C. T. Hu 張毓璋 劉心溪 月記之	Trade 商
Lung Fong 隆豐	Tientsin 津	"	$100,000		Road No. 2 I. C. 發租界二號路二號	2, 21, 1940	Y. H. Hsü 徐延榕	C. Liu C. L. Hsieh, etc. 劉 局, 謝之龍等五人	"
Hsing Sheng Yung 興盛永	Shen-Chi 深系	"	$50,000		Erh Ching Li I. C. 發租界二慶里一號	10,10,1930	C. M. Yang 楊子明	C. C. Chao, L. P. Wu, S. L. Liu 趙紫宸 吳慶伯 劉詳園	Politics and Trade 政, 商
Chung I 衆誼	"	Solo Proprietorship 獨資	$42,000		Road No. 2 I. C. 發租界二馬路七號	4, 1, 1940	H. T. Liu 劉濟濤	C. T. Hsing 邢詹淬	Politics 政
Sheng Chü 盛潔	"	"	$40,000	$20,000	Canton Road B. C. 英租界廣東路四十九號	4,15,1940	L. P. Chui 崔潞坪	H. C. Wang 王鴻釗	Trade 商
I Tung 義東	"	Partnership 合夥	$100,000		East Road I. C. 發租界東馬路樓鮑大家B字十一號	4,24,1940	C. Chang 張 焱	Y. T. Chao, T. I. Shiao, C. F. Fu 趙棟堂 蕭子樹 傅徐闢	"
Tung Chang 同昌	"	"	$50,000		Shiao Ma Road I. C. 發租界小馬路工部局十號	3, 23, 1940	T. L. Liu 劉德茂	T. Chang, S. T. Kuo, Y. C. Wang 張廷經 郭秀經 王霍泉	"
Hsin Chung 鑫忠	Shansi 山西	"	$100,000		River Bank Road I. C. 發租界河沿馬路新記木行沿廿四號	3, 17, 1940	I. S. Wang 王韭修	I. T. Chi 殷宜汸 H. M. Chang, 張向明,	"

APPENDIX V—THE TABLE OF TINETSIN NATIVE BANKS

Name of Native Bank 字號	Group 札派	Types of organization 組織	Capital 資本額	Hu Pên 護本額	Address of the business 營業所在地	Date when business started 開業日期	Manager 經理人姓名	PROPRIETORS Names 出資人 姓名	Occupation 經歷
I Feng Hou 金豐厚	Shon-Chi 深	Sole Proprietorship 獨資	$30,000		Road No. 5 F.C. 法租界五號路志成代棧	1, 1940	J. P. Tu 杜悅詳	Y. C. Li 李耀卿	Politics 政
Ho Chi 和記	"	Partnership 合夥	$50,000		River Bank Road I.C. 英租界河沿些路一十六號	2, 2, 1940	Y. T. Chang 張育德	H. C. Hu, P. S. Chang 胡祥階, 張瑞綵	Trade 商
Chung Cheng 中誠	Shansi 山西	Sole Proprietorship 獨資	$50,000		Road No. 6 I.C. 英租界六號路鮑家人摟九號	11, 15, 1939	H. F. Tien 田華川	S. F. P'ei 裴秀峯	"
Yuan Mao 源茂	Tientsin 津	"	$60,000		Yang-Fu-Yin Road F.C. 法租界楊嗣經路三十二號	3, 23, 1940	Y. P. Wu 吳調波	Y. P. Wu 吳調波	Banking 錢
Lee Hua 利譁	Shon-Chi 深	Partnership 合夥	$50,000		Road No. 2 I.C. 英法租界二號路廿三號惢泰樓內	4, 17, 1940	K. C. Wang 王拱之	H. M. Miao, etc. 苗新明筝三人	Trade & Agriculture 商農
Ho Hsiang 和祥	Tientsin 津	"	$100,000		Road No. 4 I.C. 英租界四號馬路柒市丙六號	3, 17, 1940	C. H. Yu 于治準	S. C. Meng, H. C. Jen 孟促同, 任臨卿	Trade & Banking 商, 錢
Teh Feng Lung 德豐隆	Shon-Chi 深	Sole Proprietorship 獨資	$40,000		Cheng Ho Li I.C. 英租界正和里一號	2, 1934	I. C. Wang 王毅之	S. C. Wang 王世氏	Agriculture 農
Ming Teh Lung 明德隆	"	"	$24,000		East Road I.C. 英租界東馬路四十二號	4, 1940	Y. T. Hsieh 謝禹鉦	C. N. Liu 劉禹恩	Trade 商

APPENDIX V—THE TABLE OF TIENTSIN NATIVE BANKS

Name of Native Bank	Group	Types of organization	Capital	Hu Pên	Address of the business	Date when business started	Manager	PROPRIETORS Names	Occupation
Fu Lung 福隆	Shen-Chi 深記	Sole Proprietorship 獨資	$60,000		Road No. 3 I.C. 英租界三號馬路四十六號	3, 17, 1940	B. S. Liu 劉邠生	C. S. Liu 劉拱三	Trade 商
Tung Ho 同和	"	Partnership 合夥	$100,000		Road No. 5 I.C. 英租界五號馬路二十七號	4, 17, 1940	Y. C. Li 李玉棠	T. H. Yang 楊子和, M. T. Wang 王慈庵	"
Tien Chü 天聚	"	"	$100,000		Road No. 6 I.C. 英租界六號馬路鮑家大樓	4, 3, 1940	C. C. Chen 陳樹棋	H. F. Li 李香閣, C. C. Chen 陳樹棋	"
Teh Lung 德隆	"	Sole Proprietorship 獨資	$50,000		Ta Ma Lu I.C. 英租界大馬路公和興內	3, 5, 1931	S. T. Chang 張叔逵	C. C. Chang 張介忱	"
Tung Shun Teh 同順德	"	"	$30,000		South Road I.C. 英租界南號馬路永豐裡內	5, 15, 1936	M. C. Wei 魏明久	S. N. Li 李詩年	"
Sheng Chi 盛記	"	"	$40,000		Road No. 3 I.C. 英租界三號路後排二十號後門	3, 1, 1940	M. F. Tu 杜明前	C. Y. Chang 張子珞	"
Teh Hsing Yung 德興永	"	"	$70,000		West Road I.C. 英租界西號路三十二號	4, 1940	T. Y. Chen 陳子玉	C. S. Chen 陳子緗	Agriculture 農
Yü Hua 豫華	"	"	$20,000		Road No. 3 I.C. 英租界三號路五十一號	11, 1939	M. F. Chang 張銘前	C. H. Jen 任家莶	Trade 商

APPENDIX V—THE TABLE OF TIENTSIN NATIVE BANKS

Name of Native Bank 字號	Group 帮派	Types of organization 組織	Capital 資本額	Hu Pên 護本額	Address of the business 營業所所在地	Date when business started 開業日期	Manager 經理人姓名	Proprietors Names 股資人 姓名	Occupation 經歷
Jui Tung 瑞迪	Shon-Chi 深	Sole Proprietorship 獨資	$20,000		Road No.3 I. C. 淡租界三馬路十九號三樓	1, 2, 1940	S. Y. Tung 董紹緞	Y. S. Kang 康韶珊	Banking 錢
Chong Feng Yu 正豐裕	Tientsin 津	Partnership 合夥	$120,000		Road No.4 F. C. 法租界四號路	4, 1940	Y. C. Su 蘇雨濤	P. C. Feng, C. T. Sun 馮伯卿 孫俊亭	Trade & Banking 商, 錢
Hua Sheng 華盛	Peking 京	Sole Proprietorship 獨資	$50,000		Shiao Ma Lu I. C. 淡租界小馬路工部局對過十二號	3, 29, 1940	H. M. Wang 王恩民	C. C. Kao 高敬齋	Trade 商
Fu Li 福利	"	"	$40,000		Road No.3 I. C. 淡租界三馬路十八號	1, 1940	P. S. Chang 張藻祥	W. T. Chow 周文濤	"
Chong Hsin 正信	Tientsin 津	Partnership 合夥	$160,000		East Road I. C. 淡租界東馬路三十一號	4, 2, 1940	L. M. Chow 周立勤	H. C. Liu 劉漢卿, C. P. Chai 紫竹坡	"
I Chung 徑中	Shon-Chi 深	Sole Proprietorship 獨資	$60,000		Road No.11 B. C. 英租界十一號路一〇五號鈺生樓內	4, 4, 1940	C. C. Yeh 葉卓堂	S. P. Liu 劉少瑛	"
Chū Hsing 鉅興	Peking 京	"	$50,000		Road No.23 F. C. 法租界二十三號路三十四號	3, 14, 1940	C. H. Chang 張邦祥	L. S. Chang 張閬生	"
Yu Tai 裕泰	Tientsin 津	"	$50,000		Road No.5 I. C. 淡租界五馬路路口八字三十五號	5, 6, 1940	F. H. Chang 張福軒	P. Y. Yang 楊伯翔	"

APPENDIX V—THE TABLE OF TIENTSIN NATIVE BANKS

Name of Native Bank 字號	Group 紀派	Types of organization 組織	Capital 資本額	Hu Pên 護本額	Address of the business 營業所所在地	Date when business started 開業日期	Manager 經理人姓名	PROPRIETORS Names 姓名	Occupation 經歷
Hsin Yuan 信源	Tientsin 津	Partnership 合夥	$100,000		Jui An Chioh, 2nd S.A. 特二屆瑞安街五號	5, 10, 1940	H. Y. Liu 劉夕遜	W. T. Wu, C. W. Li 武溫泰, 李郵五	Trade 商
I Sheng Yuan 義生源	Shansi 山西	"	$20,000		Road No. 11 B. C. 英租界十一號路 增盛隆內六號	5, 1, 1939	Y. C. Chang 張月村	J. C. Haw, S. Chi 郝日增, 壁三	"
Hsin Lung 信隆	Tientsin 津	"	$100,000		Road No. 6 I. C. 義租界六馬路 A字十一號	5, 22, 1940	T. Lu 陸	張靜茈, 高德林等四人 C. A. Chang, T. L. Kao, etc.	Banking 錢
Chi Chang 其昌	Shanghai 上海	"	$50,000		Road No. 5 I. C. 義租界五馬路 B字三十九號	4, 1, 1940	I. H. Ting 丁金祥	S. K. Ting, T. C. Wang 丁山祥, 王德洛	"
Yu Chang 裕昌	Tientsin 津	"	$100,000		Road No. 5 I. C. 義租界五馬路轉角廿七號	5,	T. K. Chui 崔子光	C. F. Wang, F. N. Chang, T. K. Chui 王繁封, 張恕年, 崔子光	Trade 商
Won Chi 文記	Shon-Chi 深冀	Solo Proprietorship 獨資	$30,000		Lee Chian F. C. 法租界梨棧衖沿里三號	4, 23, 1939	W. P. Liu 劉文波	W. P. Liu 劉文波	"
Yung Tah 永大	"	"	$50,000		Road No. 5 F. C. 法租界五號路三十六號	6, 9, 1940	L. H. Chao 起硯和	Y. C. Chai 蔡慾保	"
Hong Feng 恒豐	"	"	$60,000		Road No. 32 F. C. 法租界三十二號路泰景里三號	2, 24, 1938	C. K. Liu 劉兆庚	T. H. Chang 程棣華	"

APPENDIX V—THE TABLE OF TIENTSIN NATIVE BANKS

Name of Native Bank 字號	Group 幫派	Types of organization 組織	Capital Hu Pên 資本額	Address of the business 營業所所在地	Date when business started 開業日期	Manager 經理人姓名	Proprietors Names 出資人 姓名	Occupation 經歷
Ching Cheng 慶成	Tientsin 津	Partnership 合夥	$50,000	Shou-Teh Building F. C. 法租界壽德大樓八號	2, 1, 1931	C. C. Chang 張俊臣	S. F. Lung, B. C. Chao, T. C. Chang 劉少奉, 趙壁臣, 張俊臣	Trade and Banking 商, 錢
Tung Sheng 通盛	Shansi 山西	Sole Proprietorship 獨資	$50,000	South East Road I. C. 義界租界滇馬路七號二樓	3, 1940	H. T. Tuan 段鈞孚	T. Y. Chang 張子珩	Trade 商
Wen Hsing Yu 文興裕	Tientsin 津	"	$120,000	Road No. 6 F. C. 法租界六號路一百三十四號	5, 15, 1940	N. F. Iu 鳳恩輔	Y. C. Chi 祁卯卿	"
Chen Chung 振中	"	Partnership 合夥	$40,000	Road No. 4 F. C. 法租界四號路七十一號	11, 30, 1938	W. L. Ma 馬維隆	W. L. Ma, L. M. Sun, etc. 馬維隆, 係立民等四人	"
Wan Toh 萬德	Shansi 山西	Sole Proprietorship 獨資	$20,000	Road No. 30 F. C. 法租界三十號路忠厚里三號	1, 1, 1939	A. C. Li 李聲珉	C. C. Chai 祭仲堅	"
Wan Lung 萬隆	"	"	$40,000	Road No. 25 F. C. 法租界二十五號路八十七號	1, 6, 1939	F. T. Chia 賈輔廷	M. Y. Lin 林茂榮	"
Hsiang I 祥義	Tientsin 津	Partnership 合夥	$80,000	Road No. 24 F. C. 法租界二十四號路六十八號	3, 20, 1938	Y. C. Shao 邵敏珉	Y. H. Chang, Y. C. Shiao 張毓軒, 邵玉珉	Trade & Banking 商, 錢
Teh Sheng Ho 德盛合	"	"	$20,000	Road No. 6 F. C. 法租界六號路兩首一百四十八號	3, 1914	C. J. Wang 王晉榮	H. T. Tsao, Y. L. Chen 曹華庭, 陳雲樣	"

APPENDIX V—THE TABLE OF TIENTSIN NATIVE BANKS

Name of Native Bank 字號	Group 杜派	Types of organization 組織	Capital 資本額	Hu Pên 護本額	Address of the business 營業所所在地	Date when business started 開業日期	Manager 經理人姓名	Proprietors 出資人 Names 姓名	Occupation 經歷
Yuan Chang Chi 源昌	Tientsin 津	Partnership 合夥	$60,000		Road No. 3 F. C. 法租界三號路三十五號	1, 9, 1939	L. C. Ning 甯巨卿	L. C. Ning, C. H. Pian 甯巨卿, 邊日修	Banking 錢
Hsiang Feng 祥豐	"	"	$40,000		Road No. 24 F. C. 法租界二十四號路八十五號	3, 6, 1935	P. T. Ho 何渭亭	Y. C. Chi, Y. S. Shao 嵇渭洲, 邵蘭孫	"
Fu Heng 馥亨	Peking 京	"	$60,000		Road No. 5 F. C. 法租界五號路振德里	4, 1, 1935	K. Y. Han 韓冠英	S. F. Yang, S. T. Yang, S. C. Yang 楊世芳, 楊世沆, 楊世岱	Trade 商
Ta Teh Hong Chi 大德恆記	Paoting 保定	"	$50,000		Road No. 33 F. C. 法租界三十三號路仁和里十七號	1887	C. J. Lu 盧价人	C. T. Chi, S. T. Chi, etc. 嵇鶴堂, 嵇普堂等六人	"
Ta Teh Tung Chi 大德通記	"	"	$50,000		Road No. 25 F. C. 法租界二十五號路惠兵里一號	1884	C. F. Hsü 許敏齋	C. T. Chi, S. T. Chi, etc. 嵇錦堂, 嵇普堂等五人	"
Hsin Yuan 信源	Tientsin 津	Sole Proprietorship 獨資	$50,000		Road No. 1 F. C. 法租界一號路天和里十孔號	3, 1940	Y. T. Chen 陳雅亭	Y. T. Chen 陳雅亭	Banking 錢
Teh Chang Jen 德昌仁	"	Partnership 合夥	$100,000		Siao Ma Lu I. C. 義租界小馬路民德路過十四號	7, 20, 1940	T. C. Ning 甯丹忱	S. S. Yuoh, T. C. Ning 樂樹山, 甯丹忱	Trade & Banking 商, 錢
Chiu Ta 大	"	Sole Proprietorship 獨資	$20,000	$20,000	Kung Tao Chieh J. C. 日租界公道街八部地一號	3, 1, 1930	F. C. Lu 陸鳳周	F. C. Lu 陸鳳周	Banking 錢

APPENDIX V—THE TABLE OF TIENTSIN NATIVE BANKS

Name of Native Bank 字號	Group 欵派	Types of organization 組織	Capital 資本額	Hu Pên 護本額	Address of the business 營業所所在地	Date when business started 開業日期	Manager 經理人姓名	Proprietors Names 出資人姓名	Occupation 經歷
Yung Cheng 永昌	Shansi 山西	Partnership 合夥	$50,000		Road No. 32 F. C. 法租界三十二號路一百二十一號	12, 25, 1938	C. K. Chang 張兆凱	C. K. Chang, C. T. Ho, S. C. Sun	Trade 商
Tung Cheng I 同增益	Shen-Chi 深冀	Solo Proprietorship 獨資	$50,000		Road No. 31 F. C. 法租界三十一號路慶安里七號	1, 1, 1929	H. N. Chen 陳潁南	Mrs. Chia 賈潤氏	"
Tah Ho 大和	"	Partnership 合夥	$20,000		Fu Tao Road J. C. 日租界福島街	11, 3, 1937	T. C. Shia 夏經沆	H. T. Tsao, S. T. Shia, etc. 曹鴻林，及陰郜紹四人	"
Chih Cheng 志誠	"	Solo Proprietorship 獨資	$20,000		Lee Chian F. C. 法租界秋慶大慶里十四號	9, 16, 1936	P. C. Liu 劉博泉	C. C. Woi 魏志澄	Politics 政
Fu Yu Ho 福裕和	Shansi 山西	"	$20,000		Road No. 32 F. C. 法租界三十二號路泰慶里七號	6, 1938	K. T. Tion 田兆正	P. Y. Chung 宗沛然	Trade 商
Hou Feng Hung Chi 厚豐宏記	"	"	$30,000		Road No. 30 F. C. 法租界三十號路樹德里十一號	6, 1, 1931	T. H. Liu 劉子厚	C. C. Kang 鈧兌	Banking 錢
Sze Pin 四品	Shen-Chi 深冀	Partnership 合夥	$54,000		Fu Yin Li, B. C. 英租界福陰里三號	4, 1933	F. S. Li 李範四	P. N. Li, F. S. Li 李伯誠，李範四	Trade & Banking 商，錢
Chian Hsing 謙興	"	"	$100,000		River Bank Road I. C. 義租界河沿馬路興記總號內	9, 7, 1940	Y. C. Hsing 那潤川	W. C. Kao, S. C. Wang 高文佳，王仙洲	Trade 商

APPENDIX V—THE TABLE OF TIENTSIN NATIVE BANKS

Name of Native Bank 字號	Group 杜派	Types of organization 組織	Capital Hu Pên 資本額	Address of the business 營業所在地	Date when business started 開業日期	Manager 經理人姓名	PROPRIETORS 出資人 Names 姓名	Occupation 經歷
Yuan Feng 元豐	Shon-Chi 深記	Sole Proprietorship 獨記	$50,000	Road No. 32 F. C. 法租界三十二號路六十一號	4, 17, 1940	T. J. Chui 崔殿榮	M. S. Liu 劉銘三	Trade 商
Hua Chong 華成	Tientsin 津	Partnership 合夥	$150,000	Road No. 1 F. C. 法租界一號路文興里二十七號	4, 26, 1933	C. C. Kung 孔筱泉	Y. J. Cheng, C. S. Lin, etc. 程筱淞, 林竹孫等四人	Trade & Banking 商, 錢
Chung Tung 中東	Shangtung 山東	Sole Proprietorship 獨記	$100,000	Lang Shu Chih J. C. 日租界浪速街二十四號	5, 28, 1940	K. C. Sheng 盛冠中	K. C. Sheng 盛冠中	Trade 商

(being applied 在呈請中未)

Name of Native Bank 字號	Group 杜派	Types of organization 組織	Capital Hu Pên 資本額	Address of the business 營業所在地	Date when business applied 呈請日期	Manager 經理人姓名	PROPRIETORS 出資人 Names 姓名	Occupation 經歷
Tung I Hsiang 同誼祥	Shansi 山西	Partnership 合夥	$50,000	Road No. 10 B. C. 英租界十號路一百六十四號	12, 31, 1940	C. Chen 陳鑑	H. Y. Ho, T. M. Li, etc. 賀學英, 李子明等五人	Trade 商
Teh Mao 德懋	Tung-Lu 東陸	"	$60,000	West Road I. C. 淺租界兩馬路北首三號	11, 24, 1941	F. L. Chao 趙鳳樓	M. H. Chang, T. C. Liu 張慈軒, 劉子卿	"

Name of Native Bank 字號	Group 杜派	Types of organization 組織	Capital 資本額	Hu Pên 護本額	Address of the business 營業所所在地	Date when business applied 呈請日期	Manager 經理人姓名	PROPRIETORS Names 出資人 姓名	Occupation 營業
I Teh 益德	Shen-Chi 深冀	Sole Proprietorship 獨資	$70,000		River Bank Road I.C. 義租界河沿十六號 詫生大樓內	1, 24, 1941	C. H. Liu 劉慰熙	A. L. Liu 劉安淵	Trade 商
Fu Yuan 福源	Tientsin 津	Partnership 合夥	$100,000		Road No. 6 I.C. 義租界六馬路十三號	1, 24, 1941	C. L. Sun 孫家嵐	C. C. Hsü, H. S. Lin, etc. 徐傑卿, 林浩三等三人	"
Kung Hsing Yung 公興永	"	"	$120,000	$200,000	Road No. 5 F.C. 法租界六號路四十號	1, 24, 1941	S. C. Wang 王士珍	C. A. Hsü, S. C. Wang 徐家安, 王士珍	Trade & Banking 商錢
Yung Shên 永韶	"	Sole Proprietorship 獨資	$100,000	$100,000	Road No. 3 I.C. 義租界三馬路十六號	1, 31, 1941	S. F. Chang 張祚訪	C. S. Li 李靜謙	Trade 商
Teh Hung 德恆	Shen-Chi 深冀	"	$100,000		Road No. 3 I.C. 義租界三馬路 協盛里二號	2, 13, 1941	C. P. Wei 魏泵彭	T. T. Chen 陳棟材	Banking 錢
Chao Hsing 保興	Tientsin 津	Partnership 合夥	$150,000		Road No. 6 F.C. 法租界六號路 永和里四號	2, 13, 1941	C. I. Tung 濃正誼	C. Y. Tung, Y. C. Liu, etc. 濃正誼 劉渊洲等三人	"
Fu Ch'ang 孚昌	"	"	$100,000		Ta Ma Road I.C. 義租界大馬路 三益里十三號	2, 13, 1941	C. Y. Li 李任源	Y. S. Chang, P. H. Chen, etc 滋岭笙, 陳佩言等四人	Trade 商
I Lung 義隆	Peking 京	Sole Proprietorship 獨資	$50,000	$50,000	Road No. 2 I.C. 義租界二馬路九號	3, 1, 1941	P. C. Lin 林博泉	C. H. Chang 張欽軒	"

APPENDIX VI

THE TABLE OF PEKING NATIVE BANKS

as at end of April 30th 1941.

Name of Native Bank 字號	Group 幫派	Types of organization 組織	Capital 資本額	Hu Pên 護本額	Address of the business 營業所所在地	Date when business started 開業日期	Manager 經理人姓名	PROPRIETORS 出資人 Names 姓名	Occupation 職業
Ta Teh Heng 大德恆	Shansi 山西	Partnership 合夥	$10,000		Chung Wai 崇外巾帽胡同	1, 1887	H. Wang 王澄	Y. H. Chiao, Y. Y. Chiao, etc. 喬映陞 喬映元等四人	Politics 政
Ta Teh Tung 大德通	"	"	$15,000		Ch'ien Wai 前外打磨廠	1, 1886	C. C. Shên 申振技	C. T. Chiao, Y. C. Chiao, etc. 喬錦堂 喬映科等四人	Trade 商
Chung Yu 巾裕	Peking 京	"	$100,000		Ch'ien Wai 前外貨珠市	5, 1939	S. T. Wei 魏警亭	I. S. Chang, Y. C. Liu, etc. 張易三, 劉裕祥等四人	Education & Trade 學, 商
Yung Cheng Ho 永柹合	"	"	$30,000		Ch'ien Wai 前外大街	6, 1918	Y. C. Li 李福洲	C. H. Feng, S. T. Li, etc. 封竹軒, 李士通等五人	Trade 商
Yung Tung 永通	"	Sole Proprietorship 獨資	$20,000		Ch'ien Wai 前外大街	4, 1923	H. S. Liu 劉星三	Y. C. Li 李誠洲	"
Yung Tai Cheng 永泰成	"	Partnership 合夥	$ 4,000		Ch'ien Wai 前外延房二條	2, 1936	Y. H. Ku 顧義軒	Y. H. Ku, T. K. Wang 顧義軒, 王廷科	"

APPENDIX VI—THE TABLE OF PEKING NATIVE BANKS

Name of Native Bank 字號	Group 社派	Types of organization 組織	Capital 資本額	Hu Pên 護本額	Address of the business 營業所所在地	Date when business started 開業日期	Manager 經理人姓名	Proprietors Names 出資人姓名	Occupation 職業
Yung Tai Kung 永泰公	Shansi 山西	Partnership 合夥	$20,000		Ch'ien Wai 前外辟家胡衕	19. 6.	P. C. Chang 張服卿	C. C. Chang, S. T. Chang, etc. 張鞏卿劉筆十一人	Trade & Education 商, 學
Tung Teh 同德	Peking 京	"	$100,000		Ch'ien Wai 前外施家胡同	3, 1926	M. T. Lu 盧木經	H. Y. Wei, C. S. Yao 魏以榮, 姚深生	Education 學
Tung Fa Ch'ang 同發長	Shansi 山西	Sole Proprietorship 獨資	$18,000		Ch'ien Wai 前外師府胡九條	5, 1921	L. M. Li 李能吨	C. L. Wu 吳欽作	Agriculture 農
Tung I 同義	Peking 京	Partnership 合夥	$50,000		Ch'ien Wai 前外師房前條	3, 1939	H. C. Chao 趙序筬	H. L. Chao, S. C. Ch'i, etc. 峨詩臣等四人	Trade 商
Heng Yang 恆陽	"	"	$30,000		Ch'ien Wai 前外齊家胡同	9, 1938	L. C. Fu 傅運清	C. T. Peng, C. C. Chao 彭潤之, 趙仲欽	Education & Trade 學, 商
Heng Sheng 恆升	"	Sole Proprietorship 獨資	$50,000		Ch'ien Wai 前外施家胡同	5, 1939	P. S. Shang 尚聘三	H. T. Chow 周錫彤	Agriculture 農
Heng Tai 恆泰	"	"	$50,000		Ch'ien Wai 前外施家胡同	1, 1938	P. C. Chia 賈炳濟	A. T. Sun 孫安汶	Trade 商
Heng Teh 恆德	"	"	$10,000		Ch'ien Wai 前外珠市口鐵近胡同	1, 1939	H. F. Liang 梁露峯	H. F. Liang 梁鑫峯	"

APPENDIX VI—THE TABLE OF PEKING NATIVE BANKS

Name of Native Bank 字號	Group 鈙派	Types of organization 組織	Capital Hu fên 資本額	Address of the business 營業所在地	Date when business started 開業日期	Manager 經理人姓名	PROPRIETORS 出資人 Names 姓名	Occupation 經歷
Hsin Ch'êng 信誠	Peking 京	Partnership 合夥	$100,000 $200,000	Ch'ien Wai 前外施廠房頭條	5, 1933	H. C. Tu 杜賢征	H. H. Wang, C. C. Chang 王錫仇, 常錫九	Trade 商
Hsin Tai 信泰	"	Sole Proprietorship 獨資	$20,000	Ch'ien Wai 前外狚衣店	8, 1938	C. C. Ma 馬治久	C. C. Ma 馬治久	"
Hsin Yu 信裕	"	Partnership 合夥	$70,000	Ch'ien Wai 前外長巷上二條	2, 1939	H. S. Tien 田秀山	L. F. Wang, T. M. Wang, etc. 王顗竹王子明等十一人	"
Ch'un Ho 承和	"	Sole Proprietorship 獨資	$20,000	Ch'ien Wai 前外施廠房頭條	1, 1939	J. H. Kêng 耿若蘅	P. F. Chao 趙鵬飛	"
Hsiang Jui Hsing 祥瑞興	"	Partnership 合夥	$25,000	Ch'ien Wai 前外珠衣市	3, 1911	T. C. Chang 張然敬	H. T. Yang, T. C. Li, T. C. Wang 楊厚誨, 谷澤臣, 王天勉	"
Ts'un Hsing Ho 餕興和	"	"	$3,000	Tung Tan 東單四觀音寺	1, 1890	C. H. Tien 田敬先	W. H. Wang, Y. P. Chao 王文華, 趙忘平	Education & Politics 學, 政
Tai Ch'ang 泰昌	"	"	$44,000	Ch'ien Wai 前外小蒋家胡同	3, 1939	T. C. Chang 張榇江	T. C. Hsing, W. H. Li, etc. 那琛菁, 李文秀等六人	Agriculture 農
Tai Fêng 泰豐	"	Sole Proprietorship 獨資	$100,000	Ch'ien Wai 前外長巷下二條	6, 1939	Y. S. Wang 王日生	Y. S. Wang 王日生	Trade 商

APPENDIX VI—THE TABLE OF PEKING NATIVE BANKS

Name of Native Bank 字號	Group 杖派	Types of organization 組織	Capital 資本額	Hu Pên 護本額	Address of the business 營業所所在地	Date when business started 開業日期	Manager 總理人姓名	PROPRIETORS 出資人 Names 姓名	Occupation 經歷
Chin Hui Fung 晉匯豐	Shansi 山西	Sole Proprietorship 獨資	$20,000		Ch'ien Wai 前外打磨廠缺隆店內	3, 1925	Y. C. Liu 柳榮勤	P. F. Kuo 郭珮恩	Trade 商
Chi Ming 啟明	Peking 京	Partnership 合夥	$20,000		Ch'ien Wai 前外施家胡同	4, 1935	Y. C. Chao 趙潤之	Tientsin Chi Ming 天津啟明總號	"
Chi Tai 啟泰	"	"	$50,000		Ch'ien Wai 前外取燈胡同	8, 1938	M. T. Wang 王慕庭	C. J. Kao, 高濟如 H. C. Lu 盧宏儔	"
Yu Chang Ho 裕長厚	"	"	$30,000		Ch'ien Wai 前外東珠市口	1913	T. C. T'eng 滕子起	T. Y. T'eng, Y. C. Kuo, etc. 滕彤宗 郭玉潔等五人	"
Yu Ch'ang Ho 裕昌厚	Shansi 山西	Sole Proprietorship 獨資	$20,000		Ch'ien Wai 前外施家胡同	4, 1939	Y. C. Ch'en 陳棻九	T. P. Li 李竹坡	"
Hua Sheng 華盛	Peking 京	Partnership 合夥	$100,000		Ch'ien Wai 前外珠寶市	6, 1939	Y. C. Wei 魏涵洲	C. C. Kao, W. Y. Yang, etc. 高靜菁, 楊文王等七人	"
Wan I Chang 萬益長	"	"	$56,000		Ch'ien Wai 前外大蔣家胡同	9, 1910	C. C. Liu 劉晴臣	N. M. Liu, S. K. Liu, etc. 劉乃民, 劉叶科等七人	"
Wan Sheng 萬生	"	"	$100,000		Ch'ien Wai 前外坑房頭條	12, 1938	S. Y. Ch'en 陳樹慇	T. C. Li, Y. H. P'an, etc. 李梓樵, 隔英軒等三人	"

APPENDIX VI—THE TABLE OF PEKING NATIVE BANKS

Name of Native Bank 字號	Group 幫派	Types of organization 組織	Capital 資本額	Hu Pên 護本額	Address of the business 營業所所在地	Date when business started 開業日期	Manager 經理人姓名	PROPRIETORS 出資人 Names 姓名	Occupation 經歷 Trade 商
Tun Tai Yung 敦泰永	Peking 京	Partnership 合夥	$30,000		Ch'ien Wai 前外打磨廠	6, 1932	Y. C. Chang 張桂清	C. S. Ma, Mrs. Ma, etc. 馬作霖,馬本叔德等四人	Trade 商
I Chü 義聚	"	"	$80,000		Ch'ien Wai 前外打磨廠	6, 1935	C. W. Liu 劉仲五	C. W. Liu, C. S. Tien, etc. 劉仲五, 田捷三等七人	"
I Chü Ho 義聚和	"	Sole Proprietorship 獨資	$30,000		Ch'ien Wai 前外大將案胡同	10, 1938	T. P. Feng 封子平	T. P. Fung 封子平	"
I Lung 義隆	"	Partnership 合夥	$100,000		Ch'ien Wai 前外觀音寺	5, 1939	H. L. Feng 馮錫麟	C. H. Chang, J. C. Wan, etc. 張靜軒, 宛來區等五人	"
Ts'ien Ho 敦和	"	"	$40,000		Ch'ien Wai 前外師房二條	5, 1939	S. P. Li 李四平	H. F. Ning, C. T. Ning, etc. 甯心堂, 甯宗棠等五人	"
Fu Ch'ang 福昌	"	Sole Proprietorship 獨資	$60,000		Ch'ien Wai 前外師房頭條	10, 1938	C. H. Ch'ang 常仲華	H. C. Chi 李桓昌	"
Fu Li 福利	"	Partnorship 合夥	$60,000		Ch'ien Wai 前外西河沿	2, 1939	H. C. Tien 田滋章	H. L. Chow, H. H. Chow, etc. 周河惥, 周學涟等四人	"
Yuan Tung Hou 源通厚	"	"	$25,000		Ch'ien Wai 前外師房二條	7, 1939	C. T. Pan 潘林德	W. F. Kao, C. H. Chu, etc. 高魏洋, 朱淡瑞等四人	"

APPENDIX VI—THE TABLE OF PEKING NATIVE BANKS

Name of Native Bank 字號	Group 社顶	Types of organization 組織	Capital 资本额	Hu Pên 護本額	Address of the business 营業所所在地	Date when business started 開業日期	Manager 總理人姓名	Proprietors Names 出资人姓名	Occupation 職業
Chü I 聚義	Peking 京	Partnership 合夥	$120,000		Ch'ien Wai 前外珠宝市	2, 1867	P. J. Chang 张采如	Y. S. Sun, H. T. Ku, etc. 孙怡生, 顾信之等七人	Politics 政
Chü Teh 聚德	"	Sole Proprietorship 獨资	$50,000		Ch'ien Wai 前外驰河沿	7, 1934	L. A. Sun 孙禄祚	T. H. Ning 甯子衡	Education 學
Kuang Jui 廣瑞	"	"	$40,000		Chung Wai 崇外施家胡同	9, 1938	T. F. Liu 劉丹浮	N. J. Li 李愨瑞	Trade 商
Chi Sheng 祉生	"	Partnership 合夥	$100,000		Ch'ien Wai 前外施家胡同	5, 1937	P. C. Wang 王峄周	C. S. Chow, S. L. Chu, etc. 邱泉操, 朱俠黎等四人	"
Chi Ch'ang 祉昌	"	Sole Proprietorship 獨资	$40,000		Ch'ien Wai 前外哑房三條	6, 1926	T. C. Chu 朱俊卿	T. C. Chu 朱俊卿	"
Yu Ta Heng 馀大亨	"	Partnership 合夥	$15,000		Ch'ien Wai 前外施家胡同	2, 1930	T. C. Chia 贾子青	C. M. Yen, S. C. Chang, etc. 阎季民, 张世傑等五人	"
Ting Feng 鼎豐	"	"	$50,000		Ch'ien Wai 前外施家胡同	7, 1938	F. W. Chang 张范五	F. W. Chang, P. S. Wen, etc. 张范五, 文品珊等四人	Education & Trade 學, 商
Teh Yuan Ch'ang 德源長	"	Sole Proprietorship 獨资	$20,000		Ch'ien Wai 前外罗圈胡同	8, 1938	M. C. Li 李懋卿	M. C. Li 李懋卿	Trade 商

APPENDIX V—THE TABLE OF TIENTSIN NATIVE BANKS

Name of Native Bank 字號	Group 社派	Types of organization 組織	Capital 資本額 Hu Pên 護本額	Address of the business 營業所所在地	Date when business started 開業日期	Manager 總理人姓名	PROPRIETORS 出資人 Names 姓名	Occupation 經歷
Teh Yu Cheng 德裕成	Peking 京	Sole Proprietorship 獨資	$20,000	Ch'ien Wai 前外大將家胡同	5, 1939	S. J. Liang 梁式如	W. H. Wang 王惟恒	Agriculture 農
Yu Hua 豫華	"	Partnership 合夥	$50,000	Ch'ien Wai 前外長巷下二條	11, 1918	C. F. Huang 黃劍峯	C. H. Jen, C. F. Wang 任家宜, 王劍溪	Trade 商
Chi Tung 洎通	"	"	$60,000	Ch'ien Wai 前外珠寶市錢市胡同	6, 1934	J. T. Li 李瑞庭	C. W. Yang, Y. C. Li 楊集五, 李澍洲	"
Hung Ching Yu 鴻慶裕	"	"	$50,000	Ch'ien Wai 前外長巷上三條	2, 1930	Y. T. Chow 周潤德	H. L. Tien, M. C. Hsin 田蒔慾, 辛益堃	Agriculture 農
Pao Seng 寶生	"	Sole Proprietorship 獨資	$40,000	Ch'ien Wai 前外牽局胡同	11, 1926	H. C. Chu 朱仙洲	T. T. Wei 魏子丹	"
Yung Ch'ang 永昌	Shansi 山西	Partnership 合夥	$50,000	Ch'ien Wai 前外武敷九條	9, 1939	Y. J. Chang 張友仁	C.J. Chang, C.C. Li, etc. 張志仁, 李長枝 等四人	Trade 商
Yi Fung 益豐	Peking 京	"	$50,000	Ch'ien Wai 前外小鳥神胸	3, 1939	H. S. Liu 劉漢三	Y. T. Ti, C. S. Chi 邸玉堂, 祀仲石	"
Yu Lung 裕隆	"	"	$60,000	Ch'ien Wai 前外四河沿	12, 1939	C. L. Ku 顧郅隆	T. C. Wen, P. S. Yun 文子奇, 運佩珊	"

APPENDIX VI —THE TABLE OF PEKING NATIVE BANKS

Name of Native Bank 字號	Group 幫派	Types of organization 組織	Capital 資本額	Hu Pên 護本額	Address of the business 營業所所在地	Date when business started 開業日期	Manager 經理人姓名	PROPRIETORS 出資人 Names 姓名	Occupation 經應
Hua Cheng 華成	Peking 京	Sole Proprietorship 獨資			Ch'ien Wai 前外珠寶市	2, 1940	H. C. Wang 王葉溪	C. H. Hsü 許靜軒	Trade 商
I Ho 義和	"	Partnership 合夥	$50,000		Ch'ien Wai 前外長巷上上頭條	4, 1940	P. C. Sun 孫斌卿	C. T. Nai, H. F. Chao, etc. 艾芝芬 趙叙峯等四人	"
Jung Teh 榮德	"	"	$50,000		Ch'ien Wai 前外四柳樹井	10, 1939	H. C. Wang 王恕泉	T. C. Pien, H. C. Pion 邊仙洲	Agriculture 農
Hsin Feng 新豐	"	"	$50,000		Ch'ien Wai 前外廊房三條	8, 1940	K. C. Yang 楊兌忱	C. C. Chang, H. C. Li 李昆階	Trade 商
Chiu Feng 久豐	"	Sole Proprietorship 獨資	$50,000		Ch'ien Wai 前外廊房二條	6, 1940	T. S. Chang 張遊生	C. F. Chang 錦甯	"
Kai Yuan 開源	Shansi 山西	Partnership 合夥	$50,000		Ch'ien Wai 前外觀音寺	8, 1940	T. C. Yang 楊俊卿	T. M. Wang, C. C. Li 王子明 李靜之	"
Chü Hsing 聚興	Peking 京	"	$200,000		Ch'ien Wai 前外長巷下三條	7, 1940	C. C. Wang 王澍忱	H. C. Chiao, H. T. Li 喬熙卿 李熙廷	"
Tien Hsing 大興	"	Sole proprietorship 獨資	$50,000		Ch'ien Wai 前外廊房頭條	10, 1940	Y. C. Chao 趙潤川	Y. S. Li 李疆山	"

APPENDIX VI—THE TABLE OF PEKING NATIVE BANKS

Name of Native Bank 字號	Group 組派	Types of organization 組織	Capital Hu Pên 資本額	Address of the business 營業所所在地	Date when business started 開業日期	Manager 經理人姓名	PROPRIETORS 出資人 Names 姓名	Occupation 經歷
Yu Hsiang 裕祥	Peking 京	Sole Proprietorship 獨資	$100,000	Ch'ien Wai 前外珠寶市	12, 1940	H. C. Hu 呼志宸	T. T. Hsü 徐卓	Trade 商
Chung Teh 崇德	"	Partnership 合夥	$100,000	Ch'ien Wai 前外觀音寺	12, 1940	C. T. Fan 范志迿	C. C. Wang 王重臣, Y. C. Li 李榮程	"
Hua Tung 華通	"	"	$100,000	Ch'ien Wai 前外珠寶市錢市胡同	1, 1941	F. T. Kao 高輔亭	C. P. Kao 高玖桂, S. J. Hsieh 謝謝仁	"
Chin Hua 金華	"	"	$50,000	Ch'ien Wai 前外楊梅胡同	2, 1941	C. T. Wang 王振庭	C. T. Wang 王兆榮, H. W. Tu 杜顧武	"
Yu Teh 裕德	"	"	$120,000	Ch'ien Wai 前外施家胡同	2, 1941	N. P. Tu 杜藏年	C. Y. Chu 朱致遠, Y. N. Chao 趙耶農	"

APPENDIX VII

THE VOLUME OF PROFIT & LOSS IN 1940

A. Tientsin Native Banks.

Name of Native Bank 銀　　號	Volume of Profit 結盈額 (Unit: Dollar)	Volume of Loss 結虧額 (Unit: Dollar)
Ta Tê Tung　大德通	15,000.00	
Hsin Tung　信　通	20,000.00	
Tê Ch'ang Jên 德昌仁	4,000.00	
Ch'iu Ta　久　大	6,000.00	
Yung Ch'ang　永　昌	6,000.00	
T'ung Tsêng I 同增益	8,000.00	
Ta Ho　大　和	2,000.00	
Chih Ch'êng　志　誠	5,000.00	
Chih Ta　志　達	5,000.00	
Pên Li Yüan　本立源	20,000.00	
Hung Ch'ang　宏　昌	3,000.00	
P'ing Ho　平　和	5,000.00	
I Hsing　義　昌	7,000.00	
Hui Hua　匯　化	10,000.00	
Chao Feng　肇　豐	10,000.00	
Tê Ch'ang　德　昌		2,000 00
Hsiang Feng　祥　豐	15,000.00	
Yung Ta　永　大		4,000.00

Name of Native Bank 銀　　號	Volume of Profit 結盈額 (Unit: Dollar)	Volume of Loss 結虧額 (Unit: Dollar)
Chia I Kung　　甲乙公	6,000.00	
Shen Feng　　慎　豐	9,000.00	
Shên Yuan　　盛　遠	5,000.00	
I Chü　　　　義　聚	5,000.00	
Fu Chi　　　福　記	80,000.00	
I Chi　　　　益　記	2,000.00	
Tung Shên　　通　盛	8,000.00	
Wên Hsing Yu 文 興 裕	10,000.00	
Chên Chung　振　中	5,000.00	
Wan Tê　　　萬　德	10,000.00	
Wan Lung　　萬　隆	10,000.00	
Hsiang I　　　祥　義	30,000.00	
Tê Shên Ho　德 盛 和	5,000.00	
Yüan Ch'ang　源　昌	20,000.00	
Hsin Yuan　　信　遠	10,000.00	
I Shêng Yüan 義 生 源		3,000.00
Hsin Lung　　信　隆	8,000.00	
Chi Ch'ang　　其　昌	5,000.00	
Yu Ch'ang　　裕　昌	2,000.00	
Wên Chi　　　文　記	3,000.00	
Hêng Feng　　恆　豐	10,000.00	

Name of Native Bank 銀　　號	Volume of Profit 結盈額(Unit: Dollar)	Volume of Loss 結虧額 (Unit: Dollar)
Ch'ing Ch'êng　慶　　成	30,000.00	
Ming Tê Lung　明　德　隆	4,000.00	
Fu Lung　　　福　　隆	7,000.00	
T'ung Ho　　　同　　和	10,000.00	
Tien Chü　　　天　　漿	10,000.00	
Tê Lung　　　德　　隆	4,000.00	
T'ung Shun Tê　同　順　德	6,000.00	
Shên Chi　　　盛　　記	2,000.00	
Tê Hsing Yung　德　興　永	5,000.00	
Jui Tung　　　瑞　　通		2,000.00
Hua Tung　　　華　　通		3,000.00
Fu Li　　　　福　　利	5,000.00	
Cheng Hsin　　正　　信	15,000.00	
I Chung　　　溢　　中	8,000.00	
Chü Hsing　　鉅　　興	5,000.00	
Yu Jên　　　　裕　　仁	7,000 00	
Yu T'ai　　　裕　　泰	5,000.00	
Yüan Chi　　　元　　吉	2,000.00	
Yü Tê　　　　統　　德	6,000.00	
Hsin Ch'êng　信　　誠	10,000.00	
Tien Hsing Tai　天　興　泰	3,000.00	

Name of Native Bank 銀　　　號	Volume of Profit 結盈額 (Unit: Dollar)	Volume of Loss 結虧額 (Unit: Dollar)
Fu Ch'ang　　　　福　昌	8,000.00	
T'ai Chi　　　　太　極	3,000.00	
Yüan I　　　　元　一	5,000.00	
Tung Hsing　　東　興	5,000.00	
Yu Hsing　　　裕　興	80,000.00	
Jên Feng　　　仁　豐	18,000.00	
Chü Chêng　　聚　成	8,000.00	
Fu Shun　　　福　順	20,000.00	
T'ai Ho Chi　　太　和　記	30,000.00	
T'ung Feng　　桐　豐	35,000.00	
Chi T'ai　　　啟　泰	3,000.00	
T'ung Shans　同　善	6,000.00	
Yüan Hsing　　源　興	7,000.00	
Kuang Yüan　　廣　源	5,000.00	
Yung T'ai　　　永　泰	40,000.00	
Chao Feng　　兆　豐	10,000.00	
Chien Hua　　建　華	8,000.00	
Fu K'ang Jên 福康仁	50,000.00	
Yu Ch'ang Hou 裕昌厚	15,000.00	
Liu Chü　　　六　聚	5,000.00	
Tê Feng　　　德　豐	30,000.00	

Name of Native Bank 銀　　號	Volume of Profit 結盈額 (Unit: Dollar)	Volume of Loss 結虧額 (Unit: Dollar)
Hung Ch'ing Yu 鴻 慶 裕	10,000.00	
T'ung Fu Chang Chi 同孚昌記	10,000.00	
Chih Hua　　　志　華	8,000.00	
T'ung Hua　　　同　華	5,000.00	
Ho Shen　　　和　牲	5,000.00	
Hsin Tê　　　信　德	10,000.00	
Chi Shang　　　集　商	5,000.00	
Hêng Yüan I　恆 源 益	10,000.00	
Ch'ing Hsiang　慶　祥	15,000.00	
Tê Shêng　　　德　生	20,000.00	
Tien Feng　　　天　豐	10,000.00	
Tê Hsiang　　　德　祥	5,000.00	
Kuang Feng　　廣　豐	2,000.00	
Yu Tung　　　裕　東	60,000.00	
Ho Chi　　　和　記	3,000.00	
Chung Ch'êng　中　誠	5,000 00	
Yüan Mao　　　源　茂	10,000,00	
Li Hua　　　利　華	3,000.00	
Ho Hsiang　　和　祥	7,000.00	
Tê Shên Lung　德 盛 隆	2,000.00	
Fu Ting　　　蚨　亭	20,000.00	

Name of Native Bank 銀　　號	Volume of Profit 結盈額 (Unit: Dollar)	Volume of Loss 結虧額 (Unit: Dollar)
Ta Tê Hêng Chi 大德恒記	10,000.00	
Lung Feng 隆豐	10,000.00	
Hsing Shên Yung 興盛永	7,000.00	
Ch'ung I 崇義	3,000.00	
Shên Chü 盛聚	5,000.00	
I Tung 義東	10,000.00	
T'ung Ch'ang 同昌	5,000.00	
Hsin Chung 鑫忠	8,000.00	
I Feng Hou 益豐厚	10,000.00	
Fu Yu Ho 福裕和	1,000.00	
Ch'un Ho 春和	15,000.00	
Fu Feng 福豐	30,000.00	
Chi Ta 致達	15,000.00	
Hsin Hua 信華	4,000.00	
Shen Ch'ang 愼昌	2,000.00	
Fu Yü 福豫	3,000.00	
Hui Yüan Yung 匯源永	5,000.00	
Hua Feng 華豐	20,000.00	
Yu Yüan 裕源	15,000.00	
Ch'ien Feng 謙豐	30,000.00	
Chi Ch'ang 致昌	50,000.00	

Name of Native Bank 銀 號	Volume of Profit 結盈額 (Unit: Dollar)	Volume of Loss 結虧額 (Unit: Dollar)
Tê Jên 德 仁	30,000.00	
Pao Shêng 實 生	100,000.00	
T'ung Tê 同 德	25,000.00	
I Hsing Chên 益 興 珍	40,000.00	
Chung Ho 中 和	60,000.00	
Ch'ing I 慶 益	20,000.00	
Yao Yuan 耀 遠	25,000.00	
Hsiang Shêng 祥 生	30,000.00	
Ho Feng 和 豐	120,000.00	
Hung Yüan 宏 源	30,000.00	
Hung Chi 鴻 記	60,000.00	
T'ai Ho 泰 和	40,000.00	
Tien Hsing Hêng 天 興 恒	15,000.00	
I Hsin Hêng 義 興 恒	5,000.00	
I Chêng Yu 義 成 裕	60,000.00	
Hung K'ang 宏 康	15,000.00	
Hsiang Jui Hsing 祥 瑞 興	30,000.00.	
Chü I 聚 義	30,000.00	
Tun T'ai Yung 敦 泰 永	25,000.00	
Chin Shêng 晉 生	20,000.00	
Ch'ien I 謙 義	35,000.00	

Name of Native Bank 銀　　號	Volume of Profit 結盈額 (Unit: Dollar)	Volume of Loss 結虧額 (Unit: Dollar)
T'ung Shêng Hsiang 同生祥	6,000.00	
Jung Ch'ang Ho 榮昌和	2,000.00	
T'ai Hsing　泰　興	7,000.00	
Hsin Chi　信　記	8,000.00	
Chên Hsing Ch'ang 振興長	20,000.00	
Yüan Shêng　原　生		2,000.00
Chin Chi Hsing 錦記興	20,000.00	
Chü Hua Ch'ang 聚華昌	15,000.00	
Hung Hsing　宏　興	4,000.00	
T'ung Ch'ing Lung Shêng Chi 同慶隆盛記	5,000.00	
Wei Chang　維　章		1,000.00
Ch'ing Fêng　慶　豐	25,000.00	
Hsin Feng　信　豐	10,000.00	
Jui Chüan Yung 瑞泉永	30,000.00	
Chi Ming Hsin Chi 啓明新記	20,000.00	
Hsin Shêng　新　生	50,000.00	
Kuang Li　廣　利	70,000.00	
Chi Lu Chün Chi 冀魯鈞記	20,000.00	
Kuang Yü　廣　餘	80,000.00	
Jui Ch'ang Hsiang 瑞昌祥	40,000.00	
Ta Hsin Yüan　大信源	50,000.00	

Name of Native Bank 銀　　號	Volume of Profit 結盈額 (Unit: Dollar)	Volume of Loss 結虧額 (Unit: Dollar)
I Shêng　　　益　生	30,000.00	
Ch'ing Tung　　慶　通	40,000.00	
Chü Shêng　　　聚　生	20,000.00	
Hêng T'ai　　　恆　泰	10,000.00	
Chi Ch'êng　　　至　誠	10,000.00	
Hêng Yüan　　　恒　源	15,000.00	
Lao Hêng Li　老恆利	35,000.00	
Ch'ing Chü　　慶　聚	30,000.00	
Yu Min　　　　裕　民	10,000.00	
I T'ai　　　　益　泰	15,000.00	
T'ung Yu　　　同　裕	5,000.00	
Kuang Jui　　　廣　瑞	30,000.00	
Yung Tsêng Ho 永增和	30,000.00	
Chi Hsing　　　致　興	10,000.00	
Hui Ch'ang　　惠　昌	10,000.00	
Tien Yü　　　　天　鈺	10,000.00	
I Lung　　　　益　隆	25,000.00	
Ch'ien Ho　　　僉　和	8,000.00	
Shen Ch'ang　　愼　昌	7,000.00	
Hui Feng　　　惠　豐	30,000.00	
Ch'ien Shen　　謙　蚨	40,000.00	

Name of Native Bank 銀　　　號	Volume of Profit 結盈額 (Unit: Dollar)	Volume of Loss 結虧額 (Unit: Dollar)
I Hua　　　　益　華	20,000.00	
I Feng　　　　益　豐	20,000.00	
Pên Li Yung　本　立　永	15,000.00	
Yü Ta Hêng　餘　大　亨	60,000.00	
I Shêng　　　羨　勝	30,000.00	
I Ho　　　　頤　和	50,000.00	
Ta Ch'ang　　大　昌	30,000.00	
Tien Jui　　　天　瑞	40,000.00	
Yüan T'ai　　元　泰	30,000.00	
Tun Ch'ang　　敦　昌	80,000.00	
Ting Feng　　鼎　豐	8,000.00	
Chü Tê Ch'êng　聚　德　成	10,000.00	
Chih Tung　　志　通	7,000.00	
Ho Shêng　　和　生	60,000.00	
Tê Ch'êng　　德　成	10,000.00	
I Ch'êng　　　義　誠	15,000 00	
Lung Hsin　　隆　信	9,000.00	
Fu Chü　　　蚨　聚	2,000.00	
Shêng Shêng　生　生	7,000.00	
Wan Hêng　　萬　亨	8,000.00	
Fu T'ai Hêng　福　泰　恒	1,000.00	

Name of Native Bank 銀 號	Volume of Profit 結盈額 (Unit: Dollar)	Volume of Loss 結虧額 (Unit: Dollar)
T'ung Hsing 同 興	20,000.00	
I K'ang 益 康	30,000.00	
Tun Hsiang 敦 祥	10,000.00	
Hsin Ho 信 和	20,000.00	
Fu Tê 福 德	5,000.00	
Kung Hsin 洪 信	5,000.00	
Hêng Hsiang 恆 祥	5,000.00	
Wei Feng 蔚 豐	20,000.00	
Chü Ch'éng 聚 誠	15,000.00	
Chü Lung 聚 隆	3,000.00	
Ta Hêng 大 亨	3,000.00	
Tung Ch'êng 通 成	2,000.00	
Ho Hsing 和 興	5,000.00	
I Hêng 義 恒	15,000.00	
Jui Hua 瑞 華	3,000.00	
Tung Chi 通 記	5,000 00	
Yü Hua 豫 華	3,000.00	
Chêng Feng Yu 正 豐 裕	20,000.00	
Ta Fu Lai 大 福 來	80,000.00	
Total 總 額	**3,845,000.00**	**17,000.00**

B. PEKING NATIVE BANKS.

Name of Native Bank 銀　　號	Volume of Profit 結　盈　數	Volume of Loss 結　虧　數
Ta Tê Hêng　大德恒	7,967.31	
Ta Tê T'ung　大德通	29,669.09	
Chung Yü　中　裕	35,336.73	
Yung Tsêng Ho 永增合	23,266.26	
Yung T'ung　永　通	3,064.95	
Yung T'ai Ch'êng 永泰成	4,907.18	
Yung T'ai Kung 永泰公	13,614.08	
Yung Ch'ang　永　昌	13,575.87	
T'ung Tê　同　德	64,977.03	
T'ung Fa Ch'ang 同發長	1,136.17	
T'ung I　同　義	8,875.35	
Hopei Yin Ch'ien Chü　河北銀錢局		114,800.67
Hêng Yang　恒　陽	4,299.09	
Hêng Sheng　恒　升	14,756.68	
Hêng T'ai　恒　泰	66,397.11	
Hêng Tê　恒　德	1,055.25	
Hsin Ch'êng　信　誠	68,576.32	
Hsin T'ai　信　泰	5,000.00	
Hsin Yü　信　裕	51,408.74	
Ch'un Ho　春　和	4,300.35	

Name of Native Bank 銀　號	Volume of Profit 結益數	Volume of Loss 結虧數
Hou Shêng　　以　生	12,065.43	
Hsiang Jui Hsing　祥 瑞 興	4,509.84	
Chün Hsing Ho 峻 興 和	1,125.81	
T'ai Ch'ang　　泰　昌	2,551.65	
T'ai Feng　　　泰　豐		19,189.04
Chin Hui Feng　晉 睚 豐	29,363.66	
Fu Hêng　　　　扶　亨		2,281.00
I Feng　　　　益　豐	10,105.56	
Chi Ming　　　啓　明	30,144.53	
Chi T'ai　　　啓　泰	1,575.76	
Yü Ch'ang Hou 裕 長 以	160,000.00	
Yü Ch'ang Hou 裕 昌 以	15,947.05	
Yü Lung　　　　裕　隆	12,034.66	
Hua Shên　　　華　燧	20,981.99	
Hua Ch'êng　　華　成	55,541.73	
Wan I Ch'ang 萬 義 長	83,188.39	
Wan Shêng　　萬　生	7,641.86	
Tun T'ai Yung 敦 泰 永	17,194.94	
I Chü　　　　　義　聚	34,163.87	
I Chü Ho　　　義 聚 和	3,694.88	
I Lung　　　　義　隆	34,724.24	

Name of Native Bank 銀　號	Volume of Profit 結盈數	Volume of Loss 結虧數
I Ho　　　義　利	5,875.75	
Ch'ien Ho　　僉　和	2,074.74	
Fu Li　　　福　利	23,569.43	
Fu Ch'ang　　福　昌	17,495.51	
Yüan T'ung Hou 源通厚		13,723.93
Chü I　　　聚　義		3,300.00
Chü Tê　　　聚　德	22,867.61	
Jung Tê　　　榮　德	15,343.86	
Kuang Jui　　廣　瑞	62,132.29	
Chi Shêng　　積　生	90,943.96	
Chi Ch'ang　　積　昌	3,819.54	
Yü Ta Hêng　餘大亨	11,110.15	
Ting Feng　　鼎　豐	70,371.28	
Tê Yüan Ch'ang 德源長	6,269.36	
Tê Yü Ch'êng 德裕成	5,428.26	
Yü Hua　　　豫　華	876.49	
Chi T'ung　　沖　通	36,146.68	
Hung Ch'ing Yü 鴻慶裕	18,861.58	
Pao Shêng　　寶　生	32,449.00	
Hsin Feng　　新　豐	2,768.67	
Ch'iu Feng　　久　豐	2,199.93	

APPENDIX VII—THE VOLUME OF PROFIT AND LOSS

Name of Native Bank 銀　　　號	Volume of Profit 結　盈　數	Volume of Loss 結　虧　數
K'ai Yüan　　開　源		20,920.64
Chü Hsing　　衆　興	17,418.92	
Tien Hsing　　天　興		4,347.63
Yü Hsiang　　裕　祥		5,702.84
Ch'ung Tê　　崇　德		8,041.21
Total　　總　計	**1,406,582.62**	**222,015.96**

APPENDIX VIII

REGULATIONS OF THE TIENTSIN NATIVE BANKERS' ASSOCIATION

Chapter I. General Provisions

Article 1. The name of the association is Tientsin Native Bankers' Association.

Article 2. The office of the association is at the Second Floor of Hsin Hua Building, Rue de France, Tientsin. (天津法租界中街 新華大樓三樓).

Article 3. The purposes of the association are to foster the interests of the profession, to correct its deficiencies, to promote friendship and to strengthen union among the fellow-bankers, in order to develop progressively their affairs.

Chapter II. Functions

Article 4. The functions of the association are as follows:

a. To make plans for the financial circulation and the safety of transaction among fellow-bankers in this municipality and to strengthen the public credit.

b. A public assaying office is annexed to the association to probe the "Yin Sê" (銀色) circulating on the market.

c. An exchange is annexed to the association to fix the market values for purchase or sale of Shanghai exchange, silver dollars and any kind of negotiable securities.

d. To act as conciliator in the disputes among bankers, arising from their commercial activities.

e. It may transmit for decision to any legal institution of this municipality the necessary petitions concerning the commercial activities of the profession, and answer enquiries of the same institutions.

Chapter III. Officers

Article 5. The association appoints 15 executive delegates who are elected by representatives of all member-firms by using the not signed list-ballot system. The executive delegates will elect among themselves five delegates for current affairs, and from the latter one person will be elected as chairman by using the not signed ballot system.

Article 6. The association appoints 5 reserve executive delegates who are elected by representatives of all member-firms by using the not-signed list ballot system.

Article 7. The functions of chairman, delegates for current affairs and executive delegates are honorary. Travelling expenses may be allotted to them if they go outside for the association.

Article 8. The term of office of the delegates of the association is four years. Every second year, a new election will take place for one half of the number. Retiring delegates are not immediately reeligible. In the first new election, [the name of those who are to retire] will be determined by casting lots; but if the number of delegates is an odd one the number of those remaining in office shall exceed by one that of those to be replaced.

Article 9. If the chairman is prevented from fulfilling his duties the executive delegates will elect one person from among the delegates for current affairs as his substitute. If a delegate for current affairs is prevented, a substitute will be elected from among the executive delegates. If executive delegates are prevented, substitutes from among the five reserve executive delegates will replace them in the order of the number of votes they have received. The term of office of such substitutes will not be longer than the remaining part of the term of their predecessor; but as long as reserve executive delegates do not fill a vacancy, they are not allowed to attend the meetings.

Article 10. In case of change of chairman, delegate for current affairs, executive delegates, reserve executive delegates, as provided hereabove, the association should report to the Party Head-quarter for the municipality of Tientsin and to the Bureau of Social Affairs of the same municipality for record.

Article 11. Delegates of the association who have incur any of the disabilities stated in art. 22 of the Law on Chambers of Commerce must immediately resign from office.

Article 12. The chairman has power to represent the association towards third persons in the affairs of his competence. The delegates for current affairs assist him in the management of all the affairs of the association.

Article 13. The association shall have a secretary, a clerk, an accountant, and a person for social relations (交際); they will be specially engaged and appointed by the chairman in agreement with the delegates for current affairs. The employees of the public assaying office and the exchange annexed to the association shall also be appointed by the chairman in agreement with the delegates for current affairs.

Chapter IV. Meetings

Article 14. The general meeting of representatives of member-firms has the supreme authority in the association; when the general meeting is not sitting this position belongs to the executive committee.

Article 15. The meetings are divided in the 3 following classes:
　　1) General meetings of representatives of member-firms:
　　　　A. Ordinary meetings—held twice a year on the 15th of January and July.

      B. Extraordinary meetings—with no definite time; it is called by the executive committee according to circumstances, whenever this committee deems it to be necessary, or at the request of at least ten per cent of the members; but the calling of an emergency meeting should be reported to the Party Headquarter for the municipality of Tientsin, and to the Bureau of Social Affairs of the same municipality for record.

  2) Meetings of the executive committee:

      A. Ordinary meetings—held twice per month, on the 10th and the 25th.

      B. Extraodinary meetings—with no definite time, it is called by the standing committee according to circumstances whenever this committee deems it to be necessary or at the request of over one half of the executive delegates.

  3) Meetings of the standing committee:

      A. Ordinary meetings—held once a week, on Saturday.
      B. Extraordinary meetings—with no defininte time, convened by the Chairman.

Article 16. No resolution can be passed in the general meeting of representatives of member-firms unless more than one-half are present and two-thirds at least of those present give their assent.

Article 17. Those who were not present can make no objection against decisions passed by the general meeting of representatives of member-firms.

Article 18. The decisions of the general meeting of representatives of member-firms shall be recorded in detail in the "meeting records" which must be signed by the chairman or acting chairman, and kept in the association for consultation.

Article 19. The Ministry of Industry has given instruction to cancel this article [which read]: A representative who attends regularly as executive delegate or delegate for current affairs may, when he is unable to attend a metting, give under his own responsibility mandate to another person to attend as his proxy.

Article 20. Daily affairs of the association are managed by the standing committee while impentent affairs should be decided by the executive committee. The decisions of the standing and executive committees, and the votes should be recorded in the record of the meeting which should be signed by the delegates present and kept for reference.

Article 21. If the chairman cannot attend any of the meetings, one of the delegates for current affairs may be chosen by common assent as acting chairman.

Article 22. When the number of votes pro and con a proposal pending before the standing or executive committees is the same, the chairman has the casting vote.

Article 23. All members have the obligation to conform absolutely to the decisions of the association; but if a decision is detrimental to individual members they may [request] the convening of a new meeting in affording serious reasons. If the majority refuses [to cancel it], the original decision still stands.

Article 24. If members of the association have proposals, they may request the standing committee to meet to discuss them. If the standing committee cannot decide, it shoule convene a meeting of the executive committee to decide. If the executive committee is still unable to decide, it should convene a general meeting of representatives of member-firms to take the decision.

Article 25. If a member is personally interested in an affair pending before the standing committee, the executive committee or the general meeting of representatives of member-firms, he has no voting right. He may be even asked to leave temporarily the meeting if this is deemed to be necessary.

Chapter V. Joining the Association

Article 26. A firm of this profession which wishes to join the association should be introduced by two members at least and fill a written application declaring that he is willing to observe the regulations of the association and to incur all the obligations resulting therefrom. This application is handed over to the executive committee for examination. It should state in detail the following points and be signed and sealed by the introducers and the manager [of the applicant firm]:

a. name of the firm;

b. total amount of its capital;

c. full name and address of the proprietor;

d. if the business is a partnership, the number of owners and the respective amount of their shares;

e. name and address of the manager;

f. date of establishment;

g. location of the business.

Article 27. After the application has been examined by the standing committee, a general meeting of members and delegates is convened to decide, by not signed ballots whether this applicant satisfies the requirements of the association.

Article 28. All member-firms of the association may appoint their representatives to attend the meetings, but those whose average number of employees during the last year exceeded ten persons, may appoint one more representative.

Article 29. All the representatives of the member-firms have the right of vote, the right of election, and the right to be elected.

Article 30. No person being in one of the following cases may be a representative of a member-firm of the association:—

1. Any person who has opposed the [National] Revolution;
2. ,, ,, ,, ,, been deprived of civic right;
3. ,, ,, without desposing capacity.;
4. ,, ,, who has been declared bankrupt by a court, and has not yet been rehabilitated.

Article 31. Members joining the association should register in detail all the matters enumerated in art. 26 of the present Regulations in the register of members of the association, and mention the date of their joining for reference.

Article 32. If there is change in matters registered by a member, he must request the executive committee to make accordingly a change in registration. Before this is effected he cannot, set up the change against the association or third persons.

Article 33. Members who have committed any of the following acts must immediately, be expelled, if so decided by two thirds at least of those present in a meeting where two thirds at least of representatives of member-firms must be present:

a. Improper commercial acts which are detrimental to the reputation and credit of the association;

b. Loss of capacity to conduct business;

c. Indulgence in affairs which injure public welfare;

d. Infringing the regulations of the association.

Article 34. Memebers who request to leave the association should fill an "application for withdrawal" declaring the motive. After the application has been examined and approved by the executive committee, they are allowed to withdraw. The procedure of application for withdrawal is the same when a business is reorganized.

Article 35. The reasons and date of expulsion or resignation of a member should be recorded in the register of members and his membership should be cancelled. The various fees already paid by the member shall not be returned.

Chapter VI. Current Expenditure

Article 36. The current expenditure of the association is borne by the whole group of members.

1) Admission fees:　Class A　$ 200
　　　　　　　　　,,　B　$ 150
　　　　　　　　　,,　C　$ 100

2) Regular annual fees: 1st Class $ 8 per month
　　　　　　　　　2nd　,,　$ 4　,,　　,,

3) Special fees: Decided by common agreement according to circumstances.

Article 37. A budget for ordinary annual expenditure is prepared by the standing committee in the beginning of the year, and transmitted to the executive committee for examination and must be passed by the general meeting of representatives of member-firms. At the close of the business-year, at the time of the general meeting of representatives of member-firms to be held on Jan. 15th of the next year, beside the report on the various accounts of receipt and expenditures, and on important affairs concerning the management of the association to be communicated to all members, the actual amount of receipts and expenditures shall be reported to the Party Headquarter for the Municipality of Tientsin and to the Bureau of Social Affairs of the same Municipality for record.

Chapter VII. Additional Provisions

Article 38. The detailed by-laws of the association are fixed by the executing committee.

Article 39. The present regulations come into force after being submitted to the Party Headquarter for the Municipality of Tientsin for authorization, and to the Municipal Government of Tientsin for approval transmission to the Ministry of Industry for record.

Article 40. The present regulations may be amended in accordance with law if found not suitable. A report on such amendments will be made to the Party Head-quarter of the Municipality of Tientsin for authorization and to the Municipal Government of Tientsin for approval and transmission to the ministry of Industry for record.

APPENDIX IX

THE REGULATIONS OF PEKING NATIVE BANKERS' ASSOCIATION.

Article 1. The name of the association is Peking Native Bankers' Association; it is organized by the firms engaged in money business within the municipality of Peking.

2. The purposes of the association are to foster the common interests of the profession and to correct its deficiencies in business.

3. The social domicile of the association is temporarily the north part of the 1st floor of Chu'an Yeh Ch'ang, Lang Fang Tou Tiao. (廊房頭條勸業場二樓北部)

4. All Native banks which have been registered by the competent authorities of the Municipality of Peking must be members of the association, and appoint representatives to attend the meetings in accordance with art. 10 of the "Detailed Regulations for Enforcement of the Law on Industrial and Commercial Guilds".

Article 5. No person being in one of the following cases may be representative of a member firm of the Association:

1. Any person who has been deprived of civic rights;

2. Any person who has been declared bankrupt and has not been rehabilitated;

3. Any person without desposing capacity.

6. The association appoints fifteen executive delegates and seven reserve executive delegates who are elected among representatives of members by the general meeting of members. These delegates shall choose among themselves five delegates for current affairs, and shall elect among these latter delegates one person as chairman. The functions of the executive delegates, of the delegates for current affairs, and of the chairman are honorary.

Article 7. The term of office of the executive delegates, of the delegates for current affairs and of the chairman is four years. Every second year one half of the number shall be elected. Retiring delegates are not immediately reeligible. When, for any cause, the executive delegates, delegates for current affairs or chairman resign, reserve delegates fill the vacancies. If there are no reserve delegates, a meeting shall be held for an election. The term of office of the reserve delegates is only for the remaining part of the term of their predecessors.

Article 8. The meetings of the association are of three kinds: general meetings of members, meetings of the executive and of the standing committees.

Article 9. The powers of the general meeting of members include the following matters:

1. What concerns elections;
2. What concerns the approval of the budget and closing account;
3. What concerns the enactment of regulations;
4. What concerns the resignation and expulsion of members and the dismissal of officers;
5. Other important matters.

Article 10. The powers of the executive committee include the following mattes:

1. What concerns the examination of applications for membership;
2. What concerns the proposals to be submitted to the general meeting of members;

— 292 —

3. What concerns the reports and petitions to the authorities;

4. What concerns conciliation of disputes in the profession.

Article 11. The powers of the standing committee include the following matters:

1. What concerns the execution of the dicisions of the general meeting of members or of the executive committee;

2. What concerns the compilation of the budget and of the closing account;

3. What concerns the receipt or disbursement of the funds of the association;

4. What concerns the orders received from the authorities;

5. What concerns examination of the suggestions of members;

6. What concerns the preparation and convening meetings;

7. All other matters not included in the powers of the general meeting of members or of the executive committee.

In case of emergency, when it is not possible to convene the competent meeting, the standing committee may take urgent measures in the affairs mentioned in the two preceding articles; but it must [later on] request the general meeting of members or the executive committee to ratify them.

Article 12. The procedure of the meeting of the association is regulated as follows:

1. A general meeting of members shall be held in April and October every year; it shall be convened by the executive committee. But extraordinary meetings may be called whenever the executive committee deems it to be

necessary, or at the request of one tenth at least of the representatives of member-firms;

2. Meetings of the executive committee shall be held on the 1st and the 15th of every month and shall be convened by the standing committee. But an extraordinary meeting may be held whenever the standing committee deems it to be necessary or at the request of one tenth at least of the executive delegates.

3. The standing commettee is convened at any time by the chairman.

Article 13. The quorum for the above meetings is over one half of the number of members or executive delegates. The decission are taken by the consent of the majority of those present. In case of equal division of votes the chairman has the casting vote. But the matters enumerated in art. 28 of the Law on Chambers of Commerce, cannot be decided by the general meeting of members unless there is a quorum of two-thirds at least of the members and two thirds at least of those present give their consent.

Article 14. The current expenditure of the association are contributed by the members.

Article 15. Any firm wishing to join the association should be introduced by two member-firms and fill a writted application. Moreover, the manager's full name. native town and age; the full name, native town, and occupation, amount of capital of the proprietors, and the property condition of the proprietors should be filled in the form prepared by the association. After the association has sent an officer to ascertain whether everything is accurate and the application handed over to the executive committee for inspection has been accepted, it is pemitted to join the association.

Article 16. Members of the association who are in one of the following cases, in stating the motive, request their withdrawal:

    a. Those who suspend or close their business;

    b. Those who are compelled to liguidate because of the contraction of the scope of their business.

Article 17. Members of the association who are in one of the following cases, must be expelled immediately. If the case is a grievous [offence] beside the measure of expulsion, they must be dealt with in accordance with law:

    1. Those who are declared bankrupt;

    2. Those who use fraudulently the name of the association to deceive third persons, if the fact is proved with certainty;

    3. Those who infringe the regulations of the association;
    4. Those who do not pay the contribution.

Article 18. Officers of the association who are in one of the cases mentioned in No. 1 to 3 of the preceding article or who have committed another grievous [offence] must be ordered to resign.

Article 19. The association may engage salaried officers for secretarial, accounting and miscellaneous works.

Article 20. All matters not provided for by the present regulations shall be settled in conformity with the "Law on Industrial and Commercial Guilds" and the detailed "Regulations for its enforcement".

Article 21. The duration of the association has been fixed to 30 years by a resolution of the general meeting of members.

Article 22. The detailed by-laws of the association will be enacted separately.

Article 23. If the present regulations are found not suitable, they may be amended by a resolution of the general meenting of members and the amendment will be reported to the Ministries of Industry and Finance for record.

Article 24. The present regulations will come into force after being passed by the general meeting of members and having been transnulled by the Government of this Municipality to the Ministries of Industry and Finance for record.

APPENDIX X

THE REGULATIONS OF THE COMMON TREASURY OF TIENTSIN BANKERS' AND NATIVE BANKERS' ASSOCIATIONS

Chapter I General Provisions

Article 1. For the purpose of facilitating the exchanges and accomodating the circulation of money among banks and native banks, their associations organize jointly the common treasury named the Common Treasury of Tientsin Bankers' and Native Bankers' Associations and located temporarily No. 54, Consular Road, British Concession.

Article 2. Any native bank (:or banking firm) established in Tientsin by Chinese or foreigners and the Chinese Accounting Department of foreign banks, whether they are members of the Bankers' or Native Bankers' Associations or not, may join the Common Treasury as a member bank or native bank.

Chapter II Business Operated

Article 3. Whether an interest on cash deposits of the member banks or native banks should be paid or not, and the rate of interest, as well as the limitation of deposits and interest, for each depositor shall be decided in accordance with the conditions of the market, in a meeting of the Board of Directors to be held once every three months.

Article 4. When transferring his deposits, the member bank or native bank draws a check on the Common Treasury. In order to facilitate its circulation, no member bank or native bank cannot refuse to accept it. If there is some difficulty for circulation, the member bank or native bank may apply to the Common Treasury, in stating the motive, to consider some other means of accomodation.

Article 5 In case that the capacity of the premises of this Treasury is not sufficient, a part of cash received may be entrusted for custody to a bank or native bank appointed by the Board of Directors.

Article 6 To meet the demand of the market, the Common Treasury may fix daily a rate of interest, to be announced publicly in a placard, for granting call loans to member banks or native banks; but these call loans should be secured by a proper security. The kind of security as well as the procedure are decided by the Board of Directors at any time.

Article 7. The daily amount and remittance charges of Shanghai exchange (申匯)—receivable or payable in cash—which the Common Treasury operates against cash for the member banks or native banks, are decided by the President of the Treasury in consultation with the Directors for current affairs according to the market conditions, and announced publicly.

Chapter III. Board of Directors and Officers

Article 8. All the affairs of the Common Treasury are controlled by the Board of Directors, who are elected freely by ballot from among the heads of Chinese or foreign banks and native banks by member banks and native banks. There are eleven Directors and five Reserve Directors. If there is any vacancy among the directors, a Reserve Director shall take over the duties [of the retired Director].

Article 9. As regards voters, the unit is the enterprise [that is to say each bank or each native bank]. As regards candidates, any person may be elected irrespective of whether or not his enterprise has joined the Common Treasury.

Article 10. For the Common Treasury, there shall be five Directors for current affairs elected by the Directors from among them-

selves: a President shall be chosen by the Board of Directors
from among the Directors for current affairs to perform
concurrently these duties. When the President of the
Treasury is prevented to perform his duties, the Board of
Directors shall chose temporarily one of the other Directors
for current affairs to act in his place.

Article 11. The Directors for current affairs of the Treasury must go
every day to the Treasury to attend their duties. The
four Directors for current affairs other than him who is
concurrently President of the Treasury, shall fix beforehand
a weekly order of rotation for chairmanship. The Board
of Directors shall hold an ordinary meeting every Saturday.
When required by the circumstances, the chairman shall
call an extraordinary meeting (of the Board). No affair
concerning the external relations of the Common Treasury
shall be effective, unless decided by the Board of Directors.
Directors for current affairs or ordinary Directors who are
unable to attend a meeting, may delegate another Director
or Reserve Director as his proxy.

Article 12. The term of office for the Directors of the Common
Treasury is one year. At the expiration, new elections shall
take place by list ballot. [Retiring Directors] are re-eligible.
The same applies for the President.

Article 13. Under the President of the Treasury who is appointed in
the manner provided for by article 10 and who must be
concurrently Director for current affairs, there shall be
two deputy—President and a certain number of officers,
all of whom shall be chosen by the President in consultation with the Board of Directors.

Article 14. The President executes the decisions of the Board of
Directors, and in consultation with the Directors for current

affairs, manages the general affairs of the Treasury. The daily accounts and business are operated separately by the Deputy—President in Common with the various officers in accordance with the instructions of the Directors for current affairs and the President.

Chapter IV. Board of Supervisors

Article 15. Five Supervisors shall be appointed as the Board of Supervisors of the Common Treasury. They shall be elected according to the procedure provided for in articles 8 and 9. Besides, two Reserve Supervisors shall be elected. If there is any vacancy among the Supervisors, a Reserve Supervisor shall take over the duties (of the retired Supervisor).

Article 16. The Board of supervisors audits at any time all the accounts of the Treasury, checks the cash and the balance at the end of each period; it inspects concerning the affairs stated in articles 5, 6, and 7 of the present regulation, whether everything is correct or not. In case of necessity, it may submit his opinion to the Board of Directors in order to assist the latter to check and improve.

Article 17. The term of office of the Supervisors is the same as that of the Directors. They are re-eligible.

Chapter V. Meetings

Article 18. After the half-yearly settlement of accounts of the Common Treasury, the Board of Directors will fix a date for concerning an ordinary meeting of all members, in order to report on the accounts and the working conditions (of the Treasury).

Article 19. If there occurs some important affair, the Board of Directors must convene an extraordinary meeting of all the members. If three-tenths at least of the members deem it to be necessary to convene an extraordinary meeting, they shall request the Board of Directors to convene it.

Article 20. In the ordinary or extraordinary meetings of all the members, each member has one voting right. The quorum is two-thirds at least of all the members, and the decision is passed by the consent of two - thirds at least of the members who are present.

Chapter VI. The Budget and the Settlement of Accounts

Article 21. The budget of expenditures of the Common Treasury is approved by the Board of Directors. Except for the duties of the Directors and Supervisors which bring no remuneration, the salaries of the President, the Vice-presidents and other officers of the Treasury shall be decided by the Board of Directors.

Article 22. The Common Treasury settles up all accounts once every half-year. The profits and losses are shared in common by all the member banks and native banks. The respective amount and the procedure of disturibution shall be fixed separately.

Chapter VII. Additional Provisions

Article. 23 The detailed regulations for the working of the Common Treasury are fixed by the Board of Directors.

Article 24. If some of the regulations of the Common Treasury are found not be convenient in practice, they must be amended in accordance with the procedure provided by articles 19 and 20 of the present regulations.

Article 25. The present regulations come into force from the day of their approval by the competent authorities.

For Product Safety Concerns and Information please contact our EU
representative GPSR@taylorandfrancis.com
Taylor & Francis Verlag GmbH, Kaufingerstraße 24, 80331 München, Germany